Inside School Improvement

Inside School Improvement: Creating High-Performing Learning Communities

Jackie A. Walsh

and

Beth D. Sattes

AEL's mssion is to link the knowledge from research with the wisdom from practice to improve teaching and learning. AEL serves as the Regional Educational Laboratory for Kentucky, Tennessee, Virginia, and West Virginia. For these same four states, it operates the Eisenhower Regional Consortium for Mathematics and Science Education. In addition, it serves as the Region IV Comprehensive Center and operates the ERIC Clearinghouse on Rural Education and Small Schools.

Information about AEL projects, programs, and services is available by writing or calling AEL.

AEL, Inc.
Post Office Box 1348
Charleston, West Virginia 25325-1348
304-347-0400
800-624-9120
304-347-0487 (fax)
aelinfo@ael.org
http://www/ael.org

ISBN1-891677-10-1

This publication is based on work sponsored wholly or in part by the Office of Educational Research and Improvement, U.S. Department of Education, under contract number RJ96006001. Its contents do not necessarily reflect the views of OERI, the Department, or any other agency of the U.S. government.

Contents

Acknowledgments vii
About the Authors viii
Introduction: The Inside Story ix
How to Use This Book xix

Chapter One: Broadening the Learning Community 1
School and Community: A Three-Part Invention 3
School *for* Community: Tomorrow Is Another Day 5
School *within* Community: Build It and They Will Come 15
School *as* Community: The Ties That Bind 30
Processes That Involve and Build Community 51

Chapter Two: Sharing Leadership for Learning 61
The Journey from Cocksure Ignorance to Thoughtful
    Uncertainty: Reflections of an Elementary Principal 63
Through the Looking Glass: From Control to Commitment 64
The Pot of Gold at the End of the Rainbow 73
Follow the Yellow Brick Road 78
Making the Time 80
Choosing a Boat to Row: Structures to
    Facilitate Shared Leadership 86

Chapter Three: Enriching the Learning Culture 107
The Culture Puzzle: Parts, Patterns, & Possibilities 108
Creating & Nurturing a Culture for Learning:
    Lessons Learned from Three Schools 109
What If the Glass Slipper Fit Your School? 116
Crystallizing the Vision 118
Nurturing Norms and Strengthening Shared Beliefs 124
Celebrations & Rituals: Special Moments in Time 134
Stories and Storytellers: Capturing, Celebrating, and
    Learning from the Past 145
Professional Development to Enrich the Learning Culture 148
Looking at the Learning Culture in Your School 165

Chapter Four: Enabling SMART Learners 169
Developing SMART Learners: What's It All About? 170
Empowering Students to Achieve SUCCESS 175
What MOTIVATES Students to Learn—Extra Credit or
    Increased Connectedness? 195
The AUTONOMOUS Learner: Competent and Self-Directed 204
Answerable, Accountable, Trustworthy, Reliable,
    Dependable . . . RESPONSIBLE Means Much More
    than "Doing As I Say to Do" 212

Critical, Reflective, Considerate, Creative—The Many Faces of
   THOUGHTFULNESS 218
Using Assessment to Promote SMART Learning:
   The Big Picture 233

Tools
Participatory Research 51
Inside-Outside Fishbowl 54
Search Conferences 57
IQ Pairs 68
Data in a Day 96
Structured Reflection Protocol 99
20/20 Vision 120
Snowflake 123
Data on Display 127
Walkabouts 141
Storytelling 145
Collegial Investigation 151
QUILT 158
Multiple Intelligences Inventory 210
Procedures for Creating a Reflective Classroom 225
Facilitating Reflection 228
Facilitating Active Listening 230
Mindmapping 232
de Bono's Six Hats 232
Student-Led Conferences 238
Interview Design 243

Activities
Little "l" Leadership 68
Using Data on Display 91
Take a Look at Your School 103
The Important Book 125
Establishing a Shared Vocabulary 132
Tell Your Own Story 147
Looking at the Learning Culture in Your School 165
Different Perspectives on Student Success 190
Thinking about Learning Styles 212
Introducing the Art of Listening 229

Appendixes
Appendix A. Descriptions of Schools 253
Appendix B. Quest Scholars 269
Appendix C. Sample Observation Forms for Data in a Day 273
Appendix D. SMART Parenting Excerpts 283
Appendix E. Summaries of de Bono's Six Thinking Hats 295

Bibliography 301

Acknowledgments

> The future is not a result of choice among alternative paths
> offered by the present, but a place that is created—created first in
> mind and will, created next in activity.
> The future is not some place we are going to but one we are
> creating. The paths are not to be found, but made, and the activity
> of making them changes both the maker and the destination.
> —John Schaar

This book contains dozens of stories about places that were created—in mind, will, and activity—by dedicated teachers, principals, students, and parents. The activity of creating these places changed the reality of schooling for students. It also changed the individuals who were a part of the creating—including the authors, who were privileged to collaborate with these members of local school communities over the course of three years. We are grateful for the opportunity of having known and worked with this special group of people. You can learn more about the schools whose stories appear herein by turning to Appendix A.

Vision is central to creativity. Five years ago it was our challenge to create a network for school improvement as part of a long-term research and development project pursued by AEL under contract with the U.S. Department of Education. Sandra Orletsky, our long-time mentor and friend, was director of what became the Quest Network of Quality Learning Communities. Her vision shaped our work; her belief in our capacity to cocreate with member schools supported us during the project and the writing of this book.

Many other individuals within AEL contributed to this product. We are especially grateful for the efforts of Shirley Keene, who prepared the manuscript and patiently accepted "just one more edit." Additionally, we acknowledge the work of Mary George Jester, whose tenacity and good humor enabled us to complete this endeavor. Carolyn Luzader, Nancy Balow, Carla McClure, Dawn Pauley, and Marilyn Slack brought their considerable talents to the editing, proofreading, design, and layout—bringing the book to life.

Finally, we acknowledge each of you who have chosen to use this book as a resource for your own school improvement efforts. May your commitment to continuous improvement lead you to create futures of meaning for your students, your colleagues, and your community at large. May you be renewed and invigorated by your journey.

Jackie Walsh and Beth Sattes
October 2000

About the Authors

Jackie A. Walsh, Ph.D., and Beth D. Sattes have collaborated on multiple projects and publications over the past decade—Walsh as an independent education consultant living in Montgomery, Alabama, and Sattes as a research and development specialist at AEL in Charleston, West Virginia. Much of their joint work has focused on professional development, effective classroom questioning, participative assessment, and continuous school improvement.

The inspiration for this book grew out of their facilitation of the Quest Network for Quality Learning Communities. The authors designed the Network to incorporate new knowledge from the fields of business leadership, the new sciences, and education research. Through their work with the Network's educators, parents, and students, they identified characteristics of schools that function as high-performing learning communities and applied these learnings to the broader work of comprehensive school reform.

Introduction: The Inside Story

At Alexander Elementary School in Tennessee, students are leading conferences with their parents—sharing with them the work they have done and how it measures up to teacher expectations. This scene is being repeated at Natcher Elementary (Kentucky) and at Lumberport Elementary and Our Lady of Fatima (West Virginia).

Students, parents, and community members are joining teachers and other school staff to assess the extent to which schoolwide goals for learning are being met at Woodbridge Senior High and Highland Elementary (Virginia) and Alexander Elementary.

Teachers at Atenville Elementary (West Virginia), Alexander Elementary, and Woodbridge Senior High are looking collaboratively at student work to identify how well certain skills are being taught.

Schools focused on becoming high-performing learning communities are using these and other strategies to mobilize their school communities. Whether rural, suburban, or urban; large or small; elementary or secondary—these schools are bound together by a commitment to continuous improvement. Their view of continuous improvement places high value upon building connections among individuals across a wide spectrum of their school communities and finding ways to focus the resulting energy on a shared vision and goals for student performance.

Research, reflection, and systematic inquiry are at the core of teachers' work in schools that are restructuring themselves. Like their students, teachers are engaged in a process of continual learning.

—Ann Lieberman & Lynne Miller

While schools across the nation and around the world are engaged in journeys of continuous improvement, the inspiration for this book comes from work done in 18 schools across four states: Kentucky, Tennessee, Virginia, and West Virginia. AEL, a regional educational laboratory, brought these schools together in a network dedicated to continuous school improvement. Member schools were guided by a framework for continuous improvement—a theoretical construct that organizes knowledge and research for practitioner use. Parents, students, and staff in the networked schools shared their personal visions of excellence and a passion for improving learning opportunities for all of their school's students.

Framework for Continuous Improvement

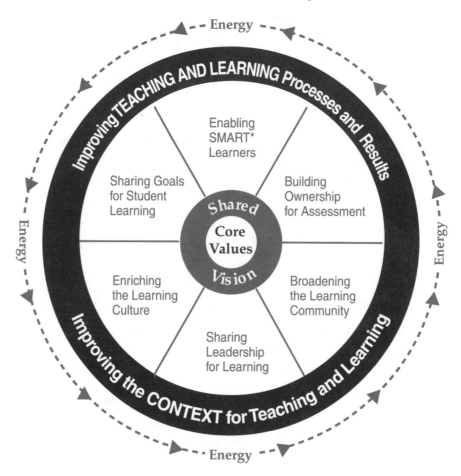

This framework emerged from a review of the knowledge base on learning communities and high-performing learning organizations—both within and outside the education arena—and of current education research and literature on high-performing schools and classrooms. The framework organizes the findings into key concepts, or constructs, that can be used by practitioners to plan and execute their own improvement initiatives. The framework captures a set of dynamic factors that are interactive and systemic in nature; it does not provide a formula or step-by-step improvement process. Network members use the framework as a point of reference in their own journeys. A school can "cut into" the framework at any one of six points, then use the selected construct as a point of departure for assessment and improvement planning.

At the heart of the framework are **vision** and **core values**. Central to any organization's attempt to become a high-performing learning community is a powerful and palpable **vision**. Such a vision permeates and guides all work within the organization and inspires and sustains all who do the work. As Peter Senge writes, "when people truly share a vision, they are connected, bound together by a common aspiration." He further suggests that one of the reasons people seek to build shared visions is their desire to be connected to an important undertaking.[1] Senge clearly articulates the power of vision and makes the case for vision being at the center of the framework for continuous school improvement. Other authors argue that shared vision is requisite to any sustained improvement effort.[2]

To be powerful and effective, the vision must be aligned with the **core values** of the broader community—surfaced and articulated by the organization's leadership. Carl Glickman makes the case for school leaders surfacing the core values of their communities

When a critical mass of people are focused on what they are trying to accomplish and have a "can-do" attitude, instead of a "can't-get-there-from-here" attitude, the impact on performance is profound.

—Ed Oakley & Doug Krug

and notes that articulation of these beliefs enables a group's members "to accomplish together what they could not do alone."[3] Others write about the potential of values to galvanize a group and promote a sense of shared ownership.[4] Examples of core values include openness and trust, respect for diversity, integrity and honesty, caring, innovation, winning and being the best, personal accountability, community involvement, social responsibility, and so forth. There is no one "right set" of core values. However, effective leaders are able to mobilize community members in support of an innovation by connecting the initiative to agreed-on core values, thereby tapping a potent resource for commitment to the change.

The three constructs comprising the bottom half of the framework address context variables—those noninstructional factors that nurture and support teaching and learning. Included among these: enriching the learning culture, sharing leadership for learning, and broadening the learning community. High-performing learning communities possess a **strong culture for learning**, a culture in which curiosity and excitement about learning abound.[5] Further, community norms support risk taking and experimentation, proactive (as opposed to reactive) approaches to change, reflection on practice, cooperative and collaborative approaches to learning, questioning, and the like.[6]

Highly compatible with the above norms is a **sharing of leadership** that rests upon a belief that "leadership is not the private reserve of a few . . . [but] a process that ordinary people use when they are bringing forth the best from themselves and from others."[7] Recent school reform efforts have given rise to numerous structures designed to encourage shared leadership, including site-based councils, school improvement councils, and faculty senates. Structures alone, however, do not ensure shared leadership; rather, its authenticity depends upon the norms, attitudes, and behaviors of both formal leaders and others in the community. Norms such as respect and trust, personal efficacy, individual responsibility, and individual initiative enable the sharing of leadership.

Leadership is not the private reserve of a few charismatic men and women. It is a process that ordinary people use when they bring forth the best from themselves and others.

—James Kouzes & Barry Posner

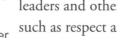

Further, community consensus that "leadership is not a zero-sum game in which one person gets some only when another loses some"[8] is essential to this approach. Critical to a true sharing of leadership are an open flow of communications, time and opportunities for involvement, shared goals for learning, and a spirit of inclusiveness.[9]

The third component of a context supportive of high-performance teaching and learning is the **broadening of the learning community**. This construct is a double-edged sword. It assumes a learning community "where students and adults alike are engaged as active learners . . . and where everyone is encouraging everyone else's learning."[10] Further, it suggests an inclusive community, one in which barriers of separation, isolation, and exclusion are eliminated. Not only do school staff join students as learners, but parents and members of the broader community are welcomed into the school family. Thomas Sergiovanni describes schools as "moral communities . . . akin to families [whose] moral connections come from the duties teachers, parents, and students accept, and the obligations they feel toward others and toward their work."[11]

The work of teachers, students, and parents in school is primarily that of teaching and learning. The top half of the framework (page x) comprises variables focused on improving teaching and learning processes and results: establishing shared goals for learning, enabling SMART learners, and building ownership for assessment. Susan Rosenholtz writes that "**shared goals** are central to the mystery of [a] school's success, mediocrity, or failure."[12] Shared goals (1) communicate expected results for students; (2) convey a hopeful message to all, i.e., that they are capable of improving; (3) enable teachers and students to gauge their success; (4) allow for meaningful feedback to all; and (5) promote professional dialogue.[13] Other criteria for effective goals are that they be limited in number and clearly focused.[14] This facilitates widespread knowledge of and conversation around the most important ends of instruction. Theodore Sizer advocates the adoption of a limited number of simple, well-formulated goals that apply to all students within the school. He acknowledges that the means to reach these goals will vary according to the varying needs and interests of students.[15]

If schools are to educate virtually all students for "knowledge work" and for complex roles as citizens in a technological world, teachers will need to know how to design curriculum and adapt their teaching so that it responds to student understandings, experiences, and needs as well as to family and community contexts.

—Linda Darling-Hammond &
Milbrey W. McLaughlin

Clearly formulated goals drive teaching and learning toward purposeful ends. The framework for continuous school improvement embodies a commitment to developing **SMART learners** who possess the skills and habits of mind required for life and work in the twenty-first century. The acronym SMART stands for Successful, Motivated, Autonomous, Responsible, and Thoughtful—traits associated with continuous, lifelong learners able to adapt to an environment marked by accelerated change. AEL staff conceived the SMART concept following a review of current literature and research related to effective teaching and learning.[16] SMART learning became a part of the Quest culture (see chapter 4). SMART is a vital part of many network schools' visions for teaching and learning—taking the emphasis away from rote memorization and accompanying passive learning behavior.

Related to shared goals and SMART learners is the third piece of the "teaching-learning pie"—**building ownership for assessment**. Central to this concept is the conviction that all members of the learning community—teachers, students, parents, and community members—need to know and understand national, state, and local standards for student performance and be involved in making meaning of assessment data emerging from all sources. Associated with this concept is an emphasis on assessment as feedback to the learning and improvement processes and on self-assessment. The challenge at the beginning of the twenty-first century is to help all stakeholders make connections between assessment as accountability and assessment as an integral part of the learning cycle.

———————— ✳ ————————

For the most part, discussions about schools, especially those concerning school reform, have centered more on what adults do than on what students do.

—Phil Schlechty

———————— ✳ ————————

Each of the six constructs within the framework emphasizes the expanded involvement of individuals from across the learning community in a school's improvement agenda. The premise of the framework is that these human interactions generate **energy** for the work of continuous improvement. This is consistent with management and organizational development theories that emphasize the role of leadership in generating and managing energy.[17] Energy generated by human connections and creative endeavors is essential for the long-term work of moving school communities to ever-higher levels of performance and effectiveness. Networking of schools is one way to facilitate connections and creativity among individual members.

The Quest Network

More than 100 people from 18 school communities across the four-state region of Kentucky, Tennessee, Virginia, and West Virginia are the inspiration and primary sources for this book. In 1997, AEL invited these schools to join a network dedicated to building quality learning communities that support high levels of student and adult performance. Over the course of three years, teachers, students, administrators, parents and community members from these school worked (1) to create communities of learners; (2) to connect with programs, strategies, and resources; and (3) to commit to continuous growth and development—individually, as school communities, and as a regional learning community. The stories that enrich this book are their stories. The network facilitated and supported their efforts to improve educational opportunities and performance for all of their students.

The Players. Each participating school recruited a leadership team to participate in network events and to take skills, strategies, and energy derived from the networking experience back to their home schools. Most elementary school teams consisted of an administrator, teachers, and parents; secondary teams added student members. Leadership teams engaged members of the larger school community in local school improvement activities. Descriptions of schools can be found in Appendix A.

The Structure. Teams came to network "rallies" that afforded opportunities to learn about strategies, tools, programs, and practices that could be adapted to their local contexts. At these events, members also had time to share effective practices and success stories with colleagues from other schools. At times, discussion focused on more effective classroom use of technology; at others on restructuring the school day or specific curricular programs. Sharing was often accomplished through *storytelling*. Over time, a network culture emerged—complete with shared norms, stories, heroes, and celebrations.

Sometimes outside networks, partnerships, or friends can serve as a constant reminder of ultimate purposes or high expectations that often get lost in the confusion of the day-to-day work of effecting change in a school—even when things are going well. Networks are important because they identify with the common struggle.

—Ann Lieberman & Lynn Miller

AEL facilitators designed rallies to incorporate not only sharing of best practice, but also reflection and dialogue. Individual reflection and writing enabled individuals to make personal meaning from information presented as well as to make connections between potential innovations and the needs and resources of their school communities. Through dialogue, individuals addressed common problems and issues. Opportunities to practice reflection and dialogue in a safe environment contributed to practitioner adoption of these habits of mind in the job setting. Leadership teams attended rallies twice annually; an annual summer symposium afforded all members of the school communities opportunities to learn about best practices from member schools and from individuals outside of the network. Additionally, AEL staff planned annual visits to member schools—called Co-Ventures in Learning—to emphasize the collegial nature of the on-site work and study.

An important component of the network was the Quest scholar program. A heterogeneous group of teachers, administrators, and students from elementary and secondary member schools served as scholars. The 17 members contributed to program design, evaluation, and research initiatives for the network. These individuals, whose names are listed in Appendix B, made significant contributions to this book. They offered their own stories and solicited stories from others. They offered suggestions as to how this work could serve the needs of those engaged in the everyday and arduous work of school improvement.

Quest has been an exciting avenue of change. It has made available many resources that would otherwise have been not only unattainable but unknown. The project has provided a method for evaluating our school and of allowing us to expand our thinking to embrace new ideas.

—Cheryl Dingess, Atenville
Elementary School

The founders of the Quest Network for Quality Learning Communities believed it was important to have a creed—something that expressed what the "important things" were. Staff felt equally strongly that the beliefs in this statement should be articulated by the network members themselves, as opposed to being written by staff and delivered to members. At an early rally, we asked network members to answer two questions, *What supports student learning?* and *What is essential in a school for successful student learning?* Through the Snowflake activity, described later in the book, we generated several categories, which were fleshed out into statements. These statements were edited by a dedicated group of two; one from the elementary school network and one from the secondary school network. They debated back and forth to determine whether we should have two creeds or one; the early creed from the elementary network was considerably different from the secondary creed. But eventually the group agreed it was important to have a single statement of beliefs. The Quest creed is a proud statement of what the network members agreed was important, indeed essential.

Lessons Learned. Scholar Connie Allen, principal of Natcher Elementary School, took a page from the opening lines of *Winnie the Pooh* in describing her experience in the Quest network: "Bump, bump, bump, bump. If only I could stop bumping long enough to think, I might be able to get myself out of this dilemma." Allen suggests that this "bumping" is an excellent metaphor for the day-to-day business of working in a school. According to Allen, educators can get so busy bumping along that there's no time for reflection and redirection. She credits the Quest network with affording her and others time for re-

The Quest Creed

SMART *learners* **are the center of the learning community.**

We believe SMART learners

- can learn
- are unique individuals deserving unconditional acceptance, attention, and encouragement
- must feel safe in the school, community, and home
- enjoy mutual trust and respect between teachers and students in open, caring classrooms
- become engaged when they have a voice in choosing and performing learning activities
- learn *how* to learn as well as *what* to learn

SMART *learning* **is meaningful and challenging.**

We believe SMART learning

- begins at the learner's level of understanding
- applies to real life
- demands open lines of communication among teachers, students, and others
- grows in a climate of curiosity, active participation, and exploration
- thrives in the presence of high standards and expectations
- requires time, resources, funding, and technology
- uses various forms of assessment as continuous feedback

SMART *teachers* **are proactive.**

We believe SMART teachers

- are passionate and knowledgeable about subject matter
- are committed, enthusiastic, and flexible
- model lifelong learning, perseverance, patience, and creativity
- use professional development for continuous self-improvement

SMART *school environments* **support learning.**

We believe SMART school environments

- include administrators who support teachers' and learners' objectives
- respect and value the uniqueness of all community members
- provide a safe place for intellectual creativity
- apply collaborative problem solving to real-life situations

SMART *school communities* **engage with learning.**

We believe SMART school communities

- commit to a shared vision of excellence
- understand that parent involvement is essential to successful learners and learning
- engage in continuous improvement

newal. Certain qualities of networks make them particularly well suited for this function.

Other authors have documented the value of networks in school improvement. Experiences in the Quest network affirm these findings.[18] More specifically, four kinds of benefits accrue to network members.

You can't replicate a school any more than you can replicate a family, but you can learn from a good school like you can learn from a good family.

—Deborah Meier

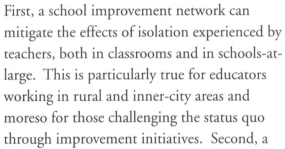

First, a school improvement network can mitigate the effects of isolation experienced by teachers, both in classrooms and in schools-at-large. This is particularly true for educators working in rural and inner-city areas and moreso for those challenging the status quo through improvement initiatives. Second, a network provides the uplifting experience of being a part of something larger than oneself. This sense of belonging and being connected to others who share a common vision provides inspiration and motivation for the sometimes lonely work of school improvement. Third, a network provides unique opportunities to learn from peers and colleagues in other schools. AEL evaluation staff noted and documented the power of cross-school sharing and mentoring. Fourth and finally, a network creates accountability between and among members. When colleagues are aware of one another's commitment, they are much more likely to follow through on that commitment.

Quest network activities followed a co-learning philosophy— AEL researchers and school practitioners studied, worked, and learned

Fundamental school reform is an essentially human process where teachers, administrators, students, parents, and community come together to think critically about what they value.

—Jeannie Oakes

together. AEL staff do not believe the "outside expert model" to be appropriate in systemic reform efforts. Rather, in seeking to build the capacity of school communities, we adopt an "inside" approach to change— developing ideas and resources from within the community. Additionally, our co-learning

proceeds from a strengths model, not a deficit model. School communities select strategies and solutions that align with their visions, goals, and human and material resources. They seek to build success into new initiatives. Hence, this book contains many success stories. Practitioner reflections provide balance and acknowledgement that the work of school improvement is not easy, nor always failure-free.

How to Use This Book

Four major constructs of the framework for continuous school improvement serve as organizers for the remainder of this book:

- broadening the learning community
- sharing leadership for learning
- enriching the learning culture
- enabling SMART learners

The focus is on what Sergiovanni refers to as the "lifeworld of schools."[19]

The chapters share common strands and formats. Each opens with a brief overview and a set of questions for reflection. The intent of these questions is to elicit the reader's current thinking regarding topics to be explored. Following the overview is a theory piece that sets the themes for the chapter and provides references to the knowledge base underpinning the selected construct. This sets the stage for the "real meat" of each chapter—school stories and the documentation of tools and strategies. School stories provide a practitioner's perspective on how to leverage a particular tool or strategy in the mobilization of community members for continuous improvement. Descriptions of tools and strategies include step-by-step directions. Sprinkled throughout each chapter are salient quotes and annotations of potentially useful books, Web sites, and other resources. At the end of each chapter is a set of questions to be used by you, the reader, in assessing your school's Improvement Quotient (IQ).

The reader can open the book to any section that appeals to a particular interest or need. Neither the chapters nor the sections within them need to be read sequentially. References to other sections can be followed according to the reader's purposes. Marginal icons enable easy identification of

Activities

Reflections

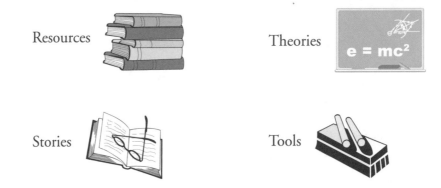

Resources

Theories

Stories

Tools

Inside School Improvement was conceived as a practical resource, a hands-on guide that will be useful to and used by individuals seeking to make a difference in their own school communities. As such, it can be used by study groups as a stimulus for developing assessment and action planning. Each chapter contains questions for reflection and/or discussion and activities that can enhance group interactions. The author and contributors hope that both the contents and the format are user-friendly and that each reader will be motivated to do something with the information provided—that at least a portion of the book will speak to you in a meaningful way. Our desire is that you will be encouraged in your own journey of continuous improvement.

The book's title, *Inside School Improvement*, is a double *entendre* of sorts. First, the stories and supporting information seek to take you inside real schools' improvement efforts. You will meet ordinary people struggling with the same kinds of problems and challenges you may face. Second, the title is intended to connote the idea that all improvement efforts begin inside individuals who commit to making a difference within their local contexts. Thus, the work of school improvement is almost always accompanied by the inner work of individuals who view their personal learning and development as continuous and lifelong. Because you are reading these words, you fit this mold. You see yourself as a continuous learner who can make a positive difference for your school and community. May the stories, strategies, and resources provided herein fuel your personal and community journeys of continuous improvement.

Notes

1. Senge, *The Fifth Discipline*, 206.

2. See Senge, *The Fifth Discipline*; Oakley and Krug, *Enlightened Leadership*; Nanus, *Visionary Leadership*; and Block, *Stewardship*.

3. Glickman, *Renewing America's Schools*, 16.

4. Nanus, *Visionary Leadership*, 51.

5. Kline and Saunders, *Ten Steps to a Learning Organization*, 44-45.

6. Kofman and Senge, *Communities of Commitment*, 21; and Handy, "Managing the Dream," 47.

7. Kouzes and Posner, "Seven Lessons for Leading the Voyage," 110.

8. Barth, *Improving Schools from Within*, 128.

9. See Sergiovanni, *Moral Leadership*.

10. Barth, *Improving Schools from Within*, 9.

11. National Staff Development Council, "Moral Purpose, Community, Must Guide School Reform," 1.

12. See Rosenholtz, *Teachers' Workplace*.

13. See Rosenholtz, *Teachers' Workplace*; Schmoker, *Results: The Key to Continuous Improvement*.

14. See Fullan, *The New Meaning of Educational Change*; Schmoker, "Setting Goals in Turbulent Times."

15. Sizer, *Horace's Hope*, 154.

16. See Elmore et al., *Restructuring in the Classroom*; Perkins, *Smart Schools*; and Goleman, *Emotional Intelligence*.

17. See Ackerman, "The Flow State"; Hawley, *Reawakening the Spirit in Work*; Oakley and Krug, *Enlightened Leadership*; and Richards, *Artful Work*.

18. Lieberman and Grolnick, "Networks, Reform, and the Professional Development of Teachers," 192-215; Sizer, *Horace's School*; and Glickman, *Renewing America's Schools*.

19. See Sergiovanni, *The Lifeworld of Leadership*.

Broadening the Learning Community

Places that hold on to narrow definitions of community not only will suffer declines in populations but will be impoverished by their lack of inclusion.

—Suzanne Morse, "Five Building Blocks for Successful Communities"

*A*s public schools confront the challenges of the twenty-first century, the issue of inclusiveness as it relates to our interpretation of school community is of tremendous importance. Inclusiveness has multiple dimensions related to the community of adults and students who inhabit a school 180 or so days each school year. Among these dimensions are: (1) the extent to which teachers are connected one to another and the extent to which they share a common purpose with the school's administration and support staff; (2) the extent to which adults in a school ensure that each child, regardless of his or her background or personal characteristics, feels valued and cared for; and (3) the extent to which students respect and care for one another. This issue also affects a school's relationship with parents and members of the broader

1

community. More inclusive school communities bring more energy, resources, and commitment to the table as they address problems critical to continuous learning and improvement. While there is no one right way to approach community building in schools, there is one sure way to assure a static, stagnant, weak community: ignore the need to reach out to all stakeholders.

Questions for Reflection

If a school is to succeed in broadening its learning community, individuals throughout the school must embrace this as a goal and be proactive and intentional in efforts to achieve this end. Up-front attention to essential questions related to this issue can enhance such efforts. The questions below may be used to begin conversations that engage different role groups.

- What is the school's responsibility to the broader community in which it is situated?

- In what ways can a school enlist individuals outside the school in its learning community?

- How do you develop a community with shared commitment to matters about which people truly care?

- In what ways does a true school community provide students with a sense of belonging and connectedness?

- Where do schools begin community building?

School and Community: A Three-Part Invention

School community. Community involvement. Community school. These three variations on the theme of school and community are inextricably linked in our democratic society. While each concept conjures a different image, the images share common threads. Primary among these is the idea of connectedness—between and among individuals and between the individual and something bigger than self. Additionally, these cojoinings of school and community are viewed as desirable ends with intrinsic value. Each of these visions is necessary, and even essential, to continuous school improvement.

Community is a word that has multiple meanings in today's society. On the one hand, the term denotes individuals who are connected by virtue of the fact that they inhabit a designated physical or geographical area. On the other, the concept suggests an emotional or psychological connectedness among individuals who hold something in common—mutual interests, a set of core beliefs, or a shared vision. Interestingly, in pre-industrial society, communities embraced both physical and psychological connectedness. The two meanings were intertwined. In these simpler times, the school was at the core of the community. The school *belonged* to the community, *served* the community, indeed *was* community. People were connected to one another and to one of their most important institutions, the school, and this connection grew out of the natural order of things. Today we yearn for this wholeness, and so we talk of "building community in school," of forging meaningful partnerships between school and community, and of community schools that serve the broader community interests. Further, we associate each of these ends with schools of continuous improvement.

The challenge of broadening the learning community is a multidimensional one. To think more clearly about community and school, we can imagine three potential relationships between the two: (1) school *for* community, (2) school *within* community, and (3) school *as* community. The first relationship is grounded in a sociological function envisioned by the founding fathers: that public schools would provide an education that enables the citizenry to sustain the nation's democratic institutions. The second relationship is, in part, a political one, which acknowledges schools' need for the public's involvement and support if they are to achieve their mission. Finally, school as community addresses the psychological and spiritual needs that are requisite to individual growth, development, and personal fulfillment.

The present-day conception of *school for community* goes beyond Jefferson's advocacy of public schools as vehicles for realizing the democratic ideal. As the nation has grown and evolved, so has our concept of the type of education appropriate to this end. At the dawn of the twenty-first century, schools are challenged to redefine their mission in view of the changing forms and roles of other societal institutions (e.g., the family, churches, economic structures) and the very scope of education itself. *School within community* refers to the relationship between the school and individuals and agencies within the broader community. This construct subsumes the notions of community involvement in schools (through such programs as Partners in Education) as well as school as a center where all in the community can gather and learn. As our society has become larger and more complex, schools have, of necessity, become more intentional about promoting the kinds of relationships with their broader communities that occurred rather naturally when communities were smaller and less complex. *School as community* refers to the relationships among individuals—young people and adults alike—who work, play, and learn together in the place called school. This has to do with the ways in which individuals are bound together by virtue of their focus on common goals, similar values and ideals, and shared experience. School as community suggests the continuous building of community within and among various stakeholders in the school—teachers, staff, students, and parents.

When communities were smaller, less transient, and more homogeneous, community and school were tightly connected. The sociological, political, and psychological functions served by the school were interwo-

Few schools know what the community wants of them; the same is true for government, healthcare, and the military. We no longer agree on what we want these institutions to provide, because we are no longer members of communities that know why they are together. Most of us don't feel as if we are members of a community; we just live or work next to each other. The great missing conversation is about why and how we might be together.

—Margaret Wheatley & Myron Kellner-Rogers

ven and mutually supportive. However, in today's society, schools have become isolated from the communities that they serve. Their core functions have become fragmented and, in some cases, forgotten. One of the primary challenges of continuous school improvement is to revitalize the school's relationships to community and thereby enrich learning and community. Schools desiring to enrich their learning communities may wish to reflect on these three dimensions of community and learn from stories shared by schools that have been working in each area.

School *for* Community: Tomorrow Is Another Day

Successful communities think as much about tomorrow as they do about today.

—Suzanne Morse, "Five Building Blocks for Successful Communities"

March 1989. Darlene Dalton, third-grade teacher at Atenville Elementary, stands before her young students with tears in her eyes. She reads an article from the *Charleston Gazette* predicting a dim economic future for these young people, some of whom are growing up in third-generation welfare households—children whose ancestors worked in now-silent coal mines. Dalton's emotions are a blend of sadness and anger out of which is born a determination. "I won't let this happen to you!" she exclaims to her third graders. Their future will be different from their parents'. Her vision is palpable.

November 1999. Dalton receives recognition at the White House as one of the nation's outstanding principals. During the past nine years, she has led this little school to new heights. Her vision that the school will prepare these children to succeed in school and beyond has been embraced by her colleagues, parents, the community, and most important, by the children themselves. To this end, the school has adopted a number of innovations specifically targeted to help students (and their parents) develop the skills and attitudes necessary to productive citizenship in our emerging global society. A nationally cited parent involvement program brings dozens of parents to school to work in various capacities toward this shared dream. In the process, many of these parents are developing new skills and a work ethic that enables them to leave the welfare rolls and seek and obtain meaningful employment. Another initiative, selected because it is aligned with this new vision, is MicroSociety.[1] This program incorporates changes in both the cognitive and affective domains. A final example of Dalton's quest to help her students dream and achieve bright, new tomorrows is the school's 21st Century Community Learning Center program, funded by the U.S. Department of Education.[2] Through these activities, students' life experiences are extended and enriched in a myriad of exciting and previously unimagined ways.

Dalton's vision of schooling to fuel a better and brighter future is a modern-day incarnation of the Jeffersonian ideal: that education should serve the needs of a democratic society. Carl Glickman writes

> The essential value of the public school in a democracy, from the beginning, was to ensure an educated citizenry capable of participating in discussion, debates, and decisions to further the wellness of the larger community and protect individual rights to "life, liberty, and pursuit of happiness." An educated citizenry and a democracy were considered one and the same; the lack of one would imperil the other. Where the public school has strayed is in its loss of focus on this central goal.[3]

Not only have schools "strayed" and experienced a "loss of focus on this central goal," the nature of the community and the American experiment continue to change at an incredible rate and in unantici-pated directions. After 200 years, the boundaries of schooling are chang-ing. The physical boundaries of schools are disappearing as information technology accelerates the movement of education beyond the walls of classrooms and schools. Likewise, the population to be served by schools is expanding: more and more schools serve the educational needs of individuals "from cradle to grave." Not only are the physical boundaries changing, but also the curricular boundaries. Educators and community leaders are challenged to "think outside the box" of the traditional curriculum. In *The Future of Work,*[4] Charles Grantham considers the integration of education, telecommunications, computers, Internet, and work practices. If we are to continue to "ensure an educated citizenry" and the "wellness of the larger community," we must grapple with the implications of the evolving digital work society for both the content and form of education.

John Naisbitt addresses some of the same ideas in *High Tech • High Touch: Technology and Our Search for Meaning.*[5] Naisbitt joins a host of other social commentators who argue that one of the greatest challenges currently facing our democratic society is to create a harmony between technology and individuals. Certainly, this is a phenomenon that must be addressed by modern schools seeking to adapt the Jeffersonian vision. As Y2K dawned, Dalton in Atenville was searching for ways to integrate technology into the school's curriculum and instruction without sacrificing the high-touch school community that has evolved there over the past decade.

After-School Smarts in Harts: 21st Century Community Learning Centers

by Darlene Dalton, Principal, and Cheryl Dingess, Speech Therapist, Atenville Elementary

The 21st Century Community Learning Centers program provides funding for schools to offer enhanced learning opportunities for students while working to decrease substance abuse and crime among young people. Atenville Elementary received a 21st Century grant in 1998 that has enabled the program described below.

> **1994:** The problem around here is they don't teach you how to dream.
> *—A parent from Big Ugly Creek in Lincoln County, West Virginia*
> **1999:** This looks like a Christmas wish list! *—Charles McCann, Director, West Virginia Dreams Project*

What a difference five years can make! Five years and a vision to move Harts school children from hopelessness to euphoria; five years and a vision to open up endless possibilities for once-dreamless children. The funding of West Virginia Dreams—a collaborative effort between Lincoln County Schools and Step by Step, Inc.—by the U.S. Department of Education's 21st Century Community Learning Centers program "put the icing on the cake" in the ongoing struggle by the Harts community to restore our children's hope.

West Virginia Dreams enriches the school day through after-school

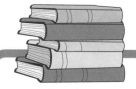

The Future of Work: The Promise of the New Digital Work Society by Charles Grantham (New York: McGraw-Hill, 2000).

Grantham, highly regarded for his applied research examining the impact of emerging work forms on individuals, writes compellingly of the need to create "new communities defined by heightened communications" as a response to changes in technology. His work is a springboard for educators engaged in futures planning. His ideas provide a focus for public dialogue, discussion, and discourse.

and summer programs that give students a place where they can be themselves. As first-round recipients of the 21st Century grants in November 1998, we had no road map to follow as we scurried about to open our centers. Miraculously, by opening day on February 8, 1999, we had enrolled 350 students, half of the students who attend school in our district, in after-school programs at four sites throughout our community. Students chose four offerings from a list that included piano, guitar, karate, gymnastics, computer, chess, creative writing, science lab, crafts, and photography.

In our first "summer of your dreams," students enjoyed field trips to the airport and the movies; they even went canoeing. They also participated in a special arts week with professional musician Rebecca Skeen-Webb and dancer Barbara Yurich. Twenty-five students attending the Big Ugly Community Center received a week of swimming lessons.

Parents also became a part of West Virginia Dreams. Twelve volunteered as regular tutors, and more than 200 attended at least one of the monthly Family Education Nights offered during 1999. During the 1999-2000 school year we used the SMART parenting materials from AEL.[6]

As students complete each year of the program, they receive a $50 scholarship that is placed in an education trust fund in their name. Community partners help with the financing of these scholarships. West Virginia Dreams participants already see positive results coming from their involvement with the program. Sixty-eight percent of the high school students who took part improved their test scores in the areas in which they were tutored. Elementary school students showed marked increases in their performance on the President's Physical Fitness test.

We envision far more long-reaching results. We know that participation in extracurricular activities is one of the great indicators of success in college, but, in an isolated rural area with no county income for extra bus runs, we have been stymied in providing these opportunities.

Through West Virginia Dreams, students experience success in a variety of arenas of their choosing, receive focused help on any academic challenges they face, and enjoy ongoing opportunities to work alongside caring adults.

MicroSociety as a Culture: Bringing the Real World into the School

by Cheryl Dingess, Speech Therapist, Atenville Elementary

A MicroSociety is a miniature community created and run by students within a school.

MicroSociety, like a master weaver, has threaded in and out of every fabric of Atenville's learning culture. It has become the thread that ties all the learning—whether in the classroom, after-school program, or home—together. Because of its relevance to the real world, students become committed to learning.

The students have become their own task-masters and must meet deadlines, fill quotas, develop business plans, pay taxes, and follow the laws of the MicroSociety. Of course, there are consequences for not managing their own learning effectively. Students may receive a ticket, appear in court, and possibly be sentenced to community service or spend time relearning decision making and/or conflict resolution.

MicroSociety brings relevancy to the day-to-day classroom curriculum. Students learn percentages so they can pay their taxes. They write business plans. They read news reports for CUB TV. For some, the daily routine includes

I served as president of the student body at Atenville Elementary for two consecutive years. Those two years were a valuable learning experience for me. I learned things about the government system that I would not have learned in a school without MicroSociety. I learned how to organize and run a successful presidential campaign. Through my campaigns, I learned critical people relation skills by talking with and working with my peers on the campaign. Being president allowed me to experience and to develop my leadership skills. I had to learn to make important decisions that affected not only me, but the entire student body. I gained valuable experience in learning firsthand how a government is organized and operated. I feel that the experience of being president for two years is something that will benefit me during my junior high and high school years. It was an experience that I will treasure for a lifetime.

—Bethany Toney,
Student, Atenville Elementary

inputting financial data into Quicken and developing graphics for the monthly newspaper. Others practice public speaking to defend a client in court or to be an anchor on the broadcast station. Students hone their Internet skills to research information for the newspaper. They also enrich their experiences through music and dance classes. The crafts they make are sold at market.

Students become so excited about learning that even the after-school program does not provide enough time to satisfy their hunger to learn. Parents often report extended conversations about their children's jobs. Students talk on the phone with their friends about new business ventures or solutions to problems that may occur during MicroSociety. The only complaint from students appears to be the need for more time.

MicroSociety is not just another program. It permeates the very fabric of our school to make learning open, honest, real-life, and challenging. Most important, MicroSociety prepares our students for citizenship in the larger community, helping them find their hidden talents and teaching them what they need to know to become productive, responsible citizens.

Becoming Good American Schools: The Struggle for Civic Virtue in Education Reform by Jeannie Oakes, Karen Hunter Quartz, Steve Ryan, and Martin Lipton (San Francisco: Jossey-Bass Publishers, 2000).

This important book addresses one of the toughest issues confronted by educators: how to actualize the belief that *all* students can learn at high levels. The authors explore the many dimensions of this issue through the stories of 16 middle schools engaged in the Carnegie Corporation-sponsored *Turning Points,* a major national reform project for middle-grades schooling of the 1990s. The major theme running through these stories is that of educators' attempts to make their schools more just, caring, and participatory in an effort to better serve the common good. The authors intertwine their findings from an extensive amount of research with poignantly human portraits from the schools investigated. Throughout they make a passionate, convincing argument for holding the public good as the measure for school effectiveness.

Service Learning for the Community

by Sandra Manning, Assistant Principal, Man High School

In the rural community of Man, many of the younger residents move away in search of better job opportunities. As the number of elderly citizens in the community increases, the need for support services also grows. One much-needed form of assistance that has occurred through the efforts of a local church is Meals on Wheels.

In the fall of 1999, Man High's 21st Century Community Learning Center program adopted Meals on Wheels, resulting in a meaningful partnership for the high school students and the elderly residents of our community. The young people prepared casseroles and desserts for their clients. Even more important, these teenagers learned the value of helping others in their community.

Both the members of the church and the recipients of the meals generously and frequently express their appreciation for our students and their assistance. The students not only feel they are helping others, they thoroughly enjoy the fun of working together to prepare the food. Meals on Wheels has become one of the most popular activities in our after-school program.

Service Learning Projects for Schools and Communities

by Terri Knight and Carol Lang, Teachers, University School

Service learning is a method by which students learn through active participation in organized service activities. These activities allow students to develop and enhance many skills taught in the regular classroom. These experiences also nourish the development of caring for others through service. A service learning project is a blending of service and learning goals in such a way that both occur and are enriched by the other. This experiential education is a focal point of the curriculum at University School, East Tennessee State University's K-12 laboratory school.

Beginning in the fifth grade, students participate in an environmental service learning project. Students run the aluminum can and plastic recycling program at the school. Not only do they collect these items, they instruct the rest of the students on the benefits of recycling. They also plan and implement the yearly Earth Week activities, during which time they conduct workshops for students in grades K-4 on different environmental topics.

Service learning operates in grades 6-8 with a project on the hazards of tobacco and smoking. Middle students create a curriculum of storybooks, skits, games, and puppet shows to teach K-5 students about the health issues of tobacco.

An intergenerational cultural exchange also provides middle school students the opportunity to meaningfully contribute to other people. Students interview older adults, take notes, and create storybooks about their lives. They then present the books to their partners as keepsakes.

These service projects were designed by students and faculty to fulfill the following goals: (1) increase young people's sense of effectiveness and their own importance in their school and community; (2) encourage responsibility, compassion, and pro-social values; (3) increase practical skills and abilities; (4) connect students to people, groups, and organizations in their community; and (5) direct efforts to generate and reinforce positive social change. Service learning projects connect the classroom to the community as they extend the classroom beyond the walls of the school for the benefit of both groups.

Resiliency Counseling at Atenville Elementary

by Michael Tierney, Codirector, West Virginia Dreams

Resiliency Dreamers reaches out to at-risk fifth through twelfth graders to engage them in constructive, safe activities. The groups meet weekly with a leader/therapist and a partner who has time to interact with the children and with their parents. Their curriculum includes such topics as anger management, tolerance for frustration, constructive use of time, drug and alcohol abuse prevention, adventure-based learning, and creative expression activities. A primary goal is to integrate students into community activities. After only one semester of activities, Resiliency Dreamers boasted a better than 70 percent attendance rate.

During the summer of 2000, in one of our communities, Big Ugly Creek, we made a particular effort to recruit some of our more troubled kids into an ambitious arts program. Many of these kids have serious problems; they receive special education services for learning disabilities or behavior disorders. During the summer program, they wrote songs and scenes for plays, performed and called square dances, played the dulcimer, and sang gospel music. I knew we had reached the students when several people commended me at the end of the summer celebration for working not only with the "toughest kids in the school" but also developing their leadership skills. Many teachers simply could not believe that these students, high on the suspension lists, had become so fully engaged by our programs.

Our play, *Bridge of Dreams,* featured performances by several learning-disabled students, young people who had never before felt they could learn lines. As we worked with them, we realized they were struggling to try to read the words on the page. We shifted gears. We used adults and peers as line coaches—reading to the young actors so they could learn their lines by ear. An extra-grueling weekend of practice with the line coaches produced a cast of confident actors.

All students who join West Virginia Dreamers sign a contract that commits them to (1) participate in the resiliency program; (2) take part in constructive, safe activities; and (3) formulate goals to improve their grades, attendance, and behavior. Successful participants receive a postsecondary education scholarship at the end of each "dream year."

Beyond funding from the U.S. Department of Education, we have several partners. Save the Children provides the student scholarships, the West Virginia Department of Health and Human Resources' Office of Behavioral Health Services conducts a self-advocacy training track, and the Department of Public Health offers programs in adventure education and nutrition. AmeriCorps workers joined us in the fall of 2000 to interact with the students and teachers during the school day, focusing on tutoring and other contract goals to help address the students' greatest resiliency challenges. AmeriCorps workers will also mentor these students who have received little positive feedback over the years.

Another effort to build resiliency in our young people centers on engaging the students' families. Family field trips provide entire families with positive, safe, drug-free experiences in new and exciting settings. While visiting Carter Caves in Kentucky, one parent exclaimed, "I'm going to get me a T-shirt, show people I've been someplace." When queried, she elaborated that she had never been farther from Lincoln County than the state capital, Charleston, and that was "only to go to the hospital." As parents support their children in exploring their dreams, we are finding many such unexpected ripples through our families and our schools. We are helping to build in these young people the stamina that will make them dare to dream dreams, dare to set goals, and dare to achieve those dreams.

Reaching Out to Families: A Rich Menu of Services for Our Community

by Janet Howell, Teacher, Atenville Elementary

President Clinton focused the nation's attention toward volunteerism and lifetime public service with the founding of AmeriCorps. Its goal was simple—to provide help where it was most needed. Atenville Elementary benefited from two Appalread[7] reading coaches, sponsored by Southern West Virginia Community College and West Virginia Reads. The reading coaches visit students' homes each week to model good homework strategies for parents as they tutor young children in reading.

A Maternal Infant Health Outreach Worker was added to our school in 1999. This AmeriCorps member visits expectant mothers as well as children from birth to age three. She provides parents with information on nutrition and child development and connects them with needed social service agencies. While on home visits, she models appropriate play activities that stimulate language development in the children. When needed, she leaves age-appropriate toys and books for the parents to use. Currently our outreach worker visits the homes of 20 babies each month.

To extend the outreach program, teachers also make home visits. They give parents information, invite them to events at school, discuss concerns about their children, and assess the family's needs for assistance in areas served by other agencies. By pulling together the total resources of our community, the program enables staff and parents to provide needed services for our children.

School *Within* Community: Build It and They Will Come

Visit Natcher Elementary on any given day, and you will find adults inside and out. Parents will be sharing lunch with their children in the inviting school cafeteria or assisting in many volunteer posts throughout the school. Fall and spring days may find parents planting bulbs or seedlings in one of the school's many gardens. Throughout the day, adults and children may be seen on the "Green Way" walking, jogging, or exercising at one of the stations constructed in cooperation with the local hospital. A closer look may find grandparents helping to maintain this expansive outdoor park that is also home to classroom gardens and a new arboretum. The grandparents may be working with other volunteers to develop the Monet Pond, which features water plants and shoreline landscaping. Or a group of students from Western Kentucky University may be participating in a special project—like the time they brought a milk cow to the front yard of the school to introduce many of the students to the first live cow they had ever met.

At Natcher, many generations come together to work and play and learn. The special places created throughout the school are the realization of a vision of principal Connie Allen. Allen values creating a physical environment that stimulates students and adults alike, and she realizes the importance of bringing the generations together in this

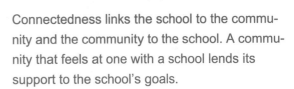

Connectedness links the school to the community and the community to the school. A community that feels at one with a school lends its support to the school's goals.

–Gene Maeroff

suburban school. Allen also understands the value of "taking the school" out to the community—especially to individuals who may be initially intimidated by school because of their own past experiences. Hence, Allen has worked with a community agency to establish a school community center in the housing project served by Natcher.

Allen is deeply cognizant of the importance of establishing a symbiotic relationship between the school and the broader community—to enrich the lives of both students and adults and to tell the school's story to the broader community. The intergenerational contacts nurtured by the Natcher community provide immeasurable benefits to the young students. Further, they serve to meaningfully engage adults in the life of the school. The serendipitous outcome is additional public support for the school—in the forms of both volunteer assistance and increased financial assistance when school bond issues are at question.

Natcher Elementary's relationship with its broader community offers evidence to support Gene Maeroff's argument that a school enhances the education of its students when it forms ties to the community. When this process draws together members of the community, chances increase that the network of support for youngsters—part of their social capital—will grow stronger. Affluent families find their own ways to make connections to schools their children attend. Less advantaged families, equally in need of such connectedness, usually require some help.[8]

The work of the Search Institute in Minneapolis, Minnesota,[9] is in keeping with this view. Since 1996 this agency has pursued its Healthy Communities/Healthy Youth initiative, which is grounded in a strong belief that intergenerational contacts are key to both the academic success and the social well-being of children and adolescents. Through an ambitious nationwide research effort, the Institute has validated the importance of 40 developmental assets to the positive development of young people.

All Kids Are Our Kids: What Communities Must Do to Raise Caring and Responsible Children and Adolescents by Peter Benson (San Francisco: Jossey-Bass Publishers, 1997).

In this book, Benson provides the theory and research underpinning the Search Institute's framework for developmental assets. Benson defines developmental assets as the core elements of healthy development; he relates these to the community actors (family, neighborhood, school youth organizations, congregations, and so forth) that are involved in promoting these building blocks. He identifies and elaborates on 40 developmental assets that research finds to be causative or predictive of healthy outcomes, including such factors as school success, affirmation of diversity, compassion for others, leadership, and choosing a healthy lifestyle.

Unfortunately, most adults are not aware of their potential importance to young people's performance. The growing isolation of schools from the communities they serve deprives students of resources that could make a critical difference in their lives. Natcher's initiatives that bring adults into contact with "other people's children" concurrently increase the number of developmental assets possessed by their students.

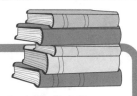

Beyond the intrinsic value to students of strong school-community relations is the long-recognized benefit of community involvement and support that increase both financial and human resources available to schools for achieving present and long-term goals. By the late twentieth century almost all schools had one or more "partners in education," a business or community organization providing financial and volunteer assistance to their adopted school. Likewise, most public schools sponsor an array of activities designed to promote parent volunteerism and involvement. Schools that increase the number of connections with their publics are more likely to have greater success in securing support for educational programs.

Inviting Family Involvement

Research confirms a strong, positive correlation between student achievement and family involvement. Many avenues are available for such involvement; Joyce Epstein's widely accepted model,[10] adapted by the National Parent Teacher Association (http://www.pta.org), categorizes strategies under the following purposes:

- regular and two-way *communication* between home and school
- development of *parenting skills* through workshops and other educational strategies
- parents supporting and assisting *student learning* at home
- opportunities to *volunteer* at the school
- participation in *decision making* and governance

Examples of these strategies for meaningful parent involvement are shared through stories from Quest schools.

Other People's Children by Lisa Delpit (New York: The New Press, 1993)

Author Lisa Delpit suggests many reasons why we have such a difficult time educating poor children, especially children of color. The author challenges the appropriateness of current classroom instructional methods—for example, process writing and whole language—as failing to meet the learning needs of most minority children. Delpit believes that adults from the children's home culture must be consulted to design appropriate and adequate instruction and makes a compelling case that, in the future, public education must accommodate diversity and eliminate all stereotypes, biased research, and racism. Only by removing these blinders will it be possible to reach and teach all children.

Book review by Pamela Dunigan, Teacher, Alexander Elementary

I have always looked at our school in terms of just my child. I now realize that our school is a community and that we all have to care about all the children for us to be successful.

—Parent, Natcher Elementary

Communicating Effectively with Parents

Communicating effectively with parents is important but extremely challenging. Most teachers don't feel skilled in this area or, if they do, fail to make it a priority. Either way, it often doesn't happen frequently or satisfactorily. Kathy Wheeler, a teacher at Natcher Elementary, discovered an innovative way around these problems.

Students write weekly letters to their parents, describing the work they have done that week and including topics such as the following: "what I really learned a lot about," "something I'm really proud of," "how I think I can do better," and "the way I think you can help me."

Speaking in Cursive

One spring, children's author Paul Brett Johnson gave a presentation to the Natcher Elementary student body. He detailed the entire process of producing an illustrated book for children, explaining such things as how four ink colors are layered to create the many colors in the illustrations. Following the assembly, a teacher asked one of the kindergarten girls if she had enjoyed Mr. Johnson's talk. She replied with an enthusiastic, "Oh, yes!" then went on to say, "but part of the time, you know . . . he was speaking in cursive." Principal Connie Allen reflected, "Several times since then I've thought how often we educators 'speak in cursive' to our students and to our parents. At Natcher, we now make special efforts to communicate in words and ways that everyone can understand.

Parents have an opportunity to write back with questions and comments. How better to enhance school-home communication than by putting students at the helm of the communication boat?

Student-led conferences are another effective way to increase communication with parents about student progress and to make students an integral part of the process.

At Alexander Elementary, parent attendance skyrocketed to nearly 95 percent when the school implemented student-led conferences instead of the more traditional parent-teacher conference. "I hadn't planned on coming, but my daughter worried the devil out of me—so here I am," one parent confessed to Principal Wiman.

In the age of instant communication, one would think that communication with parents would be a simple matter—write a note, pick up a telephone, or even send an e-mail. But in the mountains of West Virginia, communication with parents poses a difficult task for Atenville Elementary.

Our primary difficulty is simple economics. Some families within our attendance area cannot afford telephones. They depend on extended family members for telephone service. Internet access is available but not affordable for these same families. The most insurmountable difficulty, however, remains the high rate of illiteracy among our parents. We needed a way to communicate effectively with our parents and increase their involvement in their children's education.

In January 1992, the Atenville Elementary Phone Tree began service. A group of parent volunteers from each of Atenville's attendance areas meets monthly with the principal and parent coordinator to look at the upcoming month's calendar and to review information and concerns given to them by the parents in their attendance area. These phone tree parents in turn contact parents in their attendance areas to relay information from the meetings. They also mail calendars and information to parents who do not have phones. If school closes early or other emergency situations arise, the parent coordinator activates the phone tree to contact all parents.

As an extension to the phone tree, we have installed telephones in each teacher's classroom. Each day teachers call absent students. They also call parents with good news about students' behavior, as well as when students misbehave or fail to achieve their potential in class.

Vickie Luchuck, a teacher at Lumberport Elementary, contends that parents' highest interest is in knowing how they can best help their own child at home. The following story demonstrates how she helps them know.

During the course of her 23-year career, second-grade teacher Vickie Luchuck had often heard parents' concerns. "How much should I help with homework?" "I ask every night, but she tells me she doesn't have any." "What can I do to give my child some extra help?" "Does my second grader know what she should know?" With Title I monies, Vickie arranged to provide a workshop for parents in the fall of 1998. Tailored to their specific needs, the workshop

The student-led conferences have led down an avenue with which I was uncomfortable; however, I was intrigued by the empowerment and responsibility they were said to bring to the students. The benefits I have seen and the communication between student and parent are phenomenal.

—Mathew Brown, Teacher,
Natcher Elementary

Some teachers still make home visits. But it's rare, and it shouldn't be rare. It takes time in the beginning, but those teachers have a lot less trouble with discipline in the classroom and with kids feeling unknown, misunderstood, disconnected, and uncared for.

—Mary Poplin & J. Weeres,
Voices from the Inside

19

was all about homework—and what parent hasn't had questions or concerns about that? First, Vickie clarified the purposes of homework and let parents know what they could expect. For example, "If your child never has homework, you need to ask the teacher about it. The teachers at Lumberport assign some homework nearly every day." Then Vickie provided homework suggestions specific to each grade level at the school. Lots of good tips were provided, many available free from the Internet. Finally, most helpful of all, Vickie provided specific skills for parents: basic sight words for first and second graders, punctuation rules, multiplication facts, and a world map to name just a few. All comb-bound in a handy booklet, these ideas are a rich resource for families. Most important, her efforts communicate clearly: we're listening and responding to what you want!

Gwen Vance, one of many parent volunteers at Atenville Elementary, writes compellingly about her experiences as a volunteer.

I have been a parent volunteer at Atenville for about 12 years. During this time, I have witnessed many positive changes in the students as a result of an after-school tutoring program. I remember one young student who was very shy and withdrawn when she entered the modern dance class I taught. After only a couple of weeks, I watched this child gain confidence and open up to warmth and affection. She began to come to me for hugs and to tell me about things she liked and how much she enjoyed the class. Her outlook toward school, along with the attitudes of her classmates, became positive and enthusiastic.

In addition to modern dance, we offer creative writing, games, and computer instruction. We also arrange field trips, with activities such as canoeing, horseback riding, caving, college football games, musical theatre productions, and a variety of cultural events that simply are not available to most children who live in our rural area. For many children, the after-school tutoring program gives them the kind of help with their schoolwork that they don't receive at home. As tutors, we can make a big difference in their success in school and in the way they feel about themselves. Seeing a child learn how to feel good about himself makes me, as a volunteer, know I am doing something right. The rewards I receive from this work are more valuable to me than any monetary reward could ever be.

Vickie Luchuck, a teacher at Lumberport Elementary, relates the story of how she and her colleagues encouraged their students to read more books while drawing students and parents together for fun-filled activities.

In spring 1998, the staff at Lumberport struggled to discover ways to encourage our rural families to read to and with their children more often. We felt the need to get more quality literature into the homes of our children. We had already begun the Homeward Bound Books program that placed five paperback books in each child's personal home library each year. We knew this was successful because children were sometimes found reading their books in the lunchroom and on the playgrounds during recess. We still felt the need to have more involvement with parents.

We scheduled a Bingo for Books in an effort to get more parents into our school in a non-threatening way, engage parents and children in an activity together, promote the value of reading, and ensure that children had plenty of books available in their homes. We ordered books for all reading levels and interests; we borrowed the Bingo cards and materials from a local club; we advertised the event, talking it up with the students; and we waited. How many could come? Would it be successful?

Much to our amazement and delight, 120 parents and students crowded in for the two-hour bingo! Every student went home with at least one book; some took as many as five. More than 300 books found their way into the homes of our youngsters that night. The event was judged a great success, not only because so many attended, but because it brought a wider parent base into the building. We didn't have only our parent "regulars," we saw many parents we seldom see. We saw fathers. We saw grandparents. And *everyone* had fun and participated actively! Laughter and excitement glittered in the eyes of chil-

Family Connections—A Ready-Made Way to Connect with Families of Young Children

Most parents want to be involved in helping their children learn better; some don't know what to do and feel uncomfortable in the role of "teacher." To help parents—and to help schools who want to include parents in this important job—AEL has developed a series of 30 guides for parents.[11] Called *Family Connections,* the guides were designed so schools could send one home each week with young students (preschool through grade one). The colorful guides are attractive to parents and students alike; include a message for parents; have a read-aloud selection such as a poem, rhyme, or make-believe story; and include ideas for inexpensive activities that family members can do at home with their youngsters.

What I like best about using *Family Connections* is watching my children's faces light up and hearing the questions they ask.

—Parent

dren, parents, and teachers that night. Parents chatted with teachers; some stayed to help clean up; many asked when we would do it again.

Bingo for Books must become a new tradition at Lumberport. We have decided that even if we don't have money in the school budget, we will hold this activity with book exchanges, allowing students to bring in their old books and select different books for every "winning" bingo card.

Parents as Educational Partners: Improving School Climate

by Cheryl Dingess, Speech Therapist, Atenville Elementary

Parents have become such an integral part of our school that sometimes we forget the impact they have on every aspect of our school community. They help make almost all decisions concerning the day-to-day running of the school and are active in formulating the vision and goals we have for our students. At times, it seems that they are actually the ones in charge. They answer the telephone; help with playground duties; keep the lines of communication open between the school and the home; assist with MicroSociety; paint; replace bulletin boards; copy papers; make packets for presentations; clean; help organize and supervise talent shows, proms, and dances; and volunteer as tutors in the after-school program. They serve on the discipline committee, the Local School Improvement Council, the MicroSociety steering committee, the playground committee, the Quest team, and the action research team. They make home visits to help children with reading and to help new mothers feel a part of the community from the beginning. They attend professional development sessions and travel to conferences with the professional staff. They attend parent workshops to improve their computer skills and other skills necessary to help their children. The list can go on and on. But the biggest impact they have on the school is the warmth and caring that permeate the very fiber of the school community.

Because the parents are such an important part of our school community, we needed to provide a space for their activity. The faculty

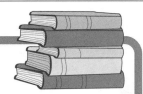

Workshop Series: Doing Your Part to Help Your Child Become SMART[12]

Parents want to help their children do better in school but often don't know what they should do. These six workshops offer tips on parenting SMART learners—continuous, lifelong learners who can adapt to rapid change and who possess characteristics associated with success in and out of school. Developed by AEL, the series provides
- information from current research and best practice
- learning activities that will actively engage parents in thinking and talking about important questions and issues
- time for parents to share with other parents
- activities to take home to use with children

Workshop 1: *What Are SMART Learners?*
Parents explore the five characteristics of SMART learners—Successful, Motivated, Autonomous, Responsible, and Thoughtful—and they learn how to support their children's development as SMART learners.

Workshop 2: *"S" is for Successful*
This session provides an introduction to brain-based learning and encourages parents to think with other parents about how to put this information into practice in the home.

Workshop 3: *"M" is for Motivated*
What can be done to help children develop internal motivation? Why do some children "self-start" and others wait for bribes or punishment before they become involved in the learning process? Participants look at current research and interact with other parents.

Workshop 4: *"A" is for Autonomous*
Parents learn how to identify and best support their children's learning strengths to help them become more independent learners.

Workshop 5: *"R" is for Responsible*
Workshop 5 addresses helping children become increasingly responsible.

Workshop 6: *"T" is for Thoughtful*
During this session, parents learn how their communications with their children can improve their ability to think through problems and topics. They consider how questioning, active listening, and modeling can encourage and support thinking.

lounge became the Family Center—a place where parents and professional staff could meet, eat lunch together, discuss school policies, problems, and cures. But it also became the heart of our school—the place students can go for a few words of comfort or for help with problems only a motherly hug could solve. It is not unusual to enter the school and see a parent, book in hand, sitting at the reading center with a small child beside her. Or to find a parent in the Family Center, helping a student with homework that had somehow been forgotten the night before. Neither is it unusual to hear a word of encouragement from a parent-tutor accompanying a student into a classroom for after-school tutoring.

Our load as educators is lightened because our parents share our vision and goals; they help with daily tasks; and they accept, along with us, responsibility to love our students and help them learn. Through our work together, we are changing the very essence of our community. Bonds have been built between community agencies and families. A way of life has been opened to the community that would have otherwise been unavailable. The Family Center has opened windows to the world, not only for our students but also for our families. Trust in education has been reestablished. High expectations for our children have been communicated to our parents and our students. Parents no longer accept the mediocre. They strive to make their children the best they can be.

Broadening the School-Community Connections

Another dimension of reaching out—beyond the immediate school family of parents, teachers, and staff—is the concept of community involvement. Pam Brown, former principal of Woodbridge Senior High, shares a story of the importance of helping teachers appreciate and honor the diversity of their student body by better understanding the communities in which their students live.

In a word, the Woodbridge Senior High neighborhood might be called *affluent*. Based on its beautifully manicured location, it is not surprising that new staff members often share a common misperception about the demographics of our student body. The largest senior high school in the state, we enroll students from 54 countries. Two teachers and a teacher assistant staff our English as a Second Language Center. Many of our students are educationally and economically disadvantaged.

I believed that it was critical for staff to understand the diversity of our student population and recognize it as an asset to our school. Three years ago, I borrowed the idea of taking new teachers on a tour of the school attendance area. Each August, the assistant principal who works with our at-risk students and I board an unairconditioned school bus with our new staff members. We leave the affluent area surrounding the school and go to areas where many of our students live—government-subsidized housing, Navy housing, low-income housing, homeless shelters, high-crime apartments, and townhouse subdivisions. This one trip speaks loudly to our teachers—certainly, it communicates about the needs of our diverse population much more clearly than my telling them.

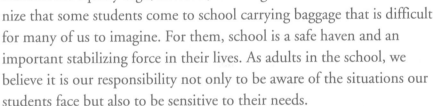

A neighborhood's connection to the school in its midst can bind children to education and lend cohesion to the community. With this sense of connectedness comes a feeling of ownership by the people whose support the school needs in order to thrive.

—Gene Maeroff

At Woodbridge, we try to ensure that the academic and behavioral expectations for all students are equally high; however, we recognize that some students come to school carrying baggage that is difficult for many of us to imagine. For them, school is a safe haven and an important stabilizing force in their lives. As adults in the school, we believe it is our responsibility not only to be aware of the situations our students face but also to be sensitive to their needs.

At the end of last year's new teacher tour, an individual who had recently retired from the military and whose children had attended our school, said in amazement, "Thank you so much. I never realized some of these areas existed in our town, much less that these students attended Woodbridge. I have worked only with the privileged through my coaching and my own children's activities. This [the tour] will be very helpful to me as I begin my teaching career."

Ann Watkins, former principal of Sewanee Elementary, writes about Friday School, a unique way to include community members with student learning.

Friday School is a four-week enrichment program held in late winter. Every student in grades K-6 gets the opportunity to interact with a talented community volunteer. Classes have included such things as puppetry, clowning, commercial writing, sculpture, cosmetology, and auto mechanics. Participation in this 20-year-old cornerstone program is eagerly anticipated not only by students, but also by faculty, parents, and community members.

Lots of preparation makes the effort successful. Months of planning go into scheduling and determining the classes that will have the greatest appeal to participants. Students make their choices for the class they will attend for one hour a week; parent volunteers coordinate the scheduling. Classroom teachers and staff help supervise the courses, some of which are held away from school grounds. Small classes of no more than six to eight students ensure individual attention.

At the close of the session, we hold an open house to celebrate our accomplishments, show the items students have made, and demonstrate new skills learned. Sewanee becomes a true community of learners. Volunteers take pride in sharing their interests and talents with the students. Students, school staff, and other citizens also revel in the fact that these Friday School sessions make learning meaningful.

Margaret Muth, a teacher at Our Lady of Fatima, shares a story of how community volunteers have enriched the lives of students.

At a board-teacher luncheon in 1996, several of our board members asked what improvement I would like to see in our school. I mentioned our playground, even though I did not think it would become a top priority. To my amazement, they established a playground committee the following year, forming a partnership with a local hospital. Through a $5,000 grant, St. Mary's Hospital helped establish a Project Fit America site.[13] Many volunteers gave countless hours to construct the fitness equipment. The playground enriches our school and our community, as children receive instruction during the school day and families enjoy it after hours.

Lives are touched by community volunteers through the mentoring program described by Janis Truex, school counselor at Alexander Elementary.

The Alexander Mentoring Program reaches students who lack a nurturing home environment and who could benefit from a weekly one-on-one visit with an adult. Academic assistance is not an essential part of this program. We focus more on building a supportive, caring relationship between each student and an adult from our community.

Teachers recommend students for participation. Once parents give permission, the counselor matches the child with a compatible mentor. Our business partners and a local sorority provide the volunteers for the "lunch buddies" program. The business partners encourage employees to participate and allow them time away from work to eat lunch at school with their buddies. The first visit takes place in the child's classroom so that student, teacher, and mentor can interact. We ask for a year's commitment in order to provide consistency for the students. Mentors plan lunch once a week with their buddies; special lunch buddy tables in the hall offer participants the chance to eat away from the noise of the cafeteria.

Our students benefit from the lunch buddy program because they develop rapport with their mentors and look forward to the special attention they receive. Often, long-term student/mentor relationships develop. Sometimes, simply having a kind, calm "buddy" to talk to means all the difference for a troubled child.

Healthy communities for children and adolescents are places with a shared commitment to care for young people.

—Peter Benson

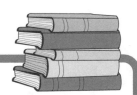

Altered Destinies: Making Life Better for Schoolchildren in Need by Gene Maeroff (New York: St. Martin's Press, 1999).

Maeroff introduces his powerful book with the following words: "Of all the riches denied to disadvantaged children, perhaps the most important have to do with the absence of a network of support that would allow them to thrive in school. The lack of this network and of the norms and values that underpin it places their education at risk from the day they first walk into classrooms across the United States." Maeroff adopts the term *social capital,* popularized by James S. Coleman, to talk about the kinds of relationships that help children develop the norms and trust that enable them to function effectively inside and outside of school. As he explores this theme, he elaborates on the concept of connectedness, which he believes critical to children's development of social capital.

27

Valuing Community—in Learning and in Celebration

The legendary Foxfire story has been touted by educators and philosophers alike as an incredible portrait of the power of celebrating the culture of a community to awaken the artist, the poet, the inventor in every child.

> Daily our grandparents are moving out of our lives, taking with them, irreparably . . . information . . . not because they want to, but because they think we don't care. And it isn't happening just in Appalachia. . . . If this information is to be saved at all, for whatever reason, it must be saved now; and the logical researchers are the grandchildren, not university researchers from the outside. In the process, these grandchildren (and we) gain an invaluable, unique knowledge about their own roots, heritage, and culture.[14]

Foxfire originated in the Rabun Gap-Nacooche School in Georgia, but this kind of learning can occur in any community, once the decision is made to ferret out the "foxfires" (tiny organisms that glow in the dark and are frequently seen in the shaded coves of the mountains) inherent to that place, to embrace their invaluable impact on its society, and to cherish their incandescent brilliance as a means of preserving what that community holds dear. Today, many educators have adopted the Foxfire concept in their classrooms.

The Appalachian Festival at South Harrison High

by Jane Byrd, Teacher, South Harrison High

In May 1998, as chair of the English department, I helped coordinate our first schoolwide Appalachian Festival. Appalachian history is part of the junior English curriculum; but, more important, it is typified by our local community's history. As I planned this first experience, I contacted local residents, inviting their participation. Stations throughout the school gymnasium contained artifacts from the past. They were designed to engage students in learning by doing. Exhibits included Appalachian clothing, food, games, wooden toys, and various arts and crafts such as quilting, canning, spinning, and glass making. There were demonstrations of mountain music, apple butter making, whittling, and folk dancing. Storytellers shared the history of Harrison County and of coal mining. The day was a great one; and students actively engaged themselves with community members, learning about their shared heritage.

Atenville Elementary takes seriously the job of connecting with families and community.

In the fall of 2000, Bridge of Dreams, a major festival at Atenville Elementary, culminated a yearlong effort to use the arts to document the community's history. The event, coordinated by an artist-in-residence, featured 25 original pieces of script and song, written and performed by students and community members to celebrate the community of Harts.

Highland County Elementary and Highland County High—the only two schools in a small, rural community—recently moved and are now consolidated on a single campus. Katherine Ralston tells how the school serves as the center of the community in an annual celebration of their maple syrup industry.

Buckwheat cakes and maple syrup. You can smell the aromas as soon as you enter the school—and thousands do during the county's annual Maple Festival that celebrates the production of maple syrup during two weekends in March. Our students are involved in the festival in various ways, but primarily through the money-making efforts of preparing and selling pancakes and buckwheat cakes. Proceeds finance the senior trip for the high school and classroom supplies for the elementary school. Each school reaps between $3,500 and $6,000, a substantial amount of money for our small schools. The schools are truly the center of this small community, where most of the land is federal forest land. But, especially during this event, schools are the center of activity. Tourists come from far and near; locals and visiting artisans sell their wares in the school gym. Student work is displayed; the school shines with pride.

School *as* Community: The Ties That Bind

Community is the tie that binds students and teachers together in special ways, to something more significant than themselves: shared values and ideals. It lifts both teachers and students to higher levels of self-understanding, commitment, and performance—beyond the reaches of the shortcomings and difficulties they face in their everyday lives. Community can help teachers and students be transformed from a collection of "I's" to a collective "we," thus providing them with a unique and enduring sense of identity, belonging, and place.

Thomas Sergiovanni makes a compelling argument for school as community. He develops a case for making "community building . . . the heart of any school improvement effort."[15] Earl Wiman, principal of Alexander Elementary, has facilitated the building of community in this inner-city school in a myriad of ways over the course of a decade. Walk into the school and you will literally feel the "we-ness" that permeates its occupants. Such has not always been the case. Wiman carefully selected and implemented a variety of instructional, professional development, and support services that enabled the emergence of the "we" over time.

Alexander Elementary is a place "where students and adults alike are engaged as active learners in matters of special importance to them and where everyone is thereby encouraging everyone else's learning"[16] in the manner envisioned by Roland Barth. For example, each morning at Alexander begins with every student and adult engaging in "AAA"— Alexander's Awesome Arithmetic. A hands-on approach to learning math facts, Wiman instituted this program in an effort to focus schoolwide attention and commitment to increasing students' mathematics competencies. Walk down the halls and you will see the walls adorned with posters featuring life-sized photographs of Alexander students. Interspersed among posters of Michael Jordan and Oprah Winfrey, the smiling faces of Alexander's students encourage one another to read and succeed. This is just one strategy employed as a part of the school's involvement in the Accelerated Reading Program. During the 1998-99 school year Alexander students read more than 13,000 books.

Alexander's learning community can also be viewed as a "community of inquirers," where "expert" and "learner" have become artificial distinctions and "everyone is asked to venture into the realm of curiosity together."[17] The professional development activities at Alexander provide poignant examples of this. Included among these have been a long-term focus on improving questioning skills of teachers and higher-order thinking skills of students through implementation of the QUILT program[18] and a focus on improving writing instruction and student writing competencies through teacher and student engagement in Structured Reflection Protocol.[19] These two programs have encouraged faculty and staff to "deprivatize their practice" via peer observations and partnering and to engage in public dialogue and reflection about instructional methods. The Alexander faculty and staff have, under Wiman's leadership, been on a journey to enrich their community and in the process have come to "value the collective process of discovery and [the] value of living with their questions."[20]

> In schools that are becoming communities, connections are based on commitments, not trades. Teachers and students are expected to do a good job not so that they can get rewards but because it is important to do so. Discipline policies are norm-based, not just rule-based as in ordinary schools.
>
> —Thomas Sergiovanni

Five Traits That Foster Community

School as community differs significantly from the traditional view of school as a hierarchical organization in many ways. Pages from the Alexander story illustrate five of the traits strongly associated with *school as community*.

1. **Shared values reflect democratic principles.** One of Wiman's greatest "prouds" is Alexander's inclusion program that intentionally places special education students into regular classrooms thus "including" them in the school community. Alexander implemented this program prior to outside mandates. According to Wiman, the school moved to truly heterogeneous classrooms "because it's the right thing to do." Observe one of special education teacher Heather Pflasterer's classes and you'll leave convinced that inclusion is not

only the right thing to do from a moral perspective, but also from an instructional perspective. Pflasterer, a QUILT-trained teacher, holds every student accountable for fully engaging in all activities. And the outside observer would be hard pressed to differentiate between the special education students and the mainstream students.

2. **Members are bound by personal relationships and ideals.**
   Sergiovanni believes that "schools are moral communities more akin to families" and that "moral connections come from the duties teachers, parents, and students accept, and the obligations they feel toward others and toward their work."[21] One crisp fall morning a nine-year-old came to Wiman's office after being tardy to school. He related his story of finding a gun on his regular pathway to school. Rather than pass by or even pick up the gun, he ran home to have his Mom call the police. As he explained to Wiman, "I was just doing what you've told us to do." Taking care of one another is a strong norm at Alexander—whether it's the principal "giving away" one of his female teachers at her wedding, teachers being available for after-school tutoring, or older students mentoring one another. Individuals are "bonded together" by a complex web of personal relationships; they are bound to "a set of shared ideals and principles."[22]

> Success must be judged in terms of schools' becoming more educative, socially just, caring, or participatory, as well as improving on the conventional indicators.
>
> —Jeannie Oakes, Karen Quarts, Steve Ryan, & Martin Lipton

3. **Students and teachers are co-learners.** Within a school community exists a number of subcommunities whose characteristics and behaviors affect the broader community. Included among these are *classroom communities* and the *professional learning community*. Schools attempting to build a learning community address the nature and extent to which community exists in classrooms and embrace a vision of "democratic classrooms."[23] "*Individual choice, responsibility, and self-control* are traits of the democratic classroom."[24] Pflasterer's inclusion classes reflect these traits. At Alexander, faculty demonstrate qualities of the type of professional learning community hailed by Shirley Hord, Linda Darling-Hammond, Milbrey McLaughlin, Judith Little, and others.[25] Grade-level groups provide a structure for experimenting with new norms and behaviors in small, safe, collegial

clusters. For example, the fourth-grade teachers at Alexander pioneered the use of Structured Reflection Protocol with Wiman's facilitation and support. Their experience with this form of learning in community was so positive that the strategy is now being used by the faculty as a whole to create more effective ways to teach higher levels of thinking.

4. **Trust and respect permeate all relationships.** Trust and respect are essential to the effective functioning of Structured Reflection Protocol, peer observations, and other processes that help build professional learning community. In the pursuit of shared goals for learning, staff use inquiry and reflection-in-action as a way of doing business—constantly seeking incremental improvements in practice that will increase successful learning for all students. A sense of true *collegiality* and *collaborative working patterns* replace congeniality and isolation. Likewise, trust and respect characterize relationships between and among teachers and students. Fourth-grade students learned to use Structured Reflection Protocol as a way to promote individual reflection and peer editing. Listening to these young students orally critique one another's work confirms the power of peer relationships in the academic arena.

> Relationships in community are characterized by the kinds of emotions—personalization, authenticity, caring and unconditional acceptance—found in families, extended families, neighborhoods, and other social organizations.
> —Thomas Sergiovanni

5. **Community boundaries are inclusive.** In schools where staff and students share a common vision for the school and a commitment to shared goals for learning, the potential is great for attracting parents and other adults outside the school—not only as volunteers for special functions, but as committed members of the learning community. The nature of this commitment is such that these adults believe deeply that they can make a difference for students. In such an environment, they—with other members of the community—ask "what if" questions as they seek to help provide those conditions that will enable continuous improvement. Because of the inclusive nature of the school community, they do not feel or act as outsiders, but as an integral part of the community.

These traits do not appear overnight; rather, they develop over time as people become bound together by a shared vision, values, beliefs, and a common and compelling set of goals focused upon increasing achievement for all students. Wiman attempted to "push the envelope" in this area in the fall of 1997, when he worked with AEL's Quest staff to facilitate a community-wide examination of the extent to which Alexander was meeting the mission and goals included in its school improvement plan. Using the Data in a Day process, Wiman brought together 28 teachers, students, support staff, parents, and community members to observe in classrooms and share and analyze their findings.[26] Among the role types included with teachers, students, and parents in this unique self-study were local ministers, the school crossing guard, and a school cafeteria worker. The trust and respect characterizing the communications among this diverse cross section of the school community were a testimony to the inclusiveness that has been cultivated over the years.

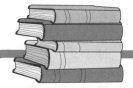

A New Vision for Staff Development by Dennis Sparks and Stephanie Hirsh (Alexandria, VA: ASCD, 1997).

The authors describe a new paradigm for staff development grounded in current research and best practice and intended to help teachers change practice. Included among the features of this new vision are learning in community, job-embedded learning, results-driven professional development, and a school-focused approach. The authors, who hold leadership positions in the National Council for Staff Development, clearly articulate the major principles of this emerging approach and illustrate these through inclusion of case studies from actual schools.

Learning in Community—Broadening the Definition of Professional Development and Collegiality

In most schools, teachers work with students but rarely with other adults. Individual teachers typically wrestle with questions and issues related to lesson designs, instructional decisions, assessment quandaries, and classroom management issues in isolation from a broader collegial group. The "egg carton" metaphor is an apt one for school organization, each teacher being separated from colleagues by classroom walls, school schedules, and time-honored norms that reinforce patterns of practice.

Two emerging themes in professional development are challenging the "Lone Ranger" approach to teacher practice: these are the deprivatization of practice and job-embedded learning. Both advance the notion of professional learning community, which is characterized by new teacher roles, relationships, and responsibilities. Deprivatization refers to practices that bring teachers out of their individual classrooms into exchanges with colleagues. For example, in professional learning communities teachers reflect together, dialogue around issues central to teaching and learning, share challenges as well as successes, focus on student work, and the like. Whether talking together about effective strategies for engaging the unmotivated student or observing and being observed for the purpose of giving and receiving feedback, teachers are beginning to look to colleagues for assistance, support, and solutions.

> As recent research has argued, the possibilities for individual teacher learning increase greatly as professional communities move from individualistic or balkanized cultures to "collaborative" cultures and towards what can be described as "learning communities."
>
> —Linda Darling-Hammond
> & Milbrey McLaughlin

Job-embedded learning integrates professional development with the daily issues of teaching and learning—centering professional learning on students and their performance. Job-embedded learning is to teachers what authentic learning is to students. In both cases, learning is problem centered and focused on real—not "made-up"—work. Job-embedded professional development moves into the mainstream of daily practice; no longer is it scheduled as 90-minute, after-school sessions or in-service days. Job-embedded learning also brings students into the loop as teachers engage them in assessment and design activities that help them think about how they best learn. The vision becomes one of individual classrooms as communities of learning and practice, each of which is a component of the larger learning organization.

Learning in community is a radical departure from traditional models of staff development, and this change doesn't "just happen" spontaneously. Rather, school leaders commit to a new philosophy and approach to professional growth and development and provide both the vision and the resources—including time, training in new strategies, and materials—to support this transformation in practice. Not only do teachers and their students benefit directly from this type of collaborative work, the nature and quality of the school community change. Stories from Woodbridge Senior High and Alexander Elementary illustrate two different models for learning in community.

Now, They're Our Kids

In high schools, it's not uncommon for teachers to be competitive, wondering, "Did 'my' students do as well as others' students?" About two years ago, the instructors of 11th-grade English at Woodbridge Senior High faced a challenge that caused them to begin working as a team—no longer seeing "my" students and "your" students—looking for ways to improve instruction that would benefit *all* students. As they struggled together, sharing ideas and learning together, they were transformed.

The story behind this community-making? The Prince William County School Board mandated the successful completion of a 14-step research paper in 11th-grade Engish as a graduation requirement beginning in 1998. Students' research papers were to be scored by external assessors. The rubric had to be learned

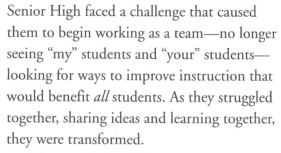

One of the things that I've learned in the last two years [being involved in protocol] is the benefits of teamwork. We take time to look at each other's papers. I'm walking away with a sheet of ideas from other teachers. Being able to work together as a team gives me so many more options.

—Dawn Moulen, English Teacher, Woodbridge High

quickly by teachers; the first papers were due a mere two months after the mandate became effective. Faced with a steep learning curve and students' graduation on the line, the school administration concurred with the teachers that they needed time for working together on this effort. Structured Reflection Protocol seemed an appropriate tool; 11th-grade English teachers used the structure as a way to talk together about fine-tuning instruction related to the 14 steps. Their concern, as they continued to work together in the second year, was "How can we help 'our' students pass and excel?" It truly became a synergistic team effort.

The winners? Certainly the teachers, because they developed trusting relationships, learned new skills, and felt a satisfying sense of accomplishment as they met the challenge. But the big winners were the students, whose achievement as a group of 11th graders sky-rocketed. Of the more than 400 research papers submitted in the spring of 1999, all but 23 passed. Of those students who did not pass on the first attempt, 15 students successfully appealed.

Protocol helps participants because they're able to draw on the expertise of the older teachers, but what you find happening is that there's a very protective atmosphere that evolves. Instead of older teachers standing aside and saying, "Oh, I remember when I did that," and "Isn't that funny?" or "Isn't that endearing?" they run to their rescue and they begin to give them support. They talk them through the difficulties they're having and provide assistance and strategies and, in some cases, materials. So, it provides a marvelous support system. For the older teachers, it acts as a sense of renewal.

—Mary Ann Hardebeck, former Assistant Principal, Woodbridge Senior High

I've never seen a group that shares as easily. Everybody helps facilitate everybody else. I've yet to go to any of my colleagues and ask a question and not get help. I think that communicates itself into the classroom.

—Jerry Cavanaugh, First-Year Teacher, Woodbridge High

Increasing Higher-Order Thinking Skills through a Community-Wide Focus

During the 1996-97 school year, teachers at Alexander Elementary embarked on a new course of professional learning that involved working with a "partner" to improve classroom questions and questioning strategies. Partners went into one another's classrooms, observed agreed-upon student and teacher behaviors, and provided feedback to one another following the observations. Partners also met with their colleagues at monthly "collegiums" where they shared successes and dialogued about problems encountered as they attempted to transform their classrooms into more interactive, inclusive arenas for student learning. How did this professional learning experience differ from most of their past staff development activities? In a number of important ways. First, everyone—all grades, both teachers and paraprofessionals—focused on the same improvement objectives. Second, teachers were leading their own professional growth experience. A team of teachers had attended a summer training-of-trainers institute that provided them with the knowledge and skills to implement this program back home with their colleagues. Third, partners learned from one another through observations and dialogue and with their colleagues during the collegiums. Finally, this professional learning experience was not a one-shot workshop; it extended over the course of an entire school year with follow-up into the future.

Another special trait of this professional learning experience was that teachers taught their students the new vocabulary and behaviors that were at the heart of this program. Alexander students know that "wait time" provides the opportunity for thinking about one's own and classmates' answers to questions. They are also aware that attentive listening will enable them to "piggyback" on a classmate's response and move a discussion to a higher level of thinking. Young students know about Benjamin Bloom's taxonomy and understand what is meant by thinking at "higher cognitive levels." In addition to these and other desired behaviors, students are learning new norms for classroom interaction: "We learn best when we formulate and ask our own questions," and "When we share talk time, we demonstrate respect and we learn from one another."

The professional development program? Questioning and Understanding to Improve Learning and Thinking (QUILT), a nationally validated program that has been adopted by hundreds of schools across the nation.[27] Teacher response to this collegial form of learning acknowledges the value of learning in community: "Being involved in QUILT has been a highlight of my 17-year teaching career. I now see more than ever that I'm not a teacher alone in the classroom, but an integral part of the whole educational system."

Five years after the initial training at Alexander, the faculty continues to draw on their QUILT experience to push their students to even higher levels of thinking. As they strive to help students increase perfor-mance on required state tests, they think together about how they can help young learners become more reflective and facile in making connections that lead to higher levels of understanding. The Alexander faculty is now using Structured Reflection Protocol to think together about how to address gaps between student achievement goals and

Available evidence suggests that students' academic achievement is greater in schools where teachers report high levels of collective responsibility for student learning.

—Judith Warren Little

student performance. Both QUILT and Structured Reflection Protocol have provided the Alexander faculty with structures that facilitate the "sharing of personal practice," a critical attribute of professional learning community.[28]

Building Classroom Community

"Who are we?" and "What matters?" are critical community-forming questions. "When we don't answer these questions as a com-munity, when we have no agreements about why we belong together, the institutions we create to serve us become battlegrounds that serve no one."[29] This is no less true for classrooms than for churches, civic clubs, governments, and other agencies. Classroom teachers who are intentional about answering these questions with their students create an environment of genuine connectedness, caring, and trust, as the two stories that follow clearly illustrate.

A Teacher Talks to Her Students About "Family"

by Katherine Ralston, Teacher, Highland Middle School

At the beginning of the school year, I talk with each of my classes about "family." Even though my students come from various kinds of families, I try to find some common ground. Then I tell my students that in the following ways we will function as a family in my classroom: we will be together several days each week; we will eat a meal together every day; we will study together; we will play together. I let them know that if I announce, "This is a family thing," everyone must participate. No one can decline.

I use the term sparingly. If the class is lethargic and I decide to break for deep breaths and knee bends, some students invariably resist, but when I announce, "It's a family thing," everybody gets up and gets energized. But there are other times when I specifically say, "This is not a family thing. Only participate if you feel like it."

I use the "family thing" all year to hold down distracting discussion. There are often a few moans at the announcement, but secretly my middle schoolers like being involved in our family.

Sometimes, when I announce a new activity, students will tell me to make it a family thing. At other times, when they are presenting their own work to their classmates, they will include "family thing" activities.

The need for community is universal. A sense of belonging, of continuity, of being connected to others and to ideas and values that make our lives meaningful and significant—these needs are shared by all of us.

—Thomas Sergiovanni

Genuine connectedness imbues students with a sense of wanting to be a part of the school.

—Gene Maeroff

"Thumper Rule" Teaches Students Respect

by Kathy Wheeler, Teacher, Natcher Elementary

Kathy Wheeler, a fourth-grade teacher at Natcher Elementary, uses the "Thumper Rule" in her classroom to help students learn to respect each other.

Most of my classes are very heterogeneous—ranging from emotionally disturbed to gifted and talented. Oftentimes, this can present imposing challenges as I seek to build community across diverse individuals. I have found that rules, roles, and responsibilities help build a sense of "we-ness" among these students while helping them develop mutual respect and understanding.

Classroom structure is very important. Everyone has a job to do: attendance clerk, paper passer, TV/VCR operator, errand runner, etc. They do these jobs well, and when we change jobs about every four weeks, they train the next person to assume their responsibilities. Students sit in groups of five, and each has a job within the group: quiet captain, coach, reader, checker, recorder. This approach works well when engaging in cooperative group activities. Since the Jaguar is the school mascot, I assign a different colored jaguar paw print to each group and place the appropriately colored paws on the students' desks.

Classroom rules are also important. We have a Thumper Rule in our room that states, "If you can't say anything nice, don't say anything at all." We don't have to share everything we think! Respect is extremely important for self and for others. Honesty is also stressed in our classroom. We are currently engaged in a program called Second Step,[30] which deals with empathy, impulse control, and anger management and helps students develop norms and behaviors consistent with our classroom rules. These strategies help develop a positive learning environment and a caring and connected community.

Success and the Human Connection

by Alice Phillips, Teacher, Sewanee Elementary

I once worked for a short time at a regional junior high school as a special education assistant. Every day we would try to work on homework or classwork that students had not done and usually did not want to do. This is not a disclosive age, so I rarely was able to tell when I was successful at teaching what I was trying to teach. But one success story came back to me through another teacher and has stayed with me for many years.

This story involves a young man in the ninth grade. He was the only student I had in this time slot. I tried to keep him focused on his work, but probably half of our time together was in conversation that had nothing to do with school. Day after day he would arrive without his work and I would sigh and shake my head and tell him I was disappointed, and then I would struggle to help him get the work done. One day I finally just ran out of patience. I was so exasperated that I paced the room, shaking my hands in the air, and raising my voice to a near shout, saying, "Why are you doing this to me? I work so hard, and you come in here every day with nothing!"

All through my tirade, he sat passively, watching me almost curiously. When I stopped, he just said, "Why do you care?" I said, "I don't know. I just like you, that's all." He never said anything else. He took his books and left without a word. The next day it was almost as if nothing had happened, but he had a little of his work done when he came to me. I just picked up where he had left off and, together, we got it done.

It must have been about a month later when, early one morning, his biology teacher appeared at my door. She said, "I don't know what you did, but whatever it was, it worked. For the first time ever, he is actually walking the halls of this school with books in his hand. And, he's getting his work done! Whatever you did, thank you!"

What had I done? I had yelled and ranted and been angry! But, most important, I had cared, genuinely cared, about him as an individual. I cared enough to get mad and let him know how his behavior affected me.

Student Assignment to Homeroom

by Annette Graves, Glenda Lewis, and Pat Jones,
Teachers, Alexander Elementary

In May of each year, grade groups meet for the purpose of making homeroom assignments for the next school year. The teachers assign the students who are in their homeroom classes in the spring to a homeroom in the next grade level. Student placement is based upon a number of considerations such as academic achievement, special education needs, discipline concerns, race, gender, and parent request.

We place high-, average-, and low-achieving students in each homeroom to foster the best classroom environment and enable the homeroom teacher to use peer tutoring, cooperative learning groups, and other strategies. Special education students are carefully placed in a limited number of homerooms to make it easier for special education teachers to meet the needs of their students as well as to assist homeroom teachers with modifications of the curriculum to meet IEP goals. We attempt to balance homerooms by gender and race and to avoid placing students with the same first names in the same homeroom.

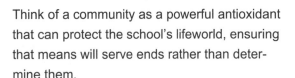

Think of a community as a powerful antioxidant that can protect the school's lifeworld, ensuring that means will serve ends rather than determine them.

—Thomas Sergiovanni

We avoid some discipline problems by placing students who do not get along in different homerooms, and we consider pairing students with special behavior problems with teachers who have had success handling similar problems. Teachers have stated that having teachers assign students to homerooms works better than having the principal make the assignments because the teachers are most familiar with student behavior and academic needs.

One advantage to placing students in homerooms before the school year begins is that homeroom rolls are available before the summer break. Even though there may be some drops and adds in the fall, having the class roll in advance makes the beginning of the school year go much more smoothly.

Our ultimate desire is to increase our students' learning to its highest potential. By carefully deciding the make-up of our homeroom classes, we are creating an environment where that potential can be realized.

Taking It to the Classroom Community: A Teacher's Story[31]

by Denise Greenhalgh, Teacher, Fairview Elementary School, Portland, Oregon

"What am I doing wrong?" was a question I found myself asking a lot. It was my first year teaching in a new school, and in a new state, for that matter. I had the most frustrating class of my short, seven-year teaching career. "Kids can't be that different from those in Arizona," I kept telling myself. I had a group of 27 fourth- and fifth-grade students who didn't let a day pass without showing some kind of disrespect.

I had many class meetings, sometimes more than one a day, to address the "issues" that plagued our room. Nothing seemed to help. I found myself questioning whether my choice to be a teacher was a good one. Classroom management has never been my strongest area, nor is it my weakest; but this year I was falling on my face. The school's veteran teachers viewed me as a new teacher with no behavior standards. I had a class that made me look like a referee instead of a teacher.

By spring, I was close to giving up trying to get into students' heads to find out what the problem was in our room. Luckily, my principal had attended a School Change Collaborative meeting where he learned about focus groups.[32] He brought back his learning to another fourth/fifth-grade teacher and myself. Together, we strategized how to use the focus group procedure with our students.

We determined we would conduct a preparatory survey, asking the kids six questions that we hoped would allow them to respond openly and honestly about their school experience. Right away, I just knew they would be negative. When the principal handed me the surveys, I wasn't sure I was ready for the truth—that I was failing miserably as a teacher.

After the surveys were completed, we asked the students to read their classmates' responses. We asked them to take notes on the things that stood out to them. Then we brought the two classes together, and they reported their findings to each other. It was an amazing process. Each child shared one response to each question until no one had anything else to say.

I was scribe, recording what the children shared and looking for themes that surfaced. The theme of *safety* surfaced. My students weren't feeling safe. Then came *relationships*—respect for gender, race, values, and loyalty. Some of these things I hadn't thought a problem in my room. Last, but not least, came the theme of *learning*. Children weren't feeling valued for their academic efforts. They wanted personal feedback on how they were doing—were their efforts good enough in the teacher's eyes? Some feelings around the theme of "learning" were based on what was taking place in other classrooms and areas of the school. I was amazed at how much this group valued having a positive learning experience. I had thought I had an apathetic bunch that just didn't care about school.

I remember sitting at my desk at the end of the focus group day with new understanding of where the kids were coming from. My eyes were opened. I finally had a glimpse into what these kids were thinking and feeling.

I would love to say that empowering the students to have voice in that focus group cured all that ailed us last year, but it didn't. However, it gave me an awareness of where my kids were; and, most important, they felt they were heard.

Half of my class returned this year; last year's fourth graders are now my fifth graders. The first class meeting of the year we came up with class agreements and consequences. It was then that I was able to see how the focus group helped my kids talk about what they needed for a positive learning experience. My fifth graders shared with our new fourth graders their experience from the previous year. When discussing class agreements, my fifth graders wanted to make sure that our room was safe and full of respect so learning could go on.

This year has been amazing. My students have taken control of their environment, and it has been wonderful. I couldn't be more pleased. I find myself using mini-versions of the focus group tool in weekly class meetings. I want the students to feel they have a voice all the time—not just once a year. Over time, I see their skills growing. They are well on their way to being better communicators and are ready to take on new challenges as a community of learners.

Win-Win: Inclusion at Alexander Elementary

by Martha Myers, Ruby Vaulz, and Cindy Hodge, Teachers, Alexander Elementary

In some schools, special and regular education personnel co-exist side-by-side but do not truly work together. Teachers have separate classrooms and work with different curricular materials, and scarce resources are hoarded rather than shared. At Alexander Elementary, special education is viewed as a service, not a place. With this idea in mind, Alexander faculty and staff began including special education students in regular classrooms in 1994. Alexander's inclusion program involves bringing the support services to the child.

The faculty and staff at Alexander work together as a team, utilizing many strategies to help all children learn cooperatively and take the threat out of the learning process. Teachers and administrators develop and use cooperative learning strategies to provide opportunities for all students. We deliver integrated support services in the general education setting. We anticipate difficult behaviors and intervene before they happen. We feel that students should learn together at their own rates. All students can learn and succeed; and we encourage parents to have hopes, dreams, and goals for their children.

Before the mandatory spring team meetings, planning of the schedule and class rosters ensures the smooth transition from the current grade and teacher to the next year's grade and teacher. By assigning students to general education classroom teachers prior to the spring planning meetings, we create a team of personnel who have current experience with a student, as well as teachers who will have future experiences with this child. Teachers share and cooperate to help the student. What could be an anxious and uncertain time for students, parents, and teachers becomes a powerful tool for successfully transitioning special education inclusion students.

Students with disabilities benefit in a number of ways from being included in the general education classroom. The special education students increase self-esteem by experiencing increased opportunities to develop meaningful friendships and appropriate social skills with peers in the general education classroom. They practice learned skills, including communication skills, in real-life situations. They learn part(s) of the general education curriculum and perhaps pursue a special interest. The inclusion students become more aware of their environment and learn to do things not typically found in the special education setting.

Students without disabilities benefit from being educated with diverse learners because they learn to understand disabilities and lose their fear of human differences. The opportunity to peer tutor a classmate with a disability increases the academic skills. By meeting the challenges of real-life situations, the general education student increases problem-solving and collaborative skills.

Parents also benefit from their children's inclusion in the general education classroom. Their children are given the same opportunities to be involved in the normal development of academics, social, or vocational skills as their peers. Parents gain a more positive view of special education services since no negative stigma is attached to a particular child or the service provided through the inclusion program. Students remain with their nonhandicapped peers in the regular classroom. Parents more readily see gains, especially when their children require decreasing amounts of special service or none at all.

Inclusion may not be the best thing for every student; that decision must be made by professional educators and parents. But for those who can be included, the program could be the key to helping them integrate into society and lead more normal, self-supporting lives in the future. The extra effort required to make inclusion work is a good investment in every student's future and society's future as well. Inclusion is an important part of community, providing a positive learning experience for all students.

Creating Connections across Classrooms: Schoolwide Community

One way to build schoolwide community is to facilitate relationships between and among students across grade levels. Mentoring programs that connect younger students to older students promote this end. The stories below relate how two schools approach mentoring. Community comes from "communion." It means "of one heart and one mind." Its symbol is the circle.

—Peter Block

Ann Watkins, former principal, and Alice Phillips, teacher, from Sewanee Elementary, describe a plan to team their lower-grade and upper-grade students to increase connectedness and enrich learning opportunities for all students.

A number of years ago a sixth-grade teacher and a third-grade teacher brought their students together occasionally to read or work on projects. Soon, other teachers began to discuss the benefits of this collaborative work. So, in the spring of 1995, the idea of pairing up classes of older and younger students was written into our school's improvement plan. The teachers made the decision to pair first with fourth graders, second with fifth graders, and third with sixth graders. The kindergarten classes were paired with both third and sixth graders. The teachers then worked collaboratively in multigrade pairs to decide what the partner classes would do together. Within each of the paired classes, individual students were assigned mentor partners. Once a week, or whenever planned, students would meet with mentors. One class would go to the partner classroom, or the classes might split so that half went into one room and half into the other.

Each six weeks, the entire school focused on one word, beginning with the word "mentor" and continuing with "courageous," "expecta-tions," "respect," "humor," and finally "reflection." The focus word for each term was highlighted on a banner flying over the Magical World of Learning castle in the school lobby. Study of the focus word took many forms. To exemplify the word "expectations," each student depicted on a paper quilt square what he or she expected to be doing in 20 years. These squares now reside in the Archives of the University of the South.

Throughout the year, a variety of events and activities provided numerous opportunities to recognize the learning that was occurring. Once, while studying about Pocahontas, John Smith, and cooperation with the native Americans, one fifth-grade student raised his hand and declared, "John Smith was a courageous mentor!"

> I learned that you can learn from younger students, too. Those you teach can teach you something. Just because you are older doesn't mean you are better.
>
> —Jesse, Fifth Grader, Sewanee Elementary

During the last six weeks, the school reflected on the year's activities. We remembered second-grade students making relief maps with the help of fifth-grade students, and sixth-grade students helping third graders with their multiplication facts. First graders borrowed science books from the fourth grade for a research project and practiced their portfolio presentations with them. Sixth graders taught science lessons to the third graders. It was so much fun to hear a sixth grader exclaim in frustration to his teacher, "How can I teach him anything if he won't listen?" and then smile as he recognized that his teacher had said the same thing about him just a few hours earlier.

> The best part [of the mentoring program] is that you make new friends. I have become a more responsible and caring person.
>
> —Katie, Sixth Grader, Sewanee Elementary

How did our students benefit? The mentoring program was not a specific academic program, but a process to enhance successful life lessons, to bond, and to develop cohesiveness between the upper and lower grades. A sense of cooperation and responsibility grew in the older students. Friendships blossomed, and a sense of "family" developed within the school, providing a vehicle for working with others and gaining insights about teaching. Teachers had the opportunity to learn about students outside their own grade, as multiage groupings interacted.

Our state department sent a team to study our mentoring program and award us a certificate of excellence that designated our program as innovative and creative. This was cause for true community celebration!

Katherine Ralston, Teacher, Highland Elementary, also relates a story of pairing students to build community in her school.

When we consolidated our elementary and high schools at one site, we had a program called Big Buddies that involved pairing sixth graders with kindergartners for a half-hour each month for various activities. The activities were designed to help the sixth graders become mentors and the kindergartners acclimate to school. After consolidation, we decided to expand the program to include K-2 and 6-8, pairing kindergarten with sixth, first with seventh, and second with eighth graders.

There was some reluctance on the part of the teachers involved because this was one more thing added to their busy schedules, but there was no reluctance on the part of the students at any level. Students became involved in planning the activities and begged for more opportunities to be with their buddies.

One of the most heartening examples [of community] we've encountered is a junior high school that operates as a robust community of students, faculty, and staff by agreeing that all behaviors and decisions are based on three rules and just three rules: "Take care of yourself. Take care of each other. Take care of this place."
—Margaret Wheatley & Myron Kellner-Rogers

The first year of the expanded program, the seventh graders were very involved in the game of checkers and decided to teach their first graders how to play the game. Our culminating activity that year was a checkers tournament that was won by the first graders! Our sixth graders put freezer paper on the floor of the gym and traced their kindergarten buddies, then helped them color and decorate their images. We displayed the finished products on the walls of the cafeteria and the entire

school population, K-12, enjoyed trying to identify "the originals." Eighth graders took their second-grade buddies on nature hikes and scavenger hunts on the campus that was new to the young students.

From a simple mentoring program, Big Buddies has become a community-building process in our school. When seniors graduate and write class histories and prophecies, we often hear stories of big buddy adventures that will never be forgotten.

Processes That Involve and Build Community

Schools that are intentional in enriching their learning communities value inclusiveness, diversity, and related democratic principles such as participation, responsibility, and egalitarianism. These qualities are embraced as core values, and leaders promote them through both word and deed. Additionally, leaders seek and use processes and strategies that bring individuals together for the purpose of talking and thinking about their collective vision. Participatory research, student focus groups, and future search conferences are among the many structures available to schools committed to strengthening the bonds between and among all segments of the community.

Participatory research is self-examination—of the school and of the individual and of relationships to the larger society and to issues of power. They can't be separated. The community or the school cannot change without the individuals inside it changing and vice versa—once the individuals in the community change, the community will change.

—Mary Poplin & Joseph Weeres

Participatory Research Develops Community through Self-Study that Includes All Members of the Community

Participatory research[33] is a process for helping all members of a school community explore the problems of a school and become empowered to take action to improve it. Participatory research is based on the following beliefs: if a school community is to change, then change must come from the commitment of individuals within it; problems are deeper than examination of quantitative data would indicate; relationships must be developed and nurtured to strengthen a school; the entire community must be involved—with equal voice; and solutions ultimately must come from within—not from outside experts.

Process

1. Develop a short questionnaire, with open-ended questions, that can be administered to every member of the school community. The three to five questions should be created by the school community; there are no established questions. Some examples include the following:

- What do you like about school?
- What do you dislike about school?
- What would make this a more effective school?
- *Teacher question:* How could this school better prepare students for the future? *Student question:* How could this school better prepare you for the future?

(continued on page 52)

What Do Our Children Say?

Four schools conducted participatory research, as described above, facilitated by professors from California's Claremont Graduate School. From their studies, they identified seven major issues for students outside the classroom.[34] The authors believe that these seven issues are universal; that is, that they would be identified in almost any school in the country. They argue that much school reform—which focuses on test scores, standards, and curriculum—misses the heart and soul of what's wrong with schools today. A summary of the seven issues follows. Strikingly, the notion of *community* is central to the resolution of most of these problems.

Only when we begin to listen to students will we be able to create real changes in schools—changes that make school relevant to students and make students want to become true participants in their own learning.

—Lynn Stewart, Teacher, El Molino High

1. **Relationships.** When members of the school community analyze school data from participatory research, the number one issue is human relationships. Do people in schools feel cared about? Do they feel understood and listened to? Respect, honesty, openness, and sensitiv-

(continued from page 51)

Parent question: How could this school better prepare your children for the future?

- If you could design the perfect school, what would it be like? You can write a description or create a graphic using pictures, words, and symbols.

2. The questionnaires should be completed anonymously; the only identifying mark is the participant's role in the school community—teacher, student, support staff, parent, or community member.

3. Completed questionnaires are duplicated so that there are three complete copies of all the data. They are distributed among the research team—which includes parents, teachers, classified staff, and students—such that every member reads some of the questionnaires from students, parents, teachers, and classified staff. It is important that everyone read part of the data from every group—and that each questionnaire is read by at least three different people.

4. Then, seated in a circle, the research team shares its findings. Typically, a group will pursue the findings from one set of data first. For example: "What did you see in the student data?" In order to ensure that all members speak and that everyone is heard with equal weight, some rules are followed.

a. First, all researchers spend a few minutes writing their answers before anyone begins speaking. This allows everyone to generate ideas independently and to listen carefully to what is being said.

b. Two members of the research team, while still active participants, serve as recorders of group comments; one writing

ity are valued and necessary for learning. The relationship issue is further clouded by racial and ethnic differences. Students of color do not feel valued or understood by teachers and other students; teachers believe they do not fully understand students from ethnic backgrounds different than their own.

2. **Race, culture, and class.** In most schools—as in most of American society—some groups are targets of discrimination. These are most likely racial minority groups (although, as the authors note, often they are not truly the "minority" of the population); culture and social class are also dividing lines for unfair treatment and perceived injustice. In every school, students could cite specific examples of racism. On the curricular side, many students of color demonstrate a great longing to know more about their own and others' cultures but report that little depthful knowledge is provided in school. The curriculum consistently represents the "majority" (i.e., European American) viewpoint to the exclusion of others.

＊

When asked, "What is the problem of schooling?" one high school student replied, "This place hurts my spirit."

＊

---

on paper, the other on a visible board or flipchart.

c. One member of the research team serves as facilitator, making sure that everyone listens attentively and that everyone gets equal opportunity to speak and be heard.

d. Each researcher, in turn, shares one idea, or theme, that came from reading the questionnaire results. Continue sharing around the circle until all ideas have been heard and recorded.

5. From this list of themes, the research team will identify problems as well as strengths of the school. It may become apparent that further questions should be pursued. For example, if students talk about the importance of "teachers caring," bringing a group of students together to talk in more depth about "What do you mean when you talk about teachers caring? What does that look like?" might help teachers better understand their students' views and needs. If support staff talk about racial inequity, several groups might be convened to follow up on this line of inquiry. These follow-up discussions are powerful when conducted in an "inside-outside" circle,[35] a format in which researchers form a circle around the circle of discussants for the purpose of listening and note taking.

Participatory research is true "community learning" because not everybody reads all the survey data. Some people have some of the information and others have different pieces of the information, but until it is all heard and discussed—put together, as pieces of a puzzle—no one has the whole picture.

3. **Values.** Shared values permeate the community but are rarely if ever discussed. Many believe that others (from different ethnic or cultural backgrounds) fail to hold these values in common. Most "parents, teachers, students, staff and administrators of all ethnicities and classes, value and desire education, honesty, integrity, beauty, care, justice, truth, courage and meaningful hard work. . . . [Students] desire a network of adults (parents and teachers) with whom they can 'really talk about important things.'"[36]

4. **Teaching and learning.** Students are bored with much of the academics of schools and see little or no relevance to their future lives. Interestingly, teachers are also bored much of the time with what they teach and have very little time to share ideas and best practices with colleagues—an activity that would no doubt energize their efforts.

5. **Safety.** Especially in secondary schools—but increasingly in elementary schools—members of the school community do not feel that schools are safe places. Incidents of physical violence, drug use, and verbal harassment are commonplace.

Inside-Outside Fishbowl

Many educators are familiar with the focus group, or structured group interview, in which a group of six to twelve individuals discuss a topic with the help of a facilitator who poses questions, probes for clarity, and maintains focus on the topic at hand. Most traditional focus groups are videotaped for later use by researchers wishing to gauge the groups' thinking to establish trends, or marketing firms testing ideas and products with groups of consumers.

The fishbowl is an adaptation of the focus group—so called because, as this group talks, its participants are observed or "watched" by a larger group. Fishbowl can be a useful strategy when a group is too large to have a discussion in which everyone can participate meaningfully. By selecting a subgroup to do the talking, the entire group stays engaged—either as discussants or observers.

The "fishbowl" arrangement generally makes people more careful of what they say and how they say it. Observers, although not talking, perform a specific role and remain engaged as they listen carefully to the discussion. Fishbowl is also a useful strategy to help a group think about the process of discussion because the setting causes people to be more mindful of how often they talk and how clearly they communicate. It is a useful tool for learning about productive ways to discuss in groups.

The "inside-outside" fishbowl is a further

6. **Physical environment.** "Students want schools that reflect order, beauty, space, and contain rich materials and media. The desire for clean, aesthetically pleasing and physically comfortable spaces is expressed by all."[37] Yet many schools have depressingly dirty or poorly maintained physical plants and rarely have adequate "personal space" for teachers or for students. Decent food is a priority for all students—and especially foods that are more reflective of the student body's cultural backgrounds.

7. **Despair, hope, and the change process.** During the process of participatory research, the authors note, community members seem to acknowledge a feeling of despair about the condition of schooling; however, through the process of discussion and dialogue, hope inevitably takes root. This note of optimism empowers research team members to take action and—through the power of community and the synergy of collective energy—this process continues to inform and improve the conditions in school that are important to improved student learning.

It's easy to read [our book] *Voices from the Inside* and say, "Oh, I'm not that kind of teacher." But you can't read *your own* students' comments and say, "I'm not that kind of teacher." I've always said that people don't need to *read Voices,* they need to *do* it.

—Mary Poplin & Joseph Weeres

adaptation. As schools in the Quest network have used it, fishbowl offers a powerful way to hear from students about what is important to them in the school environment. Basically, as eight to fifteen students sit in a circle, a number of listening adults—teachers and/or parents, depending upon the topic and purpose—surround them. As students discuss, adults carefully listen. At the end of thirty to sixty minutes of discussion among students, adults change roles. They talk as the students carefully listen. The adults review what they heard the students say and the implications for their school. Some procedural tips follow:

1. Invite students who are representative of the entire student body. Too often, when we listen to students, we hear only from the brightest or most involved. It is helpful to invite all grade levels, all socioeconomic groups, and all achievement levels.

2. Establish norms for the group, e.g., keep things confidential, listen with respect, contribute when you are moved to speak, and don't use names of teachers or students.

3. Look for volunteers to assume roles of facilitator, recorder or scribe, and monitor (so no one talks too much).

4. Clarify the role of the outside circle. They are to listen carefully throughout the discussion, not talking or interjecting until it is their turn.

5. When individuals in the outside circle speak, they say only what they have heard. They do not attempt to defend their position or react to student comments.

Student Voice at Spring Valley High

Students sat in a "fishbowl" in the school library. As they sat in a circle and talked to one another, a group of parents, teachers, and the principal sat in an outer circle. The job for this second group was to listen attentively as students talked about what's important around their school, what supports learning in their school, and what interferes with learning in their school. When the high school students finished, they changed places with the teachers and parents, who—now in the fishbowl themselves—shared at least one insight, affirmation, or surprise from listening to the students.

Predictably, the students talked about relationships—the importance of teachers caring, knowing their names, and even "the name of my sister"; they talked about the power of teacher enthusiasm and preparedness to make coursework interesting; and they talked about the importance of active learning in subjects that had relevance to their lives. One teacher, who had heard students talk about the strong influence of teacher mood, declared that she would be more mindful of the importance of bringing enthusiasm to her students daily, "checking my mood at the door," and "checking for understanding" more routinely.

Future Search: An Action Guide to Common Ground in Organizations and Communities, by Marvin R. Weisbord and Sandra Janoff (San Francisco: Berrett-Koehler, 1995).

This guide helps the abstract notion of a "future search" become concrete and takes the reader through each step of the future search process. The authors, who have facilitated several hundred groups through the process, offer specific tips for success (including the size of the room and panels on which to hang the group's products); examples of outcomes along the way; rationale for each stage in the process; and cautions about what can go wrong. The book is no substitute for attendance at a training-of-trainers conference, but it is a great resource for those who have been trained, for persons responsible for organizational development who might be considering a future search for their own organization, or for those serving on a planning committee. Another good resource, in which one can watch a three-day future search unfold, is the videotape *Discovering Community: A Future Search as a Springboard for Action in Santa Cruz County* by Blue Sky Productions, Inc., 1996.

Search Conferences: High-Touch Technology

A **future search conference** is a technology for helping large groups of people plan and create together. In the subtitle of his book *Discovering Common Ground,* Marvin Weisbord[38] talks about future search conferences as a means to "bring people together to achieve break-through innovation, empowerment, shared vision, and collaborative action." Pretty challenging task for a process, wouldn't you agree?

Several important principles underlie the organization of a search conference. First, a true search conference promotes **democratic dialogue**. As proposed by social psychologist Solomon Asch, this notion goes beyond a traditional discussion in which people fail to understand and own others' points of view. A search conference **releases human creativity** by creating "a uniquely-permissive atmosphere for cognitive restructuring, i.e., creativity."[39] Particularly important because we live in a highly fragmented world, search conferences look for **common ground** among participants, bringing diverse groups into the same room to share the same experience.

In *Discovering Common Ground,* Weisbord explores and explains many different structures and formats of the "search conference" that have evolved over the past 30 years or so. He proposes the model presented, in its simplest form, below.

The conference planners identify an issue or task, e.g., "assuring our students are prepared for the twenty-first century," "making our school safe," or "decreasing drug use by young people in this community." In five major steps or stages of the Future Search Conference, members accomplish the planning and the commitment to action.

The first step is a review of the **past**. Participants identify milestones in society, self, and the sponsoring organization over the previous three decades.

Next, they look at the **present**, brainstorming to identify the external forces that are currently shaping their lives and institution.

Continuing in the present, they identify the internal forces: things for which they are proud and sorry; ways in which they have contributed to the present status of the issue at hand.

Fourth, they look to the **future**: What would be the ideal scenario to accomplish our goal? Creativity abounds in this step of the process. People are freed to dream and imagine.

Finally, in a nontraditional manner, the group does **action planning** to accomplish its dream.

The success of a conference is predicted by the energy and time spent in the planning of the conference. Planners must determine who is to be invited (the stakeholder groups and the specific individuals to represent each group); the specific focus of the search (the topic must be chosen by the planning committee members, who typically are representative of the entire group); and the place.

Questions for Reflection

- Does our principal strive for meaningful community involvement in our school?

- Do community members who are not also parents of our students get involved in improving learning at our school?

- Are members of our community well informed about the school?

- Does the school staff work actively to stay informed about the community?

- Do multiple channels of communication keep segments of the school community well informed?

- Does the school community respect differing points of view among its members?

- In this school, are parents valued as members of the learning community?

- Do parents feel positive about our school?

- Do teachers, administrators, parents, and students work as a team to foster learning at this school?

- Do faculty and staff collaborate regularly?

Notes

1. See the story "MicroSociety as a Culture: Bringing the Real World Into the School" in this chapter for more information about the MicroSociety program at Atenville. The MicroSociety program has a Web site at http://www.microsociety.org.

2. See the story "After-School Smarts in Harts: 21st Century Community Learning Centers" in this chapter. The 21st Century Learning Center program was started in fiscal year 1998. Over $400 million were provided to schools and communities in fiscal year 2000 with the multiple goals of academic achievement, cultural and recreational activities, and lifelong learning opportunities for members of the community. To learn more about the program funded by the U.S. Department of Education, visit the Web site at http://www.ed.gov.

3. Glickman, *Renewing America's Schools*, 8-9.

4. See Grantham, *The Future of Work*.

5. See Naisbitt, *High Tech, High Touch*.

6. See Walsh, Sattes, and Hickman, *Doing Your Part*. For a more complete description, see "Workshop Series: Doing Your Part to Help Your Child Become SMART" in chapter one.

7. Appalread is a family literacy program that works with students and their families to develop readers. Through this program, Appalread brings books into the houses of students who otherwise would not have books.

8. Maeroff, *Altered Destinies*, 16.

9. See Benson, *All Kids Are Our Kids*.

10. Epstein, "School/Family/Community Partnerships," 701-11.

11. *Family Connections* guides were first developed at AEL in 1992 for four-year-olds and their families based on research conducted by AEL's Home-Oriented Preschool Education program, 1968-71. After a successful field test of the materials, *Family Connections 2*—for kindergartners and first graders—were developed in 1993. Finally, a Spanish language version, *Relaciones Familiares*, became available in 1996. Copies of these guides have been distributed in at least 46 states. They are available in sets of 25 for classroom use or in a notebook for parents. For more information, call AEL at 800-624-9120 or check the Web site at http://www.ael.org.

12. See note 6 above.

13. Project Fit America, a national nonprofit charity dedicated to getting kids fit, provides equipment specially designed to address children's fitness needs, developmentally appropriate curriculum for fitness, and in-service training for teachers and staff. The equipment, curriculum, and training are not available for sale; they are donated to schools with a commitment to integrate fitness into their entire educational experience. Donors are primarily community hospitals. For more information, visit the Web site at http://www.projectfitamerica.org.

14. Wigginton, *Foxfire*, 12-13.

15. Sergiovanni, *Building Community in Schools*, xi.

16. Barth, *Improving Schools from Within*, 9.

17. Ryan, "Learning Communities," 280.

18. Questioning and Understanding to Improve Learning and Thinking (QUILT) is a long-term professional development program codeveloped by the authors in 1991. (Visit the Web site at http://www.ael.org.) For a more complete description of the program, see the article

"Increasing Higher-Order Thinking Skills Through a Community-Wide Focus" in this chapter, and "QUILT: A Partnership to Increasing Shared Practice" in chapter three.

19. Structured Reflection Protocol is described in chapter two.

20. Ryan, "Learning Communities," 280.

21. National Staff Development Council, "Moral Purpose," 1.

22. Sergiovanni, *Building Community in Schools*, xvi.

23. See Sergiovani, *Building Community in Schools*.

24. Glickman, *Renewing America's Schools*, 85.

25. See Hord, *Professional Learning Communities*; Darling-Hammond and McLaughlin, "Investing in Teaching as a Learning Profession"; and Little, "Organizing Schools for Teacher Learning."

26. Data in a Day is described more completely in chapter two.

27. See note 18 above.

28. Shirley Hord has written about professional learning community in *Professional Learning Communities: Communities of Continuous Inquiry and Improvement* (Austin, TX: SEDL, 1997).

29. Wheatley and Kellner-Rogers, *A Simpler Way*, 17.

30. Second Step is a school-based social skills curriculum for preschool through junior high that teaches children to change the attitudes and behaviors that contribute to violence. The curriculum teaches social skills to reduce impulsive and aggressive behavior in children and increase their level of social competence.

31. Reprinted with permission from *Listening to Student Voices*, a publication of the Laboratory Network Program (Portland, OR: NWREL, 2000).

32. School Change Collaborative is the name of the national lab network program referred to in note 31 above. Denise Greenhalgh, the author of this article, and her principal, Dennis Sizemore, were both practitioner-members of the Lab Network.

33. See Poplin & Weeres, *Voices from the Inside*. The authors became familiar with Poplin's work as members of the School Change Collaborative (SCC). Poplin attended an SCC meeting to demonstrate her processes. The student-led focus group is one of the four tools in the Lab Network Program toolkit, published in 2000, available from the Northwest Regional Educational Laboratory.

34. These issues are reported in *Voices from the Inside*.

35. The Inside-Outside Fishbowl is more fully described on page 54.

36. Poplin, *Voices from the Inside*, 14.

37. Poplin, *Voices from the Inside*, 16.

38. See Weisbord, *Discovering Common Ground*.

39. Weisbord, *Discovering Common Ground*, 61.

Chapter Two

Sharing Leadership for Learning

As a principal, I used to think I shared leadership. I did. Or I should say I went as far as I could go or felt the school could go. But reflecting a decade later on my leadership, I see that I stopped well short of a community of leaders. Leadership for me was delegating, giving away, or sharing participation in important decisions so long as the curriculum, pupil achievement, staff development, and, of course, stability were not much altered. Now I see it differently. Rather, my vision for a school is a place whose very mission is to ensure that students, parents, teachers, and principals all become school leaders in some ways and at some times.

—Roland Barth

*T*o initiate and sustain continuous improvement, all members of the school community must step up to the plate—accepting both the opportunities and responsibilities associated with the sharing of leadership. This requires not only a redistribution and realignment of power and authority within a school but also a redefinition of roles so that students, parents, teachers, and administrators are willing to both share and own leadership. Such a model runs counter to the traditional hierarchical organization of most schools characterized by top-down lines of authority where control and conformity are primary values. Whether it is the principal making unilateral decisions for faculty and staff or teachers assuming autocratic control over classrooms, this governance model continues to permeate most schools. In a school community where all accept responsibility for high performance and where all are committed to continuous improvement, a more participatory and democratic model is needed.

Questions for Reflection

Sharing leadership necessitates a different way of thinking about issues of authority. By its very nature, it cannot be mandated from above. Rather, sharing leadership is a way of being together in which all members of a school community own responsibility for their own and others' performance. Sharing leadership requires collaboration and discussion of hard issues around matters of real importance. The questions that follow embody issues that all members of a community should consider as they address the extent to which sharing leadership is or might be realized in their school.

- How can a school community begin moving from a more traditional "top-down" leadership approach to this more expansive, powerful one?

- Why should individuals in a school community move toward sharing leadership as a way of doing business? What are the advantages and benefits to the school and its individual members?

- To what extent is sharing leadership practiced in my own school community?

- What if all members of my school community shared leadership one with another? What would this look and feel like?

The Journey from Cocksure Ignorance to Thoughtful Uncertainty: Reflections of an Elementary Principal

based on an interview with Connie Allen, Principal, Natcher Elementary School

> Here is Edward Bear, coming downstairs now, bump, bump, bump, behind Christopher Robin. It is, as far as he knows, the only way of coming downstairs, but sometimes he feels that there really is another way, if only he could stop bumping for a moment and think of it.
>
> —A. A. Milne, *Winnie the Pooh*

Allen identifies with Winnie the Pooh. She likens Pooh's dilemma to that of school leaders who often feel pulled along by outside forces, finding it difficult to take time for reflection and dialog that might lead to improvement. By introducing the Quest network to the idea of "finding the time to stop 'bumping' long enough . . .," she affirmed the value of reflection. Allen believes that sharing leadership is a powerful means for addressing the problem. The reflection below captures her concept of shared leadership in a school environment.

Sharing leadership means sharing information, so that other people are well informed. Sharing leadership means sharing responsibility; it means sharing problems, searching jointly for solutions. Sharing leadership means that you don't have to be all things to all people. Sharing leadership means that you don't have to have all the answers, but you have to be willing to admire all of the questions. It means involving students and parents, faculty, and staff in creating an atmosphere where everyone feels an equal part of what's going on. It means being willing to take the extra time to arrive at decisions by consensus.

Sharing leadership means sharing the results—the successes and not-our-brightest-moment times. It means building a sense of camaraderie. It means being the keeper of the vision, the carrier of the flame; but, it has to be shared vision. It means being and behaving in a way that serves as a model for the expectations that you have for others. It means thoughtful uncertainty. It means really listening to what people have to say and considering them seriously and knowing that the result of a cooperative effort is always going to be stronger and richer than if it were done singularly. It is realizing the value of combined brainpower and differing perspectives. It means cultivating the skills and talents of people in the schools; it means encouraging them to grow, to take risks, and to try new things. It means mutual respect and trust.

Moving from cocksure ignorance to thoughtful uncertainty has been a part of my professional growth experience. Through this journey I have been reinforced in the belief that there is seldom one right answer or one simple way to approach a problem. I have learned the wisdom of involving multiple perspectives when confronting difficult problems. In this context, my role is to ensure that we remain child-centered in everything we do, in every decision we make. The important thing is to always ask, "What is best for the children?" Not, "What is most expedient for adults?" or "What is the easiest way?" But, always, "What is best for these children we serve?"

For me, another important aspect of sharing leadership is to acknowledge what I call the "between-ness." The notion that I have about between-ness is that you never see or hear about it. You see the "before" and "after" pictures, but it doesn't seem to be part of our culture to talk about the between, the hard work. Seldom do we acknowledge the dedication, the staying power, the self-discipline, and the effort that it takes to reach the "after." And the reality is that one person can't do all the work that occurs "between." For success to occur, responsibility must be shared.

Through the Looking Glass: From Control to Commitment

Imagine moving through the looking glass from a traditional, hierarchical organization where leadership is associated with positions of power to a learning organization where leadership is open to all who are willing to unleash their personal potential toward attainment of widely shared goals. In this transformed state, formal leaders not only invite all community members to look for opportunities to exercise leadership, they act as if they are responsible for developing the capacity of each individual to lead where ability and opportunity intersect. Like Roland Barth, they view leadership as a dynamic force rather than as a fixed quotient. They know that sharing leadership is not about delegating or giving away, but rather about inspiring individuals to create ways and means to move together toward shared goals. The formal leader who adopts this philosophy is more concerned with building commitment to shared goals than with exercising control over events and individuals.

In the context of a school, sharing leadership is not something that administrators do to people, it is an attitude that pervades the thinking of teachers, staff, students, and parents alike. This attitude is born out of a sense of self-efficacy—"I can and will make a difference!"—and personal responsibility—"I should make a difference when and where I can." Teachers with this attitude instinctively behave in a proactive manner—seeking and finding solutions to

> When we equate the powerful concept of leadership with the behavior of one person, we are limiting the achievement of broad-based participation by a community or society.
>
> —Linda Lambert, *Building Leadership Capacity in Schools*

sticky problems and issues. One teacher might tackle the "homework issue" while another looks for a more effective means of reporting student progress. Students with this attitude assume responsibility for their own learning and become engaged in and with the broader community. Parents have a sense of belonging to the school. They look for meaningful ways to participate in the school community. The commitment created by the sharing of leadership generates a sense of ownership among diverse members of the community. This is the type of ownership that Margaret Wheatley describes as "personal links to the organization, the charged emotion-driven *feeling* that can inspire people."[1]

What, then, would one encounter in a school that is engaged in sharing leadership? While there is no one exemplar or magical model, the following are indicators of this expansive approach to leadership.

Belief in Individual Potential: *Each individual within the school is competent and capable of contributing to the good of the whole.* Because of this belief, individuals accord one another mutual respect and trust. A corollary belief relates to the primacy of individual responsibility in the community of learners and to the value of proactivity. Individuals hold high expectations for themselves and for others. These beliefs contribute to a sense of personal efficacy—the conviction that what one does truly makes a difference.

Shared Goals: *Individuals across all spectrums of the school community embrace a set of specific, compelling goals related to teaching and learning.* Thomas Sergiovanni argues that common goals and purpose are prerequisite for sharing leadership; that these serve to motivate and energize individuals to act.[2] Core beliefs provide the fuel to drive the engine of sharing leadership; shared goals represent the target or destination for action.

Sense of Community: *Individuals come together to create a vital and inclusive community that is defined by a "collective we" rather than a "collection of I's."*[3] Commitment is the glue that holds such a community together—commitment to shared goals and to one another. This commitment reinforces individual responsibility to assume leadership when challenges and opportunities present themselves. Sharing leadership is a part of the culture of the community that values cooperation and collaboration over competition.

Being a part of this leadership team has enhanced my job as a principal. My teachers and I have had the opportunity to form a team; to unite our efforts. We can see that we are all interested in the same thing: improving our school for students by figuring out where we are now and where we want to go.

—Brenda Williamson, Principal, Man High School

Restructured Time and Opportunities: *Individuals within the community make optimal use of existing time and structures as they work together to make sharing leadership a reality in their school.* Together they look for ways to create new structures to support sharing leadership, whether by redefining the role and functions of a PTA, student council, faculty senate, department or grade-level chairs, or site-based council—or through creative scheduling that provides opportunities for collaborative action. While shared leadership cannot be mandated, it can be invited, nurtured, rewarded, and celebrated within a community.

As a parent on the leadership team for my daughter's school, I came on board with a somewhat limited view of the school. I had been exposed only to those things that directly affected my children; I was unaware of the problems faced by other students, teachers, and support staff. Being a part of a leadership team has broadened my perspective. I have learned to make decisions based on the best interests of the school and community as a whole rather than specifically what is best for my child.

—Tammy Cecil, Parent, Moundsville Junior High

Participatory Strategies and Skills: *Individuals and groups are familiar with a variety of strategies that support reflection and*

interaction requisite to information exchange, planning, and decision making that precede action. Individuals have continuing opportunities to develop their own leadership skills. In a school committed to sharing leadership, individuals are engaged in continual learning about how to more effectively influence the course of events for the good of the community.

These five indicators define a school in which sharing leadership has replaced the traditional view that posits leadership in "the person at the top of the organization." In this traditional setting, those not occupying power positions tend to adopt attitudes of passivity, helplessness, and sometimes hopelessness. In the transformed setting, individuals act responsibly, proactively, and confidently as they share leadership to continuously improve learning for all members of the community.

Our deepest fear is not that we are inadequate. Our deepest fear is that we are powerful beyond measure. It is our light, not our darkness, that most frightens us. We ask ourselves, "who am I to be brilliant, gorgeous, talented and fabulous?" Actually, who are you not to be?. . . It's not just in some of us; it's in everyone. And as we let our own light shine, we unconsciously give other people permission to do the same. As we are liberated from our own fear, our presence automatically liberates others.

—Nelson Mandela, Inaugural Speech, 1994

Fusion Leadership: Unlocking the Subtle Forces that Change People and Organizations by Richard Daft & Robert Lengel (San Francisco: Berrett-Koehler, 1998).

The authors borrow terms from physics to distinguish between two types of leadership: fission leadership and fusion leadership. Fission leadership, the name the authors apply to the management style that evolved with the industrial revolution, is based upon a division of labor, individual accountability, and formal authority and control. Fusion leadership, on the other hand, is about joining people together, creating connections and partnerships, sharing information, and reducing barriers by encouraging conversations between and among all members of an organization. The authors note that when fusion occurs in physics, it produces five times the amount of energy as does fission. They argue that fusion leadership also produces substantially more energy for organizational changes than does fission leadership. The book is not only motivating and inspiring, it is also informational and instructional. The powerful ideas in this easy-to-read book are clearly presented and highly understandable.

IQ Pairs Interaction: A Strategy That Promotes Discussion

IQ Pairs is a process for facilitating structured group discussion. The "IQ" stands for Insights and Questions. The process begins by (1) having each individual find a partner to talk with about a given question or topic. The pair identifies both insights and questions. One member of the partnership takes notes. After three to four minutes (2) each pair connects with another pair and shares. Then, (3) each quartet finds another quartet with whom to share again. The group facilitator may ask for volunteers to share group thinking.

Little "I" Leadership

Current literature challenges traditional thinking that equates leadership with a position of authority. As James Kouzes and Barry Posner observe, "Myth associates leadership with superior position. It assumes that leadership starts with a capital 'L,' and that when you are on top you are automatically a leader. But leadership is not a place; it is a process."[4]

Leadership is not something that is given to an individual; rather, it is a talent that must be claimed by each individual for himself or herself. Little 'I' leadership is not about empowerment; it is about self-actualization. It begins with a belief that one can influence conditions and events in his or her environment and develops as the individual learns to use skills, strategies, and resources to that end. As Michael Fullan concludes, "Leadership with a small 'I' has to do with how we can all exert greater control in the complexities of everyday experience."[5]

Use IQ pairs to engage your faculty in thinking about the above two paragraphs. Pose the following questions:

- What does this say to you about sharing leadership for continuous improvement?

- What questions do you have about how to practice this type of leadership yourself or about how to encourage others to assume little "I" leadership?

Taking Our Cues from Nature

Next fall when you see geese heading south for the winter flying along in a V formation, you might consider what science has discovered about why they fly that way. As each bird flaps its wings, it creates an uplift for the bird immediately following. By flying in a V formation the whole flock adds at least 71 percent greater flying range than if each bird flew on its own. *(People who share a common direction and sense of community can get where they are going quicker and easier because they provide thrust to one another.)*

Whenever a goose falls out of formation it instantly feels the drag and resistance of trying to go it alone, and quickly gets into formation to take advantage of the lifting power of the bird immediately in front. *(If we have as much sense as a goose, we will stay in formation with those who are headed the same way we are going.)* When a lead goose gets tired, he rotates back in the wing and another goose flies point. *(It pays to take turns doing hard jobs—with people or with geese flying south.)* The geese honk from behind to encourage those up front to keep up their speed. *(What do we say when we honk from behind?)*

Finally *(now I want you to get this),* when a goose gets sick, or is wounded by gunshots and falls out, two more geese fall out of formation and follow him down to help and protect him. They stay with him until he is either able to fly or until he is dead, and they then launch out on their own or with another formation to catch up with the group. *(If we have the sense of a goose, we will stand by each other like that.)* (Source Unknown)

"Seven Lessons for Leading the Voyage to the Future" by James Kouzes and Barry Posner in *The Leader of the Future: New Visions, Strategies, and Practices for the Next Era* edited by Frances Hesselbein, Marshall Goldsmith, and Richard Beckhard (San Francisco: Jossey-Bass, 1996).

Kouzes and Posner argue that "leadership is everyone's business" and that effective leaders find ways to facilitate the leadership potential of all whom they serve. In this piece, they offer seven generalized suggestions to leaders attempting to accomplish this end. Included among these lessons, drawn from the authors' research, are "leaders don't wait," "shared values make a difference," and "you can't do it alone."

"Seven Lessons" is one of 31 chapters in this thought-provoking compendium that includes contributions from leading experts on leadership, including Peter Senge, Steven Covey, and Rosabeth Moss Kanter.

Demanding and Caring

"Encouraging the heart" is among five practices associated with exemplary leadership uncovered by the research of Kouzes and Posner.[6] In a book by this title, these long-time students of leadership make a case for leaders providing more positive affirmation to all in their organization. This is not to be confused with simple feedback or empty praise. Kouzes and Posner's research identifies seven essentials to effective use of this powerful strategy. The first two relate to communicating expected levels of performance among all members of the organization by first setting clear standards, and then expecting the best. Having clarified expectations, effective leaders proceed in the encouraging of the heart by paying attention to all individuals and their behavior, personalizing recognition, telling the story of individual accomplishments in a public forum, celebrating together, and setting the example. In a school setting, both administrators and teachers can use this approach to enhance performance of adults and students in the community. A story from an elementary school in West Virginia illustrates a principal's success in encouraging the heart of her faculty.

Walk through one of the halls in East Dale Elementary School and talk to the teachers. You'll hear them openly express the sentiment that their principal expects high performance; that many teachers in the district don't want to come there to teach because it's too hard; that teachers at East Dale put in extra hours and work to make learning positive and successful for all students. Then ask them to talk more about their principal, Janet Crescenzi. They'll tell you she's demanding—but she provides all the support they want and need. "We were all talking about GeoSafari last year after Christmas. We said how great it would be in the classroom. Janet said, 'Go buy them.' So we went to Hill's [department store] and bought four sets. She's like that with anything. If you can show her a need and a supporting reason, she'll find a way to get the materials you want and need. We have everything we want. And so we'll do anything for her." Indeed, their elementary science classroom has the latest equipment, from microscopes to a planetarium. Everyone feels excitement for learning at this school, and much of the reason seems to be the high standards demanded by the principal— along with the tangible support she offers for the staff's creative efforts.

The classroom is also a forum for sharing leadership with students.

Randy Meck, business teacher at Cave Spring High School, challenged his students to think of how they might improve the teaching and learning in their class. He placed no restrictions on the students as they brainstormed changes and the consequences and implications of each change. Meck dedicated two class periods to this open forum. He reports that "The results were great—each student takes more ownership and personal responsibility in the class."

In *Building Community in Schools,* Sergiovanni writes that "in communities, leadership is not defined as the exercise of power over others . . . [but] is redefined to become leadership as power to accomplish shared goals."[7] Schools that have clearly articulated goals for learning are able to focus the energy and commitment of students, parents, faculty, and staff toward attainment of these goals. In this way,

The Leadership Challenge by James Kouzes & Barry Posner (San Francisco: Jossey-Bass, 1995).

The authors used survey results from their database of 60,000 leaders and constituents and their findings from interviews of over 300 successful leaders to zero in on five fundamental practices of leadership and the 10 commitments they embody. The five key leadership practices: challenging the process, inspiring a shared vision, enabling others to act, modeling the way, and encouraging the heart. The 10 commitments of leadership: search out challenging opportunities, experiment and take risks, envision an uplifting future, enlist others in a common vision, foster collaboration, strengthen people by giving power to them, set the example by behaving in ways that are consistent with the shared values, achieve small wins and build commitment, recognize individual contributions, and celebrate team accomplishments.

The book touches the heart. Written in jargon-free language, it is an excellent guidebook for anyone who is or wants to become a leader. It is practical, easy to read and understand, and research-based in its findings. Throughout the book, the authors reiterate that we each have the potential to lead—to accept the leadership challenge everyday. The model presented in *The Leadership Challenge* is based not on power but on empowerment. Successful leaders do not command and control their people and resources (the traditional definition of management); rather, they serve and support their constituents. Successful leaders recognize that knowledge is distributed to all levels of the organization and, in order to make the organization benefit from that knowledge, the stakeholders must be empowered. It is not enough to make people feel they are part of the organization; rather, they must be made a part.

Kouzes and Posner's findings indicate that we overwhelmingly (88 percent) want our leaders to be honest and have ethics, with a large majority (63 to 75 percent) wanting leaders to be forward-looking, inspiring, and competent. Communications experts call these leadership traits *source credibility*. The authors outline many things leaders can practice to enhance their credibility, indicating that credibility is one of the hardest attributes to learn.

Case studies of people who have done "extraordinary things" illustrate the five key leadership practices throughout the book. One such story describes a California school superintendent, Charlene Mae Knight, who models the way to success through small wins. Ms. Knight, the twelfth superintendent in 10 years to tackle the job, inherited a school system struggling under a long-standing lawsuit—a system where 98 percent of the students achieved at extremely low rates, a system that received the state's lowest funding. Rats and gophers had literally taken over the schools in her system. Keeping her dream in mind, she began with small, doable tasks. She enlisted the support of community volunteers to completely refurbish one school. Gradually, she made changes that restored community confidence. Two years later, the children in her district performed in at least the 51st percentile in all areas tested, and education revenues had increased by 50 percent. Her schools were some of the first in California to use technology in every discipline, and they were among the first to use the Internet. The lawsuit disappeared, and Ms. Knight's system earned a coveted Distinguished School Award from the state! Knight credits it to the small-wins process.

Review by Vickie Luchuck, Teacher, Lumberport Elementary School suggests Sergiovanni, "schools can help all adults and youngsters who reside there learn how to lead and enjoy the recognition, satisfaction, and influence that come from serving the common interest as well as one's self-interest."[8]

Enlightened leaders operate with the knowledge that to the extent their people's needs and desires are fulfilled, they will go to extremes to serve the organization that supports them. . . . Enlightened leaders truly care about their people and want to help them grow and succeed as individuals. They know the truth behind the statement we have heard for years, "Your people don't care how much you know until they know how much you care."

—Ed Oakely & Doug Krug,
Enlightened Leadership

The Pot of Gold at the End of the Rainbow

Why would a school adopt sharing leadership as an approach to doing business? What's in it for the school at large? What are the benefits for student learning? What would motivate a principal to cultivate a community of leaders? What is the payoff for individual teachers, parents, staff, and students? We believe there are four primary benefits that accrue for schools that share leadership across all constituencies.

Benefit One: When individuals work together to find their own solutions to complex problems through the sharing of leadership, they have ownership in and commitment to the solution.

A success story from Alexander Elementary School provides a powerful illustration of this principle.

In the fall of 1998, principal Earl Wiman continued to be interested in improving fourth-grade student writing skills and scores on TCAP, a state-administered writing assessment. When the state-developed-and-scored writing assessment was first implemented in 1994, only 13 percent of Alexander's fourth-grade students scored at the proficient level. Compared to a state average of 7 percent, Alexander students' performance was adequate, but the principal was not satisfied. Wiman had tried bringing in writing consultants to provide training. The school saw some gains, but still not enough.

Wiman learned of the Structured Reflection Protocol and viewed it as an opportunity for his teachers to "discover their own answers."[9] Approaching his teachers, Wiman told them, "I'd like to try the Structured Reflection Protocol. I think it is a good approach, but if it doesn't work for us, we won't continue using it." With the power of the final decision in their hands, the fourth-grade teaching team agreed, somewhat reluctantly, to try the process as a way to focus on improved writing. Once a month, the four teachers used their weekly grade group meeting time to critically analyze student work related to a question they formulated about writing. Hesitant about this new technique and their use of it, they asked the principal, "Are we doing it right?" Wiman's response was a question: "Are you thinking more about writing instruction than you ever have in your whole life?" When they replied in the affirmative, he assured them that whether or not they were doing it "right," it was surely accomplishing what they had hoped!

People resist being told what to do and they readily commit to making their own ideas work. . . . True leaders will go out of their way to have their people discover their own answers even if the leaders already have some good ideas of their own.

—Ed Oakely & Doug Krug,
Enlightened Leadership

Throughout the year, the teachers became more skilled at using the process. Through their talking together in a focused way, they realized some of their collective needs and requested training in writing instruction. They shared the process with the third-grade teachers, who began in earnest to work on helping their students write better. The results in February, after five months of analyzing and reflecting together: 62 percent of Alexander's fourth graders scored at the proficient level, compared to 46 percent the year before. Additionally, Wiman says, "I think that it is important to note that 24 of the 32 children who were rated nonproficient scored a 3 on a scale of 1 to 6. Scores of 4, 5, and 6 are rated proficient. So we really are getting closer to where we want to score."

Following this successful use of the protocol process, Alexander made plans for

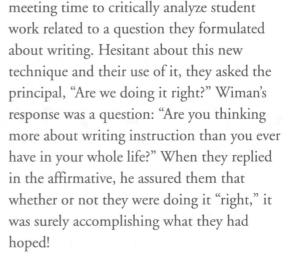

Do you believe the same results could have been achieved with a "top-down" mandate from the state, district, or school?

the next year. Every grade level team chose an area around which to conduct regular bimonthly protocol sessions. Now that other teachers have seen the power of the process, they are anxious to give it a try.

Benefit Two: Sharing leadership results in increased productivity and effectiveness for participating individuals.

Not only did the fourth-grade teachers at Alexander have more ownership and commitment to the improvement of writing than they would have implementing someone else's solution, they concurrently increased their own effectiveness in writing instruction and the effectiveness of their students as writers.

Another example of successful use of the Structured Reflection Protocol comes from Woodbridge Senior High School, where Mary Ann Hardebeck, assistant principal in charge of curriculum and instruction, likewise saw an opportunity for teachers to "grow" their own solutions. In October 1998, the district mandated that juniors successfully complete a 14-step research paper as a requirement for passing eleventh-grade English. The high-stakes nature of the requirement plus the short time line for implementation—the first class was to finish at the end of the semester in December—got the attention of the teachers, who were receptive to Hardebeck's suggestion to try the Structured Reflection Protocol as a process for reflection, analysis, and sharing. Teacher Eric Hoefler summed up his experience with Structured Reflection Protocol. "It really is an amazing team that's here. I wasn't in the process last year and coming into it this year, I can really feel that sense of camaraderie, of help and support. I think that because of that, all the teachers look forward to it and really appreciate what they get from it."

"Emotion and Hope: Constructive Concepts for Complex Times," by Michael Fullan in *1997 ASCD Yearbook: Rethinking Educational Change with Heart and Mind,* edited by Andy Hargreaves (Alexandria, VA: ASCD, 1997).

Michael Fullan, a widely recognized researcher on school change, documents the power of emotion and hope in school improvement initiatives. Beginning with a premise that top-down approaches to school change don't work, Fullan makes a compelling case for releasing the energy of adult members of a school community by attending to issues related to the heart and soul.

Benefit Three: Sharing leadership energizes and motivates individuals to work together toward attainment of shared goals.

In the spring of 1998, Brenda Williamson, then principal of Man High School, had a vision of providing after-school enrichment activities for students in this isolated, economically depressed area of the state. Aware of the 21st Century Community Learning Centers grants program sponsored by the U.S. Department of Education, Brenda assembled a team of teachers, students, and parents to explore the possibilities of such an endeavor.[10] Team members communicated with their peers in the broader school community and reached consensus regarding the kind of program that would best serve students and adults in Man. The planning for and writing of the proposal were community efforts. Involved individuals contributed many hours of personal time in pursuit of the shared goal—obtaining funding for the proposed project. The synergy created by the diversity within the group was exciting and motivated individuals to do what none of them had ever done before—develop a proposal that was ultimately funded for $300,000.

In the 25 years plus that I've been in education, I've never seen a strategy that has brought teachers together in such a way that took away the competitive nature that "my students are doing better than your students." It's the idea that our students are working together and that we are working together for the benefit of our students and we draw on each others' strengths to support our own weaknesses in teaching.

—Mary Ann Hardebeck, Former Assistant Principal, Woodbridge Senior High School

The success experienced by the Man High School team is an example of the power of creative collaboration. Hargrove suggests that creative collaboration involves "(1) different views and perspectives, (2) shared goals, (3) building new shared understandings, and (4) the creation of new value." In his studies, Hargrove found that essential to creative collaboration is a lateral leader, one who "influence[s] others less by their leadership positions than by being infused with a passion that has the capacity to ignite a shared vision." Further, the lateral leader possesses "an appreciation of the big picture and the lateral relationships they need to

Mastering the Art of Creative Collaboration by Robert Hargrove. New York: McGraw-Hill, 1998.

In this Business Week book, Hargrove gives meaningful definition to the term *creative collaboration*. He not only provides a clear rationale for this approach to leadership, but also offers a step-by-step approach to implementing it in the workplace.

create among different specialists in order to deal with complex human problems." As Williamson brought together students, teachers, and community members to create a vision of a community-school partnership that would serve the academic and social needs of youth, she created multiple lateral relationships and a highly effective work team.[11]

Benefit Four: Sharing leadership is consistent with and reinforces the democratic ideals that our public schools are intended to mirror.

It also provides a living laboratory in which students can participate with adults in shaping the school.

Peter Block argues that traditional views of leadership are based on patriarchy and self-interest and maintained by command and control; hence, they breed dependency. Conversely, stewardship is grounded in partnership and service and supported by commitment and empowerment. It promotes ownership and responsibility. Block believes stewardship to be consistent with democratic values and states that one of the goals of his book *Stewardship* is "to quicken our efforts to reform our organizations so that our democracy thrives, our spirit is answered, and our ability to serve our customers in the broadest sense is satisfied."[12]

Block defines stewardship as "hold[ing] something in trust for another" and states that the "most powerful" way of choosing service over self-interest is "by building the capacity of the next generation to govern themselves."[13] What a powerful rationale for sharing leadership in schools—particularly when students are an integral part of a partnership committed to creating more effective places for learning. At Woodbridge Senior High School, the administration and faculty provide students with multiple opportunities to assume ownership. Student governance—including the Student Council and class officers—are formally involved in annual school improvement planning. Student leaders convene in the late summer not only to

Leading Without Power: Finding Hope in Serving Community by Max De Pree (San Francisco: Jossey-Bass, 1997).

This is a small book with a big message. The potential of individuals and organizations is largely unrealized, but a true vision that touches the human spirit can unleash this considerable potential. De Pree writes eloquently and with wisdom borne out of his many years as a CEO. As he describes the power of servant leadership, the reader is convinced of his commitment to this concept and of the integrity of the idea and the man who espouses it. For those interested in exploring ways and means of inspiring all members of an organization to assume leadership, this book is a "must-read."

Students can be school leaders. When we think of student leadership, we usually think of elected student councils and other means by which students are encouraged to provide leadership for their class or school. . . . As yet, few students and schools have turned the concept of community service to improving their own school community.

—Peter Block

plan for student-focused activities, but also to engage in reflection and assessment regarding variables affecting learning. Throughout the school year students have opportunities to participate in data gathering and feedback activities. During the 1998-99 school year, 20 students participated in a Data in a Day experience designed to assess the extent to which block scheduling had achieved preestablished goals.[14] Fifteen students participated in focus groups targeted at understanding what supports and interferes with learning at Woodbridge. The commitment to provide channels for student participation and partnership is an ongoing one at Woodbridge.

Follow the Yellow Brick Road

We will view leadership as the capacity of a human community to shape its future, and specifically to sustain the significant change required to do so . . . . Leadership actually grows from the capacity to hold creative tension, the energy generated when people articulate a vision and tell the truth (to the best of their ability) about current reality. This is also not a new idea. "Leadership is vision," says Peter Drucker. Or, as expressed in Proverbs 29:18, "Where there is not vision, the people perish."

—Peter Senge

How can a school community begin moving from a top-down leadership approach to leadership to this more inclusive one? Peter Senge, the guru of learning organization theory, explores the concept and challenges of change in *The Dance of Change.* Senge and his colleagues write about "profound change," which they describe as "organizational change that combines inner shifts in people's values, aspirations, and behaviors with 'outer' shifts in processes, strategies, practices, and systems."[15] A move to the sharing of leadership in a school is an example of the profound change about which Senge writes. Such a change requires both inner shifts and outer shifts.

The outer shifts relate to restructured time and opportunities and to the adoption of participative skills and strategies. The inner shifts revolve around shared beliefs such as "Each individual within the school is competent and capable of contributing to the good of the whole"; shared goals; and a sense of community. As Senge argues, these inner shifts are inextricably connected to the "vision thing." In schools where there is a compelling vision, individuals discover the courage, heart, and intellect within to "shape their future and sustain the significant change required to do so."[16] Individuals do not find these capacities in isolation from others, rather—as did Dorothy in The Wizard of Oz—they develop these insights in a community where members share a common commitment and vision. Sharing leadership occurs only within the context of a school that has focused on articulating shared vision and core values and diffusing these throughout the community.

Unfortunately, there is no magic wand that can transform an organization from the status quo to the desired state. Given the vision and a commitment on the part of the formal leaders (e.g., the principal) a group of pioneers must be enlisted to initiate the process. Senge argues for the establishment of a pilot group that can serve as an incubator for the new way of doing business.[17] Individuals recruited to this pilot group are open to making the "inner shift"—from control to commitment. They are willing to vest time and effort in practicing this new way of relating to their school and its future.

Leadership teams in Quest schools facilitated processes, strategies, and experiences for their colleagues as part of the "outer shifts" requisite to this profound change. The Quest teams at Highland Elementary and Highland County High School, like their counterparts in other schools, used the Interview Design process to bring diverse segments of the community together in charting a new course for the future.[18] At Alexander Elementary and Woodbridge Senior High, all segments of the school community engaged in an interim assessment of instruction via the Data in a Day process. Parents at Natcher Elementary joined with educators in promoting the vision of SMART learning across the entire community. Through the network, Quest teams experienced and learned how to lead processes and strategies that enabled the desired changes. They coached one another and provided moral support to one another.

They were sustained by a community of learners who shared the same vision and goals. The network was a critical piece of the scaffolding that enabled these schools to work toward implementing profound changes.

The journey toward sharing leadership is quite analogous to Dorothy's journey through Oz. No one can do this *for* a school community; they must find within themselves the commitment to initiate and sustain their own quest. Nor will the journey be easy; there will be multiple obstacles along the way. Connectedness to others and to common goals enables and sustains progress. Perseverance is essential. Celebrations along the way are important. Many of the rewards are in the journey itself.

Making the Time

We expect that the "big L" leaders get paid to do the decision making; it's not unreasonable for them to spend time doing that because that's their job. But how do we justify "little l" leaders—teachers, students, and parents—spending time in thinking about ways to improve the school? Leadership, whether big or little L, takes time. So if we want to engage others in thinking about and making decisions that will serve students and increase learning in the school community, the challenge is to find the time for these kinds of activities.

Teaming

by Cathie DeVito, Chair, Faculty Senate, East Dale Elementary School

In schools, the schedule is too often the master of time. East Dale Elementary School took charge of time through this creative approach. In the winter of 1998, our faculty participated in a teaming day. The Benedum Collaborative[19] provided the funding for materials, preplanning, released time, and food for the full day.

Teachers and support personnel, along with central office staff and Benedum members, formed teams for the morning problem-solving exercises. After lunch, the teams realigned into primary, intermediate, and service personnel for a session. During the final session, role-alike groups (all first grade teachers, all cooks, etc.) were formed.

The common theme that echoed from our reflective exercises was the need for more time—time to plan, to coordinate materials, to reflect. To make that happen, we purchased state-of-the-art technology—a 12' x 12' screen, computer, VCR, laser disc player, Internet connection—and trained our specialist team to use the equipment.

The specialist team now prepares a weekly interdisciplinary unit for two grades at a time. While the students are with the specialists learning together, the teachers of those two grades have time together. This means that, once a month, each team has an extended period of time to work together—one week, grades 1-2; one week, grades 3-4; one week, grades 5-6; and one week, the specialist team. This innovation has resulted in quality time for reflecting and learning together in small groups.

One very specific time-related problem that arises for many teachers in sustaining continuous school improvement is the tension caused by expanding the definition of what it means to be a teacher. In the old paradigm, teachers were almost exclusively in their classrooms teaching students. In the new one, teachers are instructors, but they are also leaders, mentors, curriculum developers, and staff developers.

—Nancy Adelman & Karen Walking-Eagle, "Teachers, Time, and School Reform"

The Dance of Change: The Challenges to Sustaining Momentum in Learning Organizations by Peter Senge, Art Kleiner, Charlotte Roberts, Richard Ross, George Roth, & Bryan Smith (New York: Doubleday, 1999).

Written by the authors of the widely acclaimed *Fifth Discipline Fieldbook,* this book is a resource for those embracing the ideas associated with the *Fifth Discipline.* The major theme of *The Dance of Change* is the difficulty in accomplishing what the authors term *profound* or *deep change.* In their words, "deep changes—in how people think, what they believe, how they see the world—are difficult, if not impossible, to achieve through compliance."[20] The authors contend that this type of change, which is requisite to transformation from a traditional to a learning organization, comes only from the commitment of individuals. They offer a framework for understanding change that comprises three stages or challenges: (1) the challenges of initiating, (2) the challenges of sustaining, and (3) the challenges of redesigning and rethinking. Like its predecessor, *The Dance of Change* offers practical, hands-on strategies.

Grade-Group Meetings

by Shirley Roberts, Teacher, Alexander Elementary School

Curriculum development, implementation of local standards, new instructional methods, behavior modification plans, planning extracurricular activities—the list goes on and on. When does today's teacher find enough hours in the day to meet all of these overwhelming demands? At Alexander Elementary School, we have discovered that grade-group meetings can alleviate some of our time management problems.

Although shared lunches and planning times with a coteacher had been in place for several years, more time was needed for all teachers in grade groups to meet together on a weekly basis. At Alexander, support personnel come into classrooms to provide this extra time for teachers to meet. These staff members follow teacher-designed lesson plans. One bonus we have discovered is that utilizing grade-group meetings reduces the amount of time spent planning outside of the school day.

Through grade-group meetings, teachers have reaped numerous benefits. Better planning and pacing lead the list of positive outcomes. Teachers have a more organized approach to planning and have discovered many creative ways to present lessons. One first-grade teacher commented, "We are able to take difficult skills or concepts and work together on the best ideas to present them! I have gathered so many new ideas from my colleagues."

Learning and growth start from within; adult learning is increasingly self-directed. Adults who feel in charge of and responsible for their own development will make significant gains despite seemingly insurmountable obstacles.

—Sarah Levine

Grade-group meetings have also made us more aware of school climate. Teachers discuss upcoming events and school activities during this time and, as a result, are better informed and prepared when important events occur. Many grade groups have also reported less frustration over discipline issues.

By discussing discipline, teachers are able to brainstorm solutions that forestall critical problems. One third-grade teacher told of leaving school each day burdened by the behavior of one student. Through grade-group meetings, she learned of a new behavior modification technique that, after only one day, produced dramatic improvement in the classroom

Grade-group meetings have brought our staff closer together—to solve problems and better meet the needs of our students. These meetings allow the time needed for collaboration about curriculum, delivery, and important student issues. Through weekly grade-group meetings, Alexander Elementary School has moved one step closer to ensuring student success.

Shared Decision Making

by Jim Asplundh, former assistant principal, Moundsville Junior High School

The statewide education reforms of 1989 mandated shared decision making in our school. Subsequently, the advent of the faculty senate, school improvement councils, and curriculum teams have empowered teachers to become more and more involved in the long-term and daily operations of the school. Shared decision making requires a positive climate. As assistant principal, it is my responsibility to help create an environment where teachers, parents, students, and the community can meet for the common goal of improving education for all students.

Finding Time for Teachers

Finding time for teachers to share ideas and learn new ways of teaching is a challenge for many schools and communities. But how much time do teachers need for this? And how can that time be created?

Ideas for developing answers to those questions can be found in *Critical Issue: Finding Time for Professional Development* (1997), written by Cathy J. Cook and Carole Fine, part of the North Central Regional Educational Laboratory's award-winning *Pathways to School Improvement* Internet site.[21] This source offers descriptions of best practices, results from research, and other information on a range of issues—assessment, at-risk students, school governance, leadership, learning, math, parent and family involvement, professional development, safe and drug-free schools, school-to-work programs, science, and

technology. The article looks at obstacles and opportunities for creating more time for professional development, and it includes brief descriptions of the following:

- a partnership that is providing half a day each week for teacher meetings and professional development

- a school that used an alternative, modular-scheduling pattern to provide time for professional development and team coordination to offer additional education resources for students

- a school that has created large blocks of training and planning time during school hours

- a school district that makes time for team planning one period each day

A good example of shared decision making occurred this year when we created a new schedule for our students. Teachers agreed to start the day earlier, have an extra class period, and finish the day later, in order to allow our ninth-grade students to receive an additional elective class, our seventh- and eighth-grade students to have an enrichment period, and students needing extra help in math or reading to participate in a reinforcement class. This schedule will improve the basic skills of our seventh and eighth graders, allow for more technology electives to be taught, and provide a class on manners and civility for our students. These additions will help us meet three of our four school goals as specified in the Unified School Improvement Plan.

Clearly, this cooperative spirit between teachers, students, parents, and administration works in our school. The process is not always easy, but with clear goals and a desire to work toward these goals, our school will succeed.

Scheduling

by Diane Lay, Judy Thomas, and Heather Pflasterer,
Alexander Elementary School

Alexander Elementary School has developed a unique method for creating classroom and special activity schedules each year. Our principal appoints a committee of four teachers, at least one of whom has previous scheduling experience, to work together to ensure that schedules are made with the best interest of each classroom and each student in mind. The committee sets aside two days of uninterrupted time away from the school environment to focus on scheduling. Substitutes are provided for the teachers' classrooms during the scheduling time.

To involve all members of the faculty before the meeting, teachers have the opportunity to express their opinions in writing. They are encouraged to explain what was successful in their current schedules, as well as what was inconvenient, and to offer suggestions for next year. These requests are considered, with the understanding that not all can be honored due to the number of special needs involved.

The committee gives special attention to requests from teachers who have made certain sacrifices the previous year. For example, teachers who had to share computer lab days and attend the lab only three days a week due to scheduling conflicts are given top priority in computer lab scheduling the next year. Each committee member monitors a grade level. One person also tracks the schedules of special class teachers, such as physical education, music, art, library, guidance, and special education.

The "must haves," such as lunch, are placed on the schedule first. Blocks of academic time for reading and math are scheduled next. A well-coordinated physical education schedule allows reading and math teachers the flexibility of joint planning time.

Because a number of students are mainstreamed into our school from the West Tennessee School for the Deaf, we must accommodate their need to spend part of the day at Alexander and part at the School for the Deaf. We attempt to meet their academic and social needs through creative scheduling.

When scheduling classes such as art, music, guidance, and foreign language, we keep several details in mind. We consider the time necessary for these teachers to move from classroom to classroom. We also attempt to cut down as much as possible on the distance between the classes for special teachers, so that they do not waste precious instructional time crisscrossing the building all day long. A third consideration we make when scheduling these teachers is to allow them to flow as much as possible from level to level, rather than jumping from kindergarten to fifth grade, then back to first grade.

Scheduling by committee takes the headaches out of scheduling. Our committee approaches the table with an attitude of problem solving, allowing us to fit the pieces of the puzzle together to meet the needs of our children in every classroom.

Leadership as Spirit: Breathing New Vitality and Energy into Individuals and Organizations by Rusty S. Moxley (San Francisco: Jossey-Bass, 2000).

Written by a senior fellow at the Center for Creative Leadership in Greensboro, North Carolina, this book makes a strong case for the sharing of leadership to exercise leadership at particular times and in ways consistent with one's talents. In this setting, individuals more completely fulfill their own potential and nourish their spirit. Moxley argues that when individuals accept leadership responsibility, they participate more fully in community. This is an inspiring and motivating book for those exploring shared leadership.

Choosing a Boat to Row: Structures to Facilitate Shared Leadership

e = mc²

If sharing leadership is a stream that you want to follow, your trip will be more manageable if you travel by boat. Choose a governance structure to be your "boat." It can carry you on this trip, supporting your efforts to travel together in a common direction, to share the workload more equitably, and to safely weather the storms that are inevitable. In this section, we'll talk about the structures that facilitate sharing leadership. Whether you're talking about sharing leadership in families, schools, or businesses, it doesn't just happen.

In the Quest philosophy, sharing leadership is more a set of beliefs than a set of structures; we view structures as "necessary but not sufficient" to ensure representation and voice among the various groups in a school community. Many states and districts have mandated structures in the hopes of forcing shared decision making and shared leadership. Externally imposed structures do little to change the operation of a school if the values of the school community—and especially the school administrators—are not aligned with the intents of such laws or policies. Implementing structures for shared governance, without the belief system in place to empower the members of such a board or committee, can actually do more

We invited all members of our school community to participate in a vision-setting activity. The result was increased cohesion: the cooks and custodians became far more supportive. We heard many times how grateful they were to have been included, and we learned that they, too, were concerned about the same issues: courtesy, attitudes, and cooperation.

—Peg Webster, Teacher, Stratton Junior High School

damage than good. When parents, teachers, students, and community members are asked to contribute to governing and the work of the committee is meaningless, make work, or ignored, participants' feelings of competence and worth diminish. Their respect for the school bureaucracy and administration, likewise, decreases.

When the "big L" leaders in a school want to involve others in initiating improvements, structures can facilitate the necessary meeting, talking, planning, and doing. With such structures in place, schools can ensure equitable representation from all segments of the school community.

Principal Pam Brown has established multiple structures for shared governance because of the challenge of communicating and involving the large number of stakeholders at the 3,000-student Woodbridge Senior High School. Brown shares leadership with seven assistant principals. Although each of these assistants has responsibility for a discrete aspect of the school operation, their regularly scheduled meetings help them keep focused on the big picture—the extent to which the school is realizing their shared vision. One senses that this is a true team, where each individual is valued and where all voices are of equal importance. Large schools, like other large organizations, can easily fall into a hierarchical power structure. The team approach, with its supporting structures, assures a more democratic way of operating at Woodbridge.

Because continuous improvement is unlikely to result from a top-down mandate, an autocratic approach to leadership is not appropriate in a school committed to continuous improvement. Rather, administrators in such schools seek ways to inspire teachers, students, parents—and all others working in the school—to become school leaders, to be proactive in making things happen in which they really believe. Shared leadership puts life into faculty senates, local school improvement councils, and curriculum committees, as well as into PTOs and student governments. More important, shared leadership invites and encourages all individuals within a school community to assume responsibility for constantly looking for ways to improve their effectiveness.

I believe the experience of preparing a unified school improvement plan has helped my teachers grow; they now look beyond the classroom at the larger picture of the school. I have matured, in my role as principal, to understand that all publics have concerns about the school. Giving them a voice to talk about the issues helps us better define where the school should be.

—Brenda Williamson, Principal,
Man High School

We recently participated in an evaluation of the 4 x 4 block schedule. Over a two-day period, our 48-member team of students, parents, and teachers examined survey data, observed classes, and listened to candid focus groups. We then analyzed the data and provided our findings to the entire faculty. . . . We would like to commend Principal Pam Brown for her initiative and courage to conduct such an innovative, introspective evaluation. With total Woodbridge community involvement, teamwork, and commitment to continued evaluation of the educational process, Woodbridge Senior High will remain on the leading edge of educational excellence.

—Jeff and Linda Witherel, Parents,
Woodbridge Senior High School

East Dale Elementary School boasts a strong faculty senate. Senate chair Cathie DeVito speaks of the importance of shared leadership to her school.

We are an empowered group, making important decisions concerning such things as expenditures, field trips, and nominations of fellow teachers for awards. We have standing committee reports on discipline, technology, student assistance teams, teacher education, teacher awards, playground, and field trips. We discuss curriculum issues as well as other issues pertinent to teachers and staff (health insurance and cancer Relay for Life, for example). Teachers receive an agenda 24 hours in advance of the meetings and are free to add items as needed.

Our association with the Benedum Collaborative has also helped our staff to become empowered.[22] With their financial assistance, we have been able to send teachers to conferences and workshops. We have been able to provide released time for teachers to plan effectively, to write grants, to redesign curriculum, and to supervise preservice teachers. We have built a science/math/technology lab, the only one of its kind in West Virginia. We have also implemented the Core Knowledge sequence into our curriculum and correlated it with our state instructional goals and objectives.[23] Our faculty senate listens to the needs of our staff. Because of their input, we implemented schoolwide training on teaming; most recently, we hosted a workshop, "The Write Traits," for approximately 40 other schools.

The Kentucky Education Reform Act mandated school-based decision making councils for all Kentucky schools. Connie Allen, principal, and Maria Fernandez, parent, at William H. Natcher Elementary School reflect on the role the council plays in their school.

The Kentucky Education Reform Act of 1990 contained the requirement that schools have shared leadership through a state-mandated School-Based Decision Making Council. The council is composed of parents who are elected by the parents; teachers who are elected by the teachers; and the school principal. The purpose of the council is to establish school policy in a variety of areas—from budgeting and discipline to student class assignment and selection of instructional materials—and to offer input on the employment of staff members. Standing committees, composed of teachers and parents, address each policy area at the direction of the council. The council has a mission and responsibility to improve the performance of students. Our council has targeted several areas, such as the SMART learner theme, to fulfill the goals and to meet the school expectation of high performance and student achievement. We have also united with the PTO to obtain important feedback from our parents.

Natcher Elementary also provides opportunities for student leadership development. Allen and Fernandez describe the workings of these two groups.

Natcher boasts two student leadership groups. Our student council members are elected by their peers. The second group is composed of students who have been identified as possessing potential or demonstrated ability to perform on an exceptionally high level in social skills and interpersonal qualities such as poise, effective oral and written expression, and the ability to set goals and organize others to successfully reach these goals. The selection of the latter group of students is based on sociograms (i.e., questionnaires designed to assess leadership characteristics), peer recommendations, behavioral checklists targeting leadership behavior, and portfolio entries that display leadership qualities.

Students selected for the leadership group are mentored by the school guidance counselor. They attend leadership training workshops with students from the other elementary schools, and they perform special jobs at the school such as conducting tours for visitors and introducing programs. These students recently produced a video titled "A Day in the Life of Natcher" that introduces new students and parents to the school. Both the student leader group and the student council represent the student perspective when decisions are made on issues such as selecting playground equipment and offering special student-led activities. One of their most successful "Do Something for Someone Day" projects resulted in the planting of 300 tulip bulbs in the front yard of the church across the street from Natcher.

"The Secrets of Great Groups," by Warren Bennis, in *Leader to Leader* (San Francisco: Jossey-Bass, 1995).

This article focuses on the traits of great group leaders. Bennis notes that few great achievements have resulted from the work of great individuals, but rather from teams of great people. He adds that even Michaelangelo worked with a group of 16 to paint the ceiling of the Sistine Chapel.

Groups become great when they bring strong individual achievers to work together to get results. They provide psychic support, foster fellowship among their members, and generate courage and encouragement. Bennis cites findings from great groups such as the Manhattan Project and the Disney animators. His findings suggest the following principles common to all great groups:

- Great groups have a shared mission, a vision: their quest. That belief brings energy to their work.
- Great groups manage and resolve conflict by reminding members of their vision.
- Great groups have a leader who holds the formal leadership at bay so the group can maintain focus on its vision.
- Great groups often have an opponent or adversary.
- Great groups view themselves as the underdogs or mavericks.
- Members of great groups pay a price for their dedication and energies.
- Great groups make strong leaders. Great leaders are great because they have a great group behind them.
- Great groups are the result of carefully choosing the right people for the right jobs.
- Great groups are young in their age as well as their stamina, spirit, and culture.
- Great groups produce, or market, their work.

Review by Vickie Luchuck, Teacher, Lumberport Elementary School

Assessing the Value of Student Voice Using Data on Display

First thoughts of student leadership in schools lead one toward formal organizations such as student councils. Rarely, however, do organizations such as these focus on real school improvement. In recent years, school reformers have touted a new approach to student leadership that centers on asking students to key in on what will really improve their school. When administrators, teachers, and parents "listen to the student voice," true school improvement takes place.

Data on Display is a process that can be used to promote reflection concerning the value of student voice in school.[24] Below are suggested items for use in this activity.

1. It is essential to include student perspectives in order to achieve meaningful school improvement.

    100   90   80   70   60   50   40   30   20   10   0

2. My school routinely uses structures and processes to ensure the inclusion of student opinion.

    100   90   80   70   60   50   40   30   20   10   0

3. Leadership is open to listening to students and uses student input in decision making.

    100   90   80   70   60   50   40   30   20   10   0

4. Students in my school believe they are listened to and believe their opinions are important to teachers and administrators.

    100   90   80   70   60   50   40   30   20   10   0

5. When students are included in decision making about school improvement, they act responsibly and make substantive contributions.

    100   90   80   70   60   50   40   30   20   10   0

For more about using Data on Display, see pages 127-129.

Using Data in a Day (DIAD) to Involve All Stakeholders

"When I grow up I want to be a researcher!" announced Cherelle, a fourth-grade student at Alexander Elementary School, as she completed a morning of observing and coding in classrooms at her school. Three hours later Cherelle and seven other fourth and fifth graders took an active role in reporting to the entire faculty the findings of an intensive 24-hour study of teaching and learning. The report culminated a schoolwide learning process that was designed to examine the congruence between the mission, beliefs, and goals contained in the school improvement plan and what was actually going on in the life of Alexander on September 10, 1998.

Like other schools with a commitment to excellence, the challenge at Alexander is to maintain the focus and momentum for continuous improvement across the entire school community. To this end, the leadership at Alexander continually seeks strategies that engage individuals in reflection and self-assessment. One such strategy—DIAD—offers a number of features that distinguish it from other self-study processes and make it particularly useful to schools attempting to strengthen their capacity to act as a learning community.[25]

Principal Wiman viewed DIAD as an excellent way for the school to create a "snapshot" of how the school was doing against a predetermined set of variables. Using their mission statement and school improvement plan as springboards, the Alexander faculty chose four areas on which to focus its self-study: teaching and learning strategies that reach all children; appropriate student behavior, including responsibility for self and others and ability to work with others and conduct self appropriately; culture for learning focused on student achievement; and high expectations for all students linked with appropriate academic support-teaching for mastery.

Approximately 30 parents, community leaders, and students joined with the Alexander faculty and staff in the hands-on study of the school, observing classes and making written and oral comments on what they saw. Using the four areas of focus, the teams evaluated the performance of the school over a 24-hour period.

After the final reporting at Alexander, informal conversations continued among researchers and other members of the school community. Alyssa, a fifth-grade researcher, expressed excitement and enthusiasm about the experience and requested of an adult team member: "Please ask Mr. Wiman to let us do this again!"

DIAD can be repeated in a school on a periodic basis. It can be used as a sort of "annual checkup," a time to stop and take stock of how a school community is doing. DIAD is a tool that a learning community can use time and again to collect information that can be used to improve performance.

Special Features of the DIAD Process

1. **Focuses on teaching and learning.** Data are collected through classroom observations that focus on what is actually occurring during teaching-learning transactions. Observers record what they see during a 20-minute observation period; collectively, the observation data provide a snapshot of teaching and learning in a school during a given day. Collection of empirical data—as opposed to perceptual data so often captured in school surveys—grounds the process in the daily reality of classrooms.

2. **Involves the entire school community.** The "researchers" who collect and analyze data represent a cross section of the school. Alexander School's research team was composed of teachers, support staff, parents, and students.

3. **Emphasizes student voice.** Central to DIAD is the involvement of students. The eight fourth and fifth graders involved in the Alexander study were an integral part of the process—from beginning to end. Their perceptions enriched the definitions of the themes; they were actively engaged in the classroom observations and in the subsequent analysis of data; each student delivered a portion of the final report back to the entire community.

4. **Enables real-time learning together in community.** DIAD begins with reflection on and dialogue about the question *What do we really believe about effective teaching and learning?*, moves to data collection around themes important to the entire community, and ends with

reflection and dialogue about the question *What do teaching and learning in our school really look like?* This is a true inquiry learning process that leads to insights that are more likely to be translated to action than are recommendations made by outsiders. Furthermore, participants experience a sense of accomplishment as they move from beginning to end.

5. **Is flexible and can be used to accomplish a myriad of purposes.** Alexander Elementary used DIAD to "take a reading" on the extent to which their practice was aligned with the goals that they had set for themselves in their school improvement plan. Woodbridge High School used DIAD to assess the effectiveness of block scheduling. Many schools have used DIAD during the needs assessment phase of improvement planning.

6. **Affirms strengths and identifies areas for growth.** A serendipitous outcome of DIAD is community celebration: strengths of a school are identified and faculty and students are affirmed. At the same time, potential areas for growth and improvement are pinpointed: the community commits to continue its journey of continuous improvement and its quest for excellence.

Making the Most of Mandates

Most states now require unified school improvement plans. These mandates provide a fertile ground for experimenting with different forms of sharing leadership. Throughout this book, the reader will find strategies, tools, and techniques that can be used to involve all stakeholder groups. For example, Interview Design, Data on Display, and Snowflake could be used in the needs identification stage.[26] DIAD might be used to assess progress and gain further buy-in.

Traditional school planning, particularly as it relates to federal program monies, begins with a purpose external to a school; it begins with a federal program's purpose and a known amount of money. Once a district learns the answer to the questions, *How much money is available through the program?* and *What are we allowed to do with that money?*, they propose a program to meet the regulations in the federal program guidelines within the dollars allotted. Typically, planning for federal program money has been done at the county level. Money is distributed to schools based on a prescribed formula, a needs basis, or competitive grants. The products of this traditional planning are multiple plans at the district level—one for each of many federal and state programs.

Unified planning, posed as an alternative, results in only one plan—not multiple plans. It begins at the school level (not at the federal level) with an internal expression of need based on an assessment of needs, establishment of a vision, and the setting of improvement goals and objectives. At least in theory, this form of planning begins with the questions *What do our students really need in order to be more successful?* and *How do we define "success"?* Once the activities have been identified, the task becomes one of matching the money sources with the improvement activities. For example, if a school has decided (based on a thorough needs assessment) to offer after-school enrichment programs, in unified planning it appears to be a matter of then asking *Which of the federal programs' monies can be used to pay for such a program?*

The Unified School Improvement Plan is a mandate from the West Virginia Board of Education; every school must complete one and submit it to the district office. The rationale is clear. All schools currently have multiple plans, written to be responsive to multiple funding sources (both federal- and state-level). The idea behind the unified school planning effort is to look at the big picture—asking questions such as *What does our school need?, What are our strengths?,* and *What would best help our students?*—not the picture specific to a program or grant (e.g., technology, parent involvement, and remediation). From that big picture view, a school can more easily identify a vision that unites and energizes the entire school community; assess needs (e.g., *Where are we now compared to where we want to be?*) and then set goals to achieve that vision.

Unified planning is more than a mandate from the state board of education. It provides the **opportunity** for a school community to come together, focus on student needs, and agree to enter the journey of continuous improvement. Both as mandate and opportunity, the Unified School Improvement Plan can simplify a school's compliance with multiple required programs by eliminating duplication of efforts and focusing instead on the "big picture" or the "whole picture"—with students and student achievement at the center.

Data in a Day

Data in a Day is a 24-hour process through which a school can involve its entire community in a self-study. It is flexible and can be adapted for many purposes. It focuses on teaching and learning in the classroom, relies heavily on student voice, and has the potential to involve the entire school community. A summary of the process follows.

A. Plan and organize the DIAD process.

Allow at least two weeks, preferably more, for the following organizational tasks.

1. Communicate with the school council, parent groups, and faculty about the process and secure their commitment to participate. Recruit a design team, consisting of the school principal and two or three other people, to assist in planning.

2. Set a date. Reserve adequate space in which to meet and work.

3. Invite participants to serve on research teams. The size of the school will determine the number; six research teams of three to four members each is sufficient for a school with a faculty of 30. To assure diverse viewpoints and perspectives, research teams should include teachers, students, parents, community members, and support staff.

4. Organize teams and schedule observations, giving each team the opportunity to observe at least three classes. Recruit substitutes to cover for the faculty involved on research teams.

5. Don't forget refreshments! DIAD might begin with a dinner meeting; at the very least, refreshments should be served at the orienta-

tion meeting. Breakfast and lunch on Day Two are a necessity, as the group convenes early and continues through the afternoon. A concluding reception for all faculty is a welcome touch for Day Two's after-school meeting.

B. Identify themes for study.

Typically, the process begins at an after-school meeting on Day One, when research teams convene to identify the themes for study. In role-alike focus groups, teachers and students talk about the school and about "what's important around here." Outside facilitators, who take notes during the focus groups, consolidate the different groups' thinking and, with the help of the design team, identify themes that "define" the school's vision. The optimal number of themes for study is three or four.

Alternatively, the design team can select the themes before the first meeting of the researchers. For example, at one elementary school, the design team identified four themes that captured the essence of what was important by looking at pieces of the school improvement plan—the school vision, mission statement, and goals.

The first time you use DIAD, you'll probably find it easiest to have the design team select the themes. This is also the time when outside facilitators will be most helpful. After one experience with the process, schools can certainly conduct the study on their own.

C. Generate indicators for observations.

Teachers will be better informed about the purposes—and more interested in the results—if they can be involved in identifying what the researchers will look for. If the themes can be identified before the first meeting, then all teachers can be asked for input by identifying specific, observable examples of this theme, i.e., what it would look like—in its ideal form—in the classrooms.

The first meeting of the researchers, beginning in the afternoon or evening, provides an orientation. After introductions of all group members, review the purposes of the DIAD process and the agenda for the next 24 hours. The major purpose of this meeting is to gain a common understanding of each of the themes—as they observe on the following day, all researchers need to be looking for the same things. In role-alike groups (students, teachers, support staff, and parents/community members) brainstorm indicators—specific and observable examples—of the themes to be observed on the next day. Overnight, the design team completes a thematic analysis, summarizing the indicators into lists for each of the four thematic areas. (See sample observation forms in Appendix C.)

D. Collect data.

At a morning meeting on Day Two, researchers gather at the school to receive their assignments. During the 60 to 90 minutes after breakfast, they will observe in three classrooms each, looking for examples and nonexamples of each of the four themes.

E. Analyze data.

First, research teams summarize the data from each classroom across each theme. Researchers re-form into "theme teams" and analyze the data from all classroom observations related to a single theme. Each team prepares a summary on its theme. If time allows, teams can practice their reports.

F. Report findings.

At the end of Day Two, each theme team presents its findings to a meeting of the faculty and invited guests—parents, council, school boards, or other interested community members. The report should be visual, giving as many specific examples as possible.

G. Continue the conversations.

Follow-up is essential if this process is to result in any real change. Revisit these themes at meetings of the faculty, departments, grade-level teams, parent organizations, and school improvement councils, and use the DIAD data when making action plans.

The preparation of a Unified School Plan has been an impetus for cooperation and participation at our school. We sought and received positive input from all members of the school community. People were so pleased to have a chance to voice their opinions. Surprisingly, we found commonality in everyone's goal for our school: working together for our students. Parents and other community persons still ask what they can do to help achieve these goals! In a time of negativity in many educational systems, this has proven to be a shining ray of hope for the future of our students.

—Denise Freeland, Counselor,
Moundsville Junior High School

Getting Everyone in the Act Using Interview Design

by Cheryl Dingess, Speech Therapist, Atenville Elementary School

Recently, our local school improvement council used a new tool during its annual goal-setting conference. An informal assessment of needs and recent test scores revealed several areas of weakness that needed to be addressed. The council includes teachers, parents, service personnel, students, and business partners. In past conferences, teachers tended to control the conversation, assuming that the silence of others meant agreement. Parents, students, and service personnel often didn't have time to voice their opinions or thoughts, or they felt their views were not valued by the teachers and principal.

To give every member's thoughts and opinions equal weight, the council decided to use a process called Interview Design, which required each member to answer each question and gave everyone's answers equal weight.[27] It also provided anonymity to participants who lacked self-confidence or feared reprisals. How exciting it was to finally hear the views of our service personnel and students, as well as the parents and business partners! How exciting to see our preconceived notions crumble before the thoughtful responses to such questions as *How can we make our schools more safe?*

Interview Design helped each member to take ownership of the school community's vision and goals, thus ensuring commitment to complete the goals.

The following are questions we used during the Interview Design process with the Atenville Elementary School community:

Leadership is not the private reserve of a few charismatic men and women. It is a process that ordinary people use when they are bringing forth the best from themselves and others.

—James Kouzes & Barry Posner

1. Given the violence that recently occurred in Colorado, what can schools do to prevent violent behavior in children?
2. Nationally, many children have trouble in reading. What can we do to make certain that all children are reading by third grade?
3. Math is critical to performance in the real world. How can we better integrate Micro math into the classroom?

Structured Reflection Protocol[28]

Conducting a protocol puts people in charge of their own learning. When teachers or students use it, they begin to see how they can improve their work. Both students and teachers can begin to define the kinds of lessons and professional development they need. When you have used the Structured Reflection Protocol process for a while, you will see some changes in the way that staff members and students talk and listen to each other.

Protocol Teaches Important Skills

- Careful listening—Users become more aware of how people use words and what assumptions lie behind certain words.
- Expressing—Users get better at explaining what they mean.
- Clarifying—Users begin to take time to ask questions, to get clarification, and to arrive at mutual understanding.
- Generating—Users learn to offer different perspectives. New meanings emerge, and users propose new actions.

How to Do It

Advance preparation: prepare the question and select student work. In advance of the protocol session, participants should agree on the topic they want to address and prepare a focusing question to guide their discussion. Then they should select an analysis team (2 to 6 members), a feedback team (the same size or larger than analysis team), and a facilitator. Analysis team members will select examples of student work and consider how to present their thoughts about the work as it relates to the focusing question.

Setting up on the day of the protocol. The facilitator reviews the steps of the protocol process and informs the group he or she will keep an eye on the time spent on each part of the process. The facilitator posts the focusing question on a blackboard or a piece of paper. The analysis team members sit together so they can maintain eye contact during their conversation. Their peers in the feedback team are seated close enough to listen. The analysis team members introduce the work they have selected.

Analysis. (15-30 minutes) The facilitator starts the discussion by asking members of the analysis team to discuss their response to the focusing question and refer specifically to their examples of student work. Time allotted for the analysis will depend on the complexity of the question and the number of team members. To assist in the discussion, the facilitator may offer these generic questions to help guide the discussion after looking at the student work that has been gathered:

- What can you say about this work?
- Why are you getting student work in this form?
- What can be done to help improve the work?

Feedback. (15-20 minutes) The feedback team has been listening carefully and making notes for its response. The feedback can begin immediately, unless the team is not familiar with details of the assignment. Then, if team members need more information before they can provide feedback, the facilitator might allow a few minutes for clarifying questions.

Warm feedback comes first and consists of supportive statements.

Structured Reflection Protocol

(continued from page 99)

Usually about half the feedback time is devoted to warm feedback. Example of warm feedback:

I liked how Gary helps students improve their math expression—he has students rewrite their problems using appropriate language. I already require students to explain the process they used to get the answers, but he has them working with each other in small groups until they improve their language; he takes the students a step further.

Cool feedback comes next and takes two forms. It includes statements that start out by saying "I wonder what would happen if we tried . . ." or it might raise a question about something that should still be considered. Examples of cool feedback:

1. *I wonder if the kids are able to respond to all those writing prompts the same way. I once read that it is best to have prompts that have been used before and have worked with this age group. Have you found a good source for proven prompts?*

2. *What do you do with those students whose work shows they just don't care, who just do the minimum? Have you found anything that works with them?*

Reflection. (5-15 minutes) During the feedback, the analysis group quietly listens and reflects. Analysis team members do *not* respond to each comment or question as posed, but simply take in all that is said. Once the feedback time is over, the analysis team members talk among themselves about what they heard from the feedback group. Their dialogue centers on

- new ideas or strategies provided by the feedback

- actions the analysis team might try next
- answers to selected questions raised by the feedback team

During reflection, it is tempting to abandon the protocol format and move to a whole-group discussion. It is the facilitator's job to ensure that only the analysis team talks during this phase of the process. During this time, the feedback group members have an important task. They observe how the analysis team is using the feedback provided and consider how to give better feedback in the future.

Debriefing. (5-10 minutes) Individuals in both groups share their perceptions about the work they were shown and about the protocol process itself. The conversation here should not be targeted at any one person but, instead, be a discussion about what was learned.

Examples of debriefing statements:

1. *One of the things I've learned today is that we've come a long way this year. We now are doing some analysis and assimilation of ideas.*

2. *When students created their own math problems, I noticed that everybody seemed to learn more and it was more fun, too.*

Sample Debriefing Questions

- How did the process go?
- What have we learned?
- What would you change next time?
- Did you think of something you had not thought of before, or think of something in a different way?

Determining next steps. Members of the analysis team should leave the protocol with a "plan of action." This is often a new approach to try during the next week. The new plan may itself suggest a follow-up question for another protocol. Usually, the end of one protocol is an ideal time to generate a question for the next protocol.

Examples of next steps:

1. *I definitely think we all need to look at how to teach the students to analyze their progress and make connections between their ideas. At our next protocol session, I suggest we look at how students are connecting ideas in their science project.*
2. *Now that students have written thesis statements and collected evidence, how are we going to help them put all the ideas in a logical sequence on their lab reports? Let's address that at our next protocol.*

What Comes Next?

After completing several protocols, the "protocol-ers" may be ready to branch out. Here are some examples of the ways schools have used the protocol experience:

- Some schools have found the process is particularly helpful when school data of any kind are being examined. The whole school can use the process to look at student achievement or survey data, for instance.

- Schools have used the process to discuss diverse topics, such as state standards or the way teachers respond to a new attendance policy.

- The protocol process can be used in connection with action research being collected.

- The protocol can be used on an ongoing basis to help the school tackle issues of concern.

Structured Reflection Protocol for Student Use

Getting Ready

The class is divided into small groups. Each small group has

- two or more students who will analyze their work. This is the **analysis team.**
- two or more students who will listen and then share their thoughts. This is the **feedback team.**

Analysis Time

Analysis team members will have 10 minutes to talk about their work. Each member of the analysis team has a turn doing each of these steps:

1. First, read your answer aloud.
2. Next, read the focusing question aloud.
3. Now, describe how your work addressed this focusing question. If there were things you could have done differently on this assignment, you describe that also.

If there is time left for analysis, the analysis team members should talk about what their thinking was when they were doing this work and how they made a decision to do the assignment in this way.

Feedback team members listen and take notes while analysis team members talk.

Feedback Time

When the teacher or timekeeper says the analysis time is over, then it is the feedback team's turn to talk with each other.

Feedback team members ask questions or provide suggestions for ways to improve the work while the analysis team members just listen—the analyzers will have a chance to talk when the teacher says the feedback team time is over.

Once students are familiar with the process, they should be able to select their own facilitator or work without one.

Does Our School Community Share Leadership?

Use the following items to reflect on your own school community:

• All members of the school community believe that what they do makes a difference.

• Leadership is not associated with particular positions or roles, but is open to all who are willing to assume responsibility.

• Formal leaders communicate shared goals that mobilize and energize the entire school community.

• Those who are affected by a decision play a significant role in the decision-making process.

• School administrators share information freely with all members of the community.

• Individuals are encouraged to exercise initiative in making changes that will improve their personal performance and contribute to student learning.

• School administrators understand that they do not have all the solutions, rather they facilitate others (parents, teachers, students, and staff) in solving problems.

• School administrators facilitate two-way communications between and among all members of the community.

• Opportunities are provided for all members of the community to develop leadership skills.

If you want people to think differently, don't tell them how to think, give them a tool.

—Buckminster Fuller

Ways to use the preceding questions as a stimulus for individual reflection:

A. Write in a journal in response to the items that especially trigger your thinking. Remember and record specific examples that illustrate your school community's performance in this area, recalling the accompanying sounds, sights, and feelings of these experiences.

Consider how your own perceptions and assumptions color your views of leadership opportunities in your school. In what ways can you demonstrate leadership, invite others to share in this leadership, and generate enthusiasm for continuous school improvement?

B. For each area, give a grade (A, B, C, D, F) to your school community. What is your school's shared leadership GPA? How can you work to improve your school community's grade in any of these areas?

Take a Look at Your School

In which of the above areas does your school community most need to improve? How would these improvements make a difference for student learning? In what areas can you personally make a difference?

Group discussion:

Use Data on Display as a structure to promote group discussion on this topic with a school governance group, a faculty committee, a student leadership team, or a heterogeneous group representing the entire school community.[29] The use of this kind of structure will enable people to make their ratings anonymously and honestly and yet concentrate on the group's views as opposed to staying focused on their own individual perspectives. Select up to five items for rating and

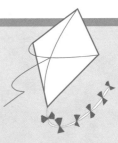

discussion, framing some of them as ideals and others as queries about "our own school." Sample items:

1. Every member of a school community has the potential to make a difference in the overall effectiveness of a school.

2. In our school, all members of the school community—parents, students, teachers, and support staff—are willing to assume responsibility.

3. Open communication is important to an effective school community.

4. Individuals in our school community regularly engage in open and honest two-way communication between and among all members of the community.

Notes

1. Wheatley, *Leadership and the New Science,* 66.

2. See Sergiovanni, *Building Community in Schools.*

3. Sergiovanni, *Building Community in Schools,* xiii and xvi.

4. Kouzes and Posner, *Encouraging the Heart,* 108.

5. Fullan, "Emotion and Hope," 225.

6. See Kouzes and Posner, "Seven Lessons."

7. Sergiovanni, *Building Community in Schools,* xix.

8. Sergiovanni, *Building Community in Schools,* 171.

9. See story about Structured Reflection Protocol at Woodbridge Senior High School in "School as Community," a section in chapter one. A story about using protocol with students at Alexander Elementary School can be found in "Building Ownership for Assessment" in chapter four. The process is more fully described later in this chapter.

10. See the story, "After-School Smarts in Harts: 21st Century Community Learning Centers" in "School for Community," a section of chapter one. The 21st Century Learning Community Center was begun in fiscal year 1998. Over $400 million were provided to schools and communities in fiscal year 2000 with the multiple goals of academic enrichment, cultural and recreational activities, and lifelong opportunities for members of the community. To learn more about the program as funded by the U.S. Department of Education, visit their Web site at http://www.ed.gov/21stcclc.

11. Hargrove, *Mastering the Art of Creative Collaboration,* 97.

12. Block, *Stewardship,* 3.

13. Block, *Stewardship,* 41, 27.

14. The process of Data in a Day is described later in this chapter along with stories about the use of the process in two schools.

15. Senge et al., *The Dance of Change,* 15.

16. Senge et al., *The Dance of Change,* 16.

17. Senge et al., *The Dance of Change,* 39.

18. The process of Interview Design is more fully described in chapter four.

19. The Benedum Collaborative is a joint venture between West Virginia University and selected West Virginia public schools to create and implement the reform of education in the state, using public schools and teacher education, based on the best research and practice available.

The Collaborative has been funded with grants from the Claude Worthington Benedum Foundation of Pittsburgh, Pennsylvania, to the College of Human Resources and Education at West Virginia University and 21 professional development schools. For more information, visit http://www.wvu/edu/~benedum/bcabout.html.

20. Senge et al., *The Dance of Change*, 13.

21. See Cook and Fine, *Critical Issue*, in the Pathways to School Improvement section of North Central Regional Educational Laboratory's Web site. Visit http://www.ncrel.org/sdrs/pathwayg.htm.

22. See note 19 above.

23. The Core Knowledge curriculum is based on work by E. D. Hirsch, Jr., a professor at the University of Virginia and founder of the Core Knowledge Foundation, an independent, nonprofit, nonpartisan organization. Hirsch is the author of many books, including *Cultural Literacy: What Every American Needs to Know*, the sequence of books that form the basis of the curriculum: *What Your Kindergartner Needs to Know* through *What Your Sixth Grader Needs to Know*. Many schools across the country use this work as the basis for their curriculum. For more information, see http://www/coreknowledge.org/CKproto2/index/htm.

24. For complete instructions on the Data on Display activity, see "Clarifying Beliefs in Community" in chapter three.

25. More complete instruction about Data in a Day (DIAD) follows this story. Earl Wiman, principal, first learned about DIAD through his work with AEL and the School Change Collaborative. The partnership among the nation's 10 regional educational laboratories developed a *Self-Study Toolkit* (2000), produced and distributed by the Northwest Regional Educational Laboratory in Portland, Oregon. AEL produced a video (2000) about DIAD, *Stop, Look, Listen: Using Data in a Day to Assess Your School Community*, which is part of the toolkit. For more information, visit the collaborative's Web site at http://www.nwrel.org.

26. These tools are described throughout this book: Interview Design is in chapter four; Data on Display and Snowflake are in chapter three.

27. See note 26 above.

28. Adapted and reprinted by permission from the Laboratory Network Program's *Listening to Student Voices Self-Study Toolkit*.

29. See note 26 above.

Enriching the
Learning Culture

Parents, teachers, principals, and students have always sensed something special, yet undefined, about their schools—something extremely powerful but difficult to describe. This ephemeral, taken-for-granted aspect of schools is often overlooked and consequently is usually absent from discussions about school improvement. For decades the terms climate and ethos have been used to try to capture this powerful, pervasive, and notoriously elusive force. We believe the term culture provides a more accurate and intuitively appealing way to help school leaders better understand their schools' own unwritten rules and traditions, norms, and expectations that seem to permeate everything: the way people act, how they dress, what they talk about or avoid talking about, whether they seek out colleagues for help or don't, and how teachers feel about their work and their students.

—Terrence Deal & Kent Peterson

*T*he intangibles that comprise the culture of a school are perhaps the strongest motivators of individual and collective performance. Culture is the factor that nourishes or poisons the efforts of teachers, students, parents, and other members of a school community—day in and day out. Because culture is an intangible, it cannot be mandated; it must be cultivated over time. One individual alone cannot cultivate a positive culture; this is the work for a community. Where individuals within a community share leadership, together they can forge a rich and vibrant school culture—one in which learning and continuous improvement of practice are expected norms.

Questions for Reflection

Schools can inventory their cultures by reflecting on the extent to which the various contributors to culture are developed within their school communities. The questions below focus attention on component parts of culture.

- Do all members of your school community share a sense of "how things are done around here"?

- Is there widespread agreement that learning is "what's really important" in your school?

- Are there tangible signs and symbols incorporating your school's character and values?

- Do members of the school community share stories that convey the essence of the school?

- Is there individual commitment to learning, growing, and becoming the best one can be?

The Culture Puzzle: Parts, Patterns, and Possibilities

Culture is the context in which individuals work and relate one to another. Culture is more related to the spiritual or emotional side of our being and behavior than to our intellectual or rational self—more to be felt or sensed than touched or analyzed. Because culture is composed of intangible, ephemeral, abstract pieces, it is not subject to objective analysis or traditional research methods.

Something is lost when one attempts to identify culture's discrete parts and separate these for study. On the other hand, current literature provides a language that facilitates thinking and talking about culture. Terry Deal suggests five phenomena related to culture.[1] Applied to the school setting, these are

- the *vision* that people have of what learning looks, sounds, and feels like
- the *norms,* or shared beliefs, that affect "how the business of teaching and learning" is done around here
- the *rituals or ceremonies* that mark important events in the school
- the *heroes and heroines* that are held up as role models
- the *stories and legends* surrounding teaching and learning

Every school has a culture. The issue is whether it is a culture for learning that has been cultivated and nourished over time or an incoherent or even toxic one that has been allowed to evolve willy-nilly. By focusing on vision, norms, rituals, heroes, and stories, school leaders can harness culture to support learning and continuous improvement.

Creating and Nurturing a Culture for Learning: Lessons Learned from Three Schools

Imagine a school where culture encourages everyone who walks its hallways to become excited about learning and to set high expectations for their own and others' achievement. What would such a school look and feel like? What kinds of voices would you hear in the classrooms? In the teachers' workrooms? On the buses? In the carpool lines? What would motivate the students, teachers, staff, and parents? How would individuals relate to one another? A multitude of different images come to mind—because there is not one right answer to any of these questions. A strong learning culture is customized to the school community that it supports. One size does not fit all. No two are exactly alike. Consider the following three school stories.

Lagniappe: The Practice of Giving an Extra Measure

Connie Allen, principal of Natcher Elementary School, talks with passion about *lagniappe* (the practice of "giving a little something extra") as the defining characteristic of "The Natcher Way." This word conveys a powerful message to members of the Natcher community who encounter it daily in the school bulletin: Always do more than what is expected of you. *Lagniappe* manifests itself in the beautifully landscaped grounds; in the welcoming lobby with running fountain and green plants, comfortable chairs, and meaningful artwork; in special events and celebrations; in extra phone calls and notes to parents; in continual striving for more effective strategies for reaching and teaching all children; in all that is undertaken by this school community. In Allen's words, "Nothing is taken for granted; no one is taken for granted. And behind all of this is a lot of love and passion for children. Without them, nothing else happens or matters."

A case in point from the history of Natcher occurred in 1997, when renowned children's author Paul Brett Johnson visited the school to read his widely acclaimed book, *The Cow Who Wouldn't Come Down.* On this day everyone got into the act: students, teachers, and staff dressed in black and white. The black and white "cow pattern" bedecked the walls and bulletin boards throughout the school. The cafeteria servers dressed in farmers' overalls and procured inflatable plastic cows to march across the serving counter. Students from Western Kentucky University's School of Agriculture brought a huge black-and-white dairy cow to pasture in the front of the school and presented "lessons" to all classes on cows. Alecia Marcum, the school librarian who orchestrated this event, subsequently received the Exemplary Library Service for Children and Young Adults Award from the Kentucky Library Association—a well-deserved award for doing "a little something extra." More important, *lagniappe* from each member of the school community contributed to a highly enriched, motivating, and memorable learning experience.

The Little School That Could: Raising Community Expectations

Nestled in the hills of West Virginia is Atenville Elementary School, where students, parents, teachers, and staff exude a "can-do" attitude as they engage in exciting new ventures in teaching and learning. Faculty and staff are continually learning and incorporating best practices into daily instruction. From a focus on brain-based learning to more effective questioning strategies, teachers seek ways to more actively engage students in learning; students move about with a sense of confidence and purposefulness—especially as they engage in learning through participation in Atenville's MicroSociety.[2] A virtual army of parent volunteers assumes myriad roles in support of teaching and learning.

Things were not always thus at Atenville. Darlene Dalton, principal, recalls the days when the little school reflected the low self-esteem and low expectations of the surrounding community, which is beset with high levels of unemployment and poverty. In Darlene's words, "Our school was a 'gray school,' infected with complacency and defeatism." This spunky lady—driven by love and passion for these children— determined that these young people would and could "get to the other side of the mountain." They would develop a vision for their future; they would believe in themselves; they would develop a work ethic; they would be nurtured by adults who held high expectations for their performance and who also provided high levels of support; they would experience success in school so that they could build on this in their futures. Darlene's vision for the children and the school is palpable—a striking example of "vision as a field of energy" that engages individuals within an organization to work together to achieve shared goals.[3]

Eating Fried Worms: A Celebration of Student Success

March 30, 1999. Jackson, Tennessee. Principal Earl Wiman, radiant in his Dr. Seuss hat, looks over the audience of eager faces—young and old—awaiting his promised performance: eating worms in celebration of an incredible feat accomplished by the 530 young students at Alexander Elementary School. These students read more than 13,000 books over the course of 12 months. They did it in response to Wiman's

Culture is generally thought of as the normative glue that holds a particular school together. With shared vision, values, and beliefs at its heart, culture serves as a compass setting, steering people in a common direction.

—Thomas Sergiovanni

challenge related to the students' participation in the Accelerated Reading program. The high school band is playing; television cameras are recording this moment in time; students and adults are cheering; excitement is building. Principal Wiman eats the three worms specially prepared by a Nashville chef. The students cheer! The celebration is on! Although Wiman is clearly the hero of the day to those gathered in the school auditorium, the real focus is on the students and their accomplishments. Wiman, as always, tells them how special they are; how great their talents and accomplishments; how bright their future. They listen and believe.

Alexander Elementary is an inner-city school, and its students bring with them all the usual factors that hinder inner-city children. The difference at Alexander: these are special students who do believe, as does their principal, that they can meet extraordinary goals; that hard work is necessary to achievement; that learning and work can be fun; and that hard-sought-after accomplishments are worth celebrating.

The Lifeworld of Leadership: Creating Culture, Community, and Personal Meaning in Our Schools by Thomas J. Sergiovanni (San Francisco: Jossey-Bass, 1999).

Sergiovanni opens this thought-provoking book with the following: "Most successful school leaders will tell you that getting the culture right and paying attention to how parents, teachers, and students define and experience meaning are two widely accepted rules for creating effective schools." He proceeds to introduce two facets of school life to which leaders must attend: the "lifeworld" and the "systemsworld." He contrasts these one to another. The lifeworld—composed of culture, meaning, and significance—focuses on individuals and their personal needs, human relationships, and the emotional and spiritual sides of organizational life. The systemsworld encompasses the organizational structures, the management systems, and other material and resource considerations. Sergiovanni contends that effective leaders attend to both of these worlds and are able to create symbiotic relationships between the two. The focus of this book is, of course, on the lifeworld; however, the author conveys throughout the book connections that leaders must make between this "human side of the organization" and the concrete world of school schedules, budgets, accountability demands, and so forth.

Lessons Learned

Three different schools. Three different images. The patterns and strokes are different, but the principles, tools, and techniques are very similar. Five common threads emerge from these school tapestries and are applicable in other school settings.

1. *Strong learning cultures don't emerge spontaneously. They are cultivated and nourished by visionary leaders.* Allen, Dalton, and Wiman hold compelling visions for the students they serve. Each of these leaders is passionate about the vision and about the children. For Allen, the vision is for each member of the school community to do and be more than is expected; for Dalton, that each child in her school develop a strong work ethic and belief in self; for Wiman, that each child feel special, cared for, and capable of achieving at high levels. In each case, the leader articulates the dream and carries the torch. These are the individuals Deal and Peterson had in mind when they wrote of "leaders [who] shape culture, creating cohesive places that help teachers teach and students learn."[4]

2. *The norms and values supporting the vision (and overall culture) are meaningfully connected to the communities served by the school.* Natcher Elementary serves a suburban population; Atenville, an isolated, rural community low on the socioeconomic scale; and Alexander, an inner-city, minority population. The term *lagniappe* might not be so eagerly embraced by members of a community existing on the edge. Emphasis on the development of a strong work ethic would not be so compelling in an upper socioeconomic community. A focus on "making students feel special and cared for" might not be so critical in more traditional neighborhoods. An important key to strengthening the learning culture is the choice of language in which a compelling idea is framed. Norms must be expressed in terms that speak to people where they are.

3. *Ordinary events are transformed to an extraordinary and memorable level through careful orchestration. These technicolor happenings provide the stuff from which stories are crafted and shared throughout the*

community. How many students are so special that they cause their principal to eat worms, and, as a result, be featured in *The Weekly Reader* and on CNN News? For how many generations will this story be passed down? And how many children have seen a cow milked on the front lawn of their school? How many of these children might have lived a lifetime without witnessing such an event save for their principal's passion to provide *lagniappe*? Finally, how can children at Atenville Elementary ever forget the business they ran, the money they made, and the pride they had in a job well done? How much impact will this first job have upon their lives and the lives of those who follow in their school?

> We dance with change . . . and when we dance with change, we dance with life. . . . It's what energizes our staff.
>
> —Darlene Dalton, Principal, Atenville Elementary School

4. *Tangible signs, symbols, routines, and rituals are adapted to represent and reinforce intangible norms and shared values.* Each school day at Natcher begins with a recitation of the Natcher student resolution:

> **I believe I can be a good student at Natcher Elementary School.**
> **I believe I can achieve and excel.**
> **Therefore, I will work hard each day to do my best.**
> **I can learn.**
> **I will learn.**
> **Because I am a SMART learner.**

Alexander students also begin their day by reciting a student creed; then they turn their attention to "Triple A Math"—Alexander's Awesome Arithmetic—a hands-on, game-type approach to the review of basic mathematical skills. Atenville students value "cub bucks," the currency in their MicroSociety. Each of these school cultures is rich with artifacts unique to the school community.

5. *The community comes together to celebrate one another and individual and collective accomplishments.* Pride permeates the fabric of each of the three schools. This pride is manifest through everyday behaviors but is particularly evident in community celebrations. Each school vignette features a community celebration that typifies the enthusiasm and excitement rippling through the schools' learning cultures.

How are these common threads woven together to create different patterns and vignettes in different school cultures? Master weavers know that looms are all-important; that strong structures support and enhance daily efforts to strengthen the fabric of an organization's culture. Hence, they are continuously searching for new and different structures and processes with which to sustain and extend their work. This is the theme that emerges from an analysis of the culture of these three schools: the work is never done. To strengthen the learning culture, the leader must continuously seek and find strategies that will induct each new generation to the manners, mores, and myths of their community.

Knitting the elements of culture into an artistic tapestry is like creating a word from the letters of the alphabet. Juxtaposed with one another the letters form a meaningful expression, just as combining the elements of culture creates a cohesive school identity.

—Terrence Deal & Kent Peterson

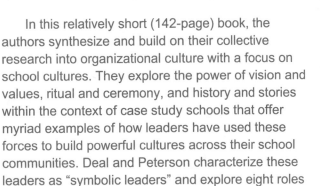

Shaping School Culture: The Heart of Leadership by Terrence E. Deal & Kent D. Peterson (San Francisco: Jossey-Bass, 1999).

In this relatively short (142-page) book, the authors synthesize and build on their collective research into organizational culture with a focus on school cultures. They explore the power of vision and values, ritual and ceremony, and history and stories within the context of case study schools that offer myriad examples of how leaders have used these forces to build powerful cultures across their school communities. Deal and Peterson characterize these leaders as "symbolic leaders" and explore eight roles that they assume. Finally, the authors explore the roots of what they call "toxic" school cultures and offer strategies for turning these cultures around.

What If the Glass Slipper Fit Your School?

What if you had a fairy godmother who could turn a pumpkin into a glittering horse-drawn coach? Or a toxic school environment into a strong learning culture? What would you wish for if the glass slipper fit your school? Is there a prototype or model to which you might turn? If you had a fairy godmother who could wave a magic wand, what type of culture would you have her create?

Vision

The magic would begin with a compelling vision embraced by all members of the school community—teachers, staff, students, and parents alike. This is the seed from which a strong learning culture develops and blossoms. This vision might paint a picture like this:

> All adults and students in our school are excited about learning. They are curious and routinely ask questions for which they do not have the answers. They are seeking better ways to do their jobs, always striving to improve their performance. They are working together to learn from their own and others' knowledge and experience. They are continually trying out new ways of doing things and collecting and using evidence to determine effectiveness. They do not fear failure, but rather view mistakes as an opportunity for learning.
>
> —Quest Vision Statement

Norms or Shared Beliefs

Embedded in any vision are norms or shared beliefs that guide the behavior of community members. A hallmark of a learning community is the *curiosity* that pervades its members, who intentionally and routinely employ inquiry as a way of searching for new knowledge. Individuals possess the courage to ask questions from a position of not knowing; they give up the need to be certain, to expect that there is only one "right answer." Those in positions of authority tolerate ambiguity and uncertainty long enough to discover something new. They encourage others to *suspend judgment* for the sake of searching and creating. They also *support experimentation* and risk-taking and establish a zone of comfort and trust that encourages these norms. Individuals shed their fear regarding mistakes and failures. Instead they seek to learn from mistakes.[5]

Norms that support curiosity and risk-taking begin with the assumption that all community members are *competent,* capable of learning and improving, and can perform at high levels. Students and adults alike are encouraged to give up the belief that the "right answers" are outside in some "expert."[6] To honor this belief, leaders of this learning community encourage all members to *reflect* on their practice, experience, and performance—and they provide time for this to happen. These practices support the *proactivity* of individuals who are consciously moving away from reactive behaviors. Although we "have grown accustomed to changing only in reaction to outside forces . . . the wellspring of real learning is aspiration, imagination, and experimentation."[7]

While high respect for the individual is essential to a learning community, the individual is not an island unto herself or himself. Rather, we see ourselves as *interdependent* with the entire community. We learn from one another and find strength in *diversity.* There is a sense that "people who collaborate learn from each other and create synergy."[8] Supporting this connectedness among individuals is a norm of honest and open communication. *Authenticity* and candor are valued; *trust* and respect enable these.

Rituals, Heroes, and Stories

The school's leadership employs rituals, heroes, and stories in an effort to strengthen the culture for learning. Ceremonies that honor individuals who exemplify norms, celebrations of community success in reaching established goals, weekly inquiry sessions that encourage faculty to question and learn together—these are examples of rituals that reinforce cultural norms. Through this process, heroes are recognized and held up as role models for others. And storytelling regarding individual and collective successes and failures is facilitated and applauded. These devices help anchor emerging norms in the learning culture.

. . . The clock strikes midnight, and all return to the real world. No magic wand can instantly change the culture of a school. Culture building is hard work that occurs over time. However, schools dedicated to enriching or strengthening their cultures in support of continuous learning and improvement can consider how vision, norms, rituals, heroes, and stories can support the new culture.

What's Important in Your School

Is the emphasis in your school on

- asking the right questions or having the right answers?
- being good or looking good?
- taking risks or playing it safe?
- cooperation or competition?
- searching or knowing?
- individual understanding or expert knowledge?

Crystallizing the Vision

Just about every person in the world has ideas about what a school should be. From the butcher to the baker, from the doctor to the lawyer, from the student to the teacher, from the parent to the principal, everyone seems to take a stand on what should and should not be happening inside the school walls. How, then, does a school create a unified, working vision that will propel faculty, staff, and, most important, students, toward an energized, focused dream that will create total school revitalization?

Pulling the vast array of opinions together into a crystallized vision demands gargantuan feats of leadership, incredible persistence, boundless tact, and sheer hard work. The process does not happen by magic; but the power of a shared vision may be said to be "magical."

A shared vision connects people in the school community around a common idea. A strong, shared vision actually helps us focus our attention on the possibilities and potentials—not the problems and pitfalls. The vision lays the foundation block for the culture of the school; it has great power to energize and mobilize.

A colleague recently shared a saying she had learned in a graduate class: "The main thing is to remember that the main thing is the main thing." Vision mobilizes a school

Few, if any, forces in human affairs are as powerful as shared vision. At its simplest level, a shared vision is the answer to the question, "What do we want to create?"

—Peter Senge

community to focus on the "main thing." In the following story from Lumberport, we learn how the faculty found the "main thing" in their school.

What's Important Around Here, Anyway?

by Vickie Luchuck, Teacher, Lumberport Elementary School

A couple of years ago, our faculty was demoralized. Although we had lots of good things going on in the school, we lacked a sense of direction. We got "stuck" thinking about all the things we didn't have: we didn't have many parents involved with the school; we lacked a true sense of community among our faculty; we didn't have strong and committed leadership.

At our first Quest rally, our school team was inspired to think about the potential of our school—and we individually and collectively pledged to help create this "better" school. One of the most moving experiences of the rally was the closing videotape. *It's In Every One of Us* was a simple, five-minute video with a beautiful musical background and video of humans—mostly faces—of all ages, nationalities, and ethnic groups. It was a poignant reminder of our common humanity.[9]

As we struggled with ideas about how to bring the Quest experience back to our faculty, we wanted to focus on the "main thing." We created a video, like the one from the rally, that was a collage of Lumberport: our students, bus drivers, teachers, cooks,

A vision presents a challenge to go where no one has gone before, to struggle and to risk failure in seeking success. It appeals to the adventurer within. A vision encourages nonconformity, asks for change, and leaves the old way behind. It is an invitation to achieve something great.

—Richard Daft & Robert Lengel,
Fusion Leadership

aides, parent volunteers, prominent community members, and our principal with his grandson. We added inspirational background music, and the powerful visual brought tears to our eyes! Seeing our children and the other members of our learning family made us proud and even more determined to work to change our school.

The day to share these ideas with other staff came quickly, and our anxiety rose just as quickly. Would they be excited and motivated too? Would they bring positive energy to add to ours—or would they drag us

> Vision gives an organization a glimpse of its collective potential. It gives meaning to why you belong to an organization. It answers the question, "Where are we going?" It defines direction.
>
> — Bob Boylan, *Get Everyone in Your Boat Rowing in the Same Direction*

down with negative energy and talk? We worked hard to establish a positive and festive climate in the school cafeteria. We encouraged everyone to bring a dish; it was our first covered-dish luncheon in many years. We tried to break up the usual cliques and groups by assigning seating. As we began, it seemed that everyone was having a good time talking and being together.

But as we began our presentation, we sensed some resistance. We were talking about change, and we realized that many teachers thought our school was just fine the way it was. We were working from two different assumptions. They equated change with "fixing" something that was broken; we saw change as a way to grow and continue to improve.

20/20 Vision: Creating a School of Continuous Improvement

Many techniques exist to help people sharpen their mental image of what they want for their school and, through honest sharing and discussion, to create a vision that all can share or claim as their collective vision. This tool, 20/20 Vision, is suggested as the first of a two-part strategy. Initially, it is important for individuals to reflect on and gain clarity about what is important to them in an "ideal" school. Teachers, parents, students, and community members can all profitably be involved in this activity, a quick way for people to begin to understand what is most important to them.

This activity should be followed by an activity (such as Snowflake) that promotes sharing among members of the group and the identification of collective, shared values with which to begin to identify common themes for a shared vision or statement of beliefs.

The 20/20 Vision activity requires 60 to 90 minutes and can be completed with a group of between 20 and 50 people. If more people participate, the ensuing conversation will be richer, but it will require more time. Prepare a handout with about 6 to 10 prompts; use or adapt the Sample Prompts handout (included on page 122), which was designed for use in a generic setting. Under each prompt on the handout, allow ample space to write.

Individual reflection. Be sure the setting is quiet and that participants respect the time to think and write without interruption. Allow at least 15 minutes; these prompts require thoughtful responses. Some people may prefer to receive the prompts in advance so that they have time to think about their answers. Make sure that people understand that no one will be reading their responses, so grammar and spelling don't count. They'll be sharing their

The highlight of our session was showing our homemade, but priceless, video. Our students made us smile, then chuckle aloud. We even heard some "ahhh's" and watched a few in the group wipe tears from their eyes. No one talked about "being bored with this movie." The only conversation was reflective and excited as we all realized why we were there...and why we needed to continuously strive for total school improvement. Doors were opened and some of our most negative teachers said things like, "You know, we do have good kids!" or "Yeah, we do some pretty cool projects here." Progress had begun. We had set our sights on the "main thing."

Just as personal visions are pictures or images people carry around in their heads and hearts, so too are shared visions pictures that people throughout an organization carry. They create a sense of commonality that permeates the organization and gives coherence to diverse activities.

—Peter Senge

responses orally in small groups after the initial time to write.

Identifying common themes. After people have completed their individual reflections, have them number off or somehow form into groups, one for each reflective prompt. Their assignment, in this new heterogeneous group, is to share individual responses and look for common themes, writing them legibly on easel paper that can be posted on the wall. For example, if a group had responded to the sample prompts, the small group assigned to the first prompt would gather together, read through the goals that "20/20 School" has for students, and record their responses on an easel sheet. Likewise, other groups around the room would be simultaneously sharing their responses to other numbered prompts.

After a sufficient amount of time (5 minutes or so), groups will move in a clockwise direction to the next station, reading through the posted responses and adding any from their individual reflections that are not represented on the list. At three-minute intervals, the groups will continue to rotate to at least three other stations, eventually moving back to their original easel paper.

Finding the common core or essential elements. Individuals and groups have now considered their own dreams and reviewed parts of the dreams and visions of others. The time has come to formulate a shared vision. Ask individuals to think about what they have seen as they walked around and then to answer the following kinds of questions: What ideas are recurring? What elements are absolutely essential for the collective "picture" the group holds for this school? Participants should write down 5 or 6 of these key ideas and then participate in Snowflake, or some other activity that will facilitate the categorization of these key ideas.[10]

Finally, a small group should be named to put this vision into a written statement. All members of the large group should have an opportunity to revise or edit the statement, but it is challenging, if not impossible, to write a meaningful statement as a large group.

Sample Prompts (Handout)

Directions: Imagine you are a part of "20/20 School" and are joining other members of the school community to celebrate 20/20's continued journey toward excellence. This is an opportunity for reflection on your personal growth as you have worked with others in this school to attain common goals. It is also an opportunity to hear from those who have shared this journey with you. Respond to the stems ending each of the eight scenarios in keeping with your philosophy and ideals regarding school improvement and school excellence.

1. You engage in an opening session that focuses on "All Students Reaching Their Potential." A large number of current and former students are talking about the *goals that 20/20 School has for all students*. You take note of the most frequently mentioned ones:

2. As you reflect on what these students have said, you remember a school rally held five years ago. This was a kickoff event for 20/20 School's recommitment to continuous improvement. In your mind's eye you can see and hear the *various groups who came together* for this event and the dreams that each had for 20/20. Included among these were:

3. You walk out of this forum with a group of parents whose pride and gratification in their children's accomplishments are apparent. The parents seem to have a great deal of ownership in 20/20 School, and they mention the following specific *ways parents are involved* in making 20/20 a place "where everyone is responsible for the total development of all students":

4. Your next stop is a classroom where a teacher and students are engaged in a regular day's work. You take a seat in the back of the room where you remain for the next hour. As you get into the flow of the class, you observe that almost all of the students are enthusiastically engaged in learning. You begin identifying the *factors that seem to contribute to student engagement*. Among the things you note are:

5. Walking out of the classroom with a smile on your face, you encounter two teachers who have been on 20/20 School's faculty "forever." They return your smile and begin talking about what's happening in the classroom you just visited. You mention that five years ago they probably wouldn't have had a clue as to what was happening outside their own classrooms. They agree. They also share with you *the excitement for learning that permeates the school and the norms that support these new behaviors,* including:

6. You continue your conversation with these teachers and turn to the high level of energy and enthusiasm for learning and teaching that they seem to exude. You ask *how they retain such high levels of energy* and excitement after all these years. You could have almost predicted they would say:

7. The conversation turns to the issue of leadership and the *kind of leadership that has made good things happen* at 20/20. Highlights of this conversation include:

8. You reflect on your part in making 20/20 such an ideal place for students and adults alike. You recall the dream you share with those you've encountered today. You also recount what you yourself have done to make this dream a reality. *Your dream? What you've done?*

Snowflake: A Process for Group Consensus[11]

Snowflake helps a large group answer a question through a highly structured process. Everyone participates equally and owns the product. Ideas quickly become anonymous—not attached to a particular "donor"—and the entire group participates throughout the entire process. At no time does the facilitator take responsibility for making decisions about categories for ideas.

Snowflake might be used to address or answer such questions as these: (1) What are the most important needs facing our school? or (2) What should our students know and be able to do when they leave our school?

The process consists of the following three steps:

1. **brainstorming**
2. **ordering** the brainstormed data into categories
3. **naming** the categories formed through ordering

Although the Snowflake process can be used in many different contexts, in this description it will be described to develop consensus on the essential elements of a vision statement for a school.

Start by dividing participants into small groups of five to eight members each.

Step 1. Brainstorming

The purpose of brainstorming is to elicit as much information and data as possible. In brainstorming, all ideas are accepted as valid; no criticism or evaluative comments are made about individual ideas.

After individuals have silently generated their ideas, ask members within each small group to share their ideas. Give each group 10 or more 5" x 7" cards and a marker. Having found many similarities among the ideas presented by group members, the job of the group is to write each discrete idea onto a card, using **no more than four words** to present each idea. It is important that the writing on the cards be large enough to be seen from across the room.

This process requires at least 20 cards, so if you have a small number of groups you may want to designate a minimum number that each group must contribute.

Step 2. Ordering

The purpose of this step is to bring order to the brainstormed characteristics by identifying similarities among the various items and organizing them by their common traits.

a. Post a set of 5" x 7" cards across a wall as column headers. On each card, draw an arbitrary symbol (circle, triangle, X, star, #, %, &, *, @, (), square, etc.).

b. Ask each group to identify the two cards from their group of cards that they feel are most important. Collect these cards. Then ask the group to identify the card that would be "easiest to implement." Collect this card from each group. This step gives the group a way to quickly arrive at some "shared understanding" because people have had to look through their cards and think about each one in comparison to the others. Most likely, they will also have lively discussions about their relative importance.

c. Once you have collected two or three cards from each group, the process of posting them begins. Read a card aloud to the group and tape it under the first symbol. In turn, read each card and tape it under the next symbol. As you post the cards, ask participants to identify any common traits or relationships among the cards that might serve to help organize them. If you read a card that seems very much like a previous card, for example, you may ask the group if it should be posted in its "own category" or under the category of a previously posted card.

d. Once categories have clearly begun to emerge, ask each group to read through its remaining cards, decide into which category each belongs, and draw the symbol of the corresponding "header" card onto the idea card. If they cannot find an appropriate already-existing category, they should draw a question mark on the card.

e. Once the cards are turned in, the facilitator continues to read each one aloud and post (with approval of the entire group) where indicated. When all cards are posted, ask all participants to deal with any cards not yet organized into a group. Move and combine cards in an attempt to eliminate any that are alone in a group of one. Do not force cards to fit into existing categories; if they do not fit, leave them as a new group rather than adding them to an existing group.

Step 3. Naming

In this step all participants arrive at consensus regarding the meaning of items that were coded to have similar properties.

a. Assign one (or more) categories to each group. Group members' job is to review the set of cards in order to come up with a suitable name for the category. As they work, suggest that they ask the following questions:

What are all of these items about?
What do they all have in common?

b. As a group suggests a name, check it out with the entire group. Ask them to reflect by asking these questions:

Is this name inclusive?
Does the name describe all of the items in the category?

Nurturing Norms and Strengthening Shared Beliefs

Providing opportunities for faculty, staff, parents, and students to reflect on their personal beliefs regarding important issues related to teaching and learning can serve as a powerful stimulus for individual and organizational change. This cannot be done as a one-time event, but requires continual revisiting and ongoing confirmation. While it is difficult to take time out from the press of daily activities and events to do this kind of work, the potential benefits to be derived are significant. Structured processes can facilitate the work and optimize results.

The Important Book

Margaret Wise Brown wrote a delightful children's book that goes by the simple name *The Important Book*.[12] In it, Brown names the essential characteristic, or "important thing," about an everyday object—a shoe, for instance. One colleague Jody Westbrook first introduced us to this book as a way for people to meet others in a group. She had people, in pairs, interview one another and then write a ditty that began and ended (as did Brown's book) with the phrase, "The important thing about Susan is . . ."

We find this book a great way for people to focus on the "main thing" about a school. Read the book to a school faculty or a student advisory homeroom or a school improvement council. Then ask listeners, in pairs or triads, to compose a page for the book about their school. It would begin and end with the phrase, "The important thing about [name of] School is . . ." Give it a try! You don't know what inspired statements are waiting to be expressed!

Following are excerpts from Lumberport Elementary School's "Important Book" and "The Important Thing about Central."

The important thing about Central High
School is our pride.
Our doors are always open wide.

Day and night,
We work until it's right.

Purple and gold, we strive to compete,
Our teams might not always win, but
we can't be beat.

Our school is known for its sharing,
Teaching, learning, helping, and caring.

Orderly and neat, our school we must
keep,
Treasures for the future that we will
reap.

Keeping everyone on the winning side.
The important thing about Central is
our pride.

The important thing about Lumberport Elementary
    School is the students
the students are like limbs on a tree in a forest
they are all shapes and sizes
they continuously grow
some have small holes (knots) in their bark
some are rough, some smooth
some grow quicker than others
they all take root and grow
the important thing about Lumberport Elementary
    School is the students

The important thing about Lumberport
    Elementary is that we *try*.
Sometimes we need encouraged a little . . .
sometimes a lot . . .
each day is new, each day is different
but we really try.
The important thing about Lumberport
    Elementary is that we *try*.

Yes, It Really Is Up to Us

Brenda Williamson, former principal of Man High School, tells a story of her successful attempt to open up the conversation and have teachers confront the discrepancies between their beliefs—mostly unspoken—and their actions.

I knew that our staff needed to spend time clarifying beliefs and setting a new vision for our school. The new strategy I had learned at a recent Quest rally, called Data on Display, seemed likely to be able to help us do that. But, I was worried. All too often, I had heard teachers shift blame to the home by saying things like, "If parents valued education, then we might see improvements in student learning." This kind of finger-pointing was not going to solve our problems. What would happen if I encouraged teachers to honestly voice their opinions? If the "same-old, same-old" attitudes were expressed, I was worried that I might be up the creek without a paddle. I wondered if teachers truly believed that what we did at school made little real difference. Could they believe that what really made the most difference was what students had, or didn't have, at home?

The day came, and we plunged in. Teachers were so involved with assessing their own beliefs, they forgot to look around or listen to what others were saying. They took their jobs seriously. There were no side conversations. The concentration was nearly tangible. Teachers bustled about, putting their yellow, green, pink, and blue Post-it notes on each graph. Again, I felt the potential results of this project weigh heavily upon me. What if they all abdicated their responsibility? Could I ever help to change their feelings?

After the data collection and analysis were finished, the results revealed that staff believed teachers made the difference! Over 85 percent believed that strong, caring teachers could help students believe in themselves, even students from economically and educationally disadvantaged backgrounds. As we discussed these beliefs, we moved to adopt a new teacher faculty motto:

Success. If it is to be, then it's up to me!

Data on Display: Clarifying Beliefs in Community

Too often, important beliefs and values are not articulated and discussed within a school community. Consider the teacher who asks more questions of high-achieving students than low-performing students. This teacher acts on a deep-seated belief about ability, based on any number of personal and academic factors, which affects his own expectations for students' performance and which, in turn, affect the actual performance of many of the students in a given class.

This belief would, undoubtedly, be uncomfortable to voice aloud; it might go something like this: *This group of students will make it. They have a supportive home environment, a track record of success, and the proper attitude. However, those other students may not make it. I'd be surprised if they could overcome the obstacles in their paths.*

A school that boasts a strong culture for learning sets the clear expectation that *all* students will succeed. No student "gets by" without extra effort on the part of the school community to ensure his success. No teacher is allowed to "give up" on any group of students.

Data on Display: The Process

Data on Display helps a school establish a risk-free environment in which members of the school community can reflect individually on core issues, see how their opinions compare to those of the group as a whole, and think about and discuss issues deeply—all within a short period of time.

Purpose: To generate data quickly from a large group of people and move individuals from thinking about their own responses to thinking about implications of the groups' responses. This approach may prompt participants to form hypotheses about the data and to examine assumptions (their own and others').

Time required: The process can be completed in 40 to 60 minutes, depending on the size of the group and the number of issues examined.

Group size: 20-100 participants

Materials: Each participant will need a pen or pencil, a copy of the statements being examined, and several 1" x 3" Post-it notes (a different color for each statement). The facilitator will need several sheets of poster paper or chart paper for the data charts.

Rationale: The process allows for individual response and reflection but does not strengthen participants' attachment to individual responses. Individual responses are represented by colored Post-it notes that anonymously mark positions on a scale ranging from 0 to 100. After everyone contributes a blank Post-it note to the data chart, individuals immediately see a graphic representation of the thinking of the group. Participants are given time to reflect individually and in groups on the meaning of the data.

Preparation: Develop a handout with 4 to 6 statements on issues to be examined. The purpose of these statements is to elicit opinions about core ideas. (See example that follows.) Charts should be posted around the room. Each chart displays one statement across the top. Down the left edge of the chart, marked off in 10-point increments, is a scale from 0 to 100.

There should be sufficient room between numbers (3 inches) to allow for the colored Post-its that will be placed on the chart.

Sample Individual Worksheet for Data on Display

Successful Learners—What's the Potential for Influence?

I. **Directions:** For each statement below, decide the extent to which you agree by circling one of the percentages—from 100 percent to 0 percent—following the statement. Use your own personal experience and observations; there are no "right" answers in this activity.

1. In my opinion, students at my school are successful learners.

    100   90   80   70   60   50   40   30   20   10   0

2. What teachers in my school do, or fail to do, determines how successful students are as learners.

    100   90   80   70   60   50   40   30   20   10   0

3. Parents' and other family members' attitudes and involvement in students' education account for their success as learners.

    100   90   80   70   60   50   40   30   20   10   0

4. The school itself—its climate, policies, rules, procedures, structures, and physical facilities—impacts students' success as learners.

    100   90   80   70   60   50   40   30   20   10   0

5. What students do themselves, or fail to do, is responsible for their success as learners.

    100   90   80   70   60   50   40   30   20   10   0

II. **Directions:** When you have completed your ratings, use the colored strips to record your responses (percentages) on the wall charts for each question.

III. **Group Discussion:** When everyone in your group has completed recording their responses on the wall chart, begin discussing the five statements and the patterns of response that have been posted by the group. As you look at the data, what questions do you have? What inferences can you make?

Sample Wall Charts for Data on Display

In my opinion, students at school are successful learners.

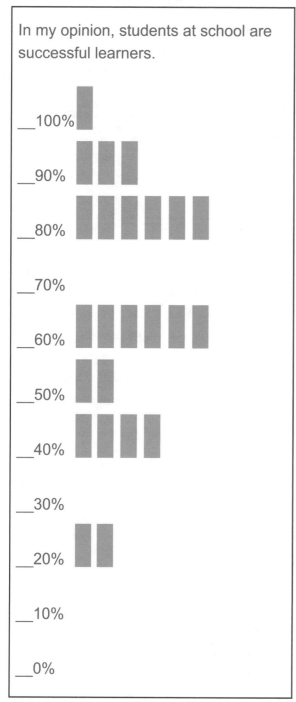

What students do themselves, or fail to do, is responsible for their success as learners.

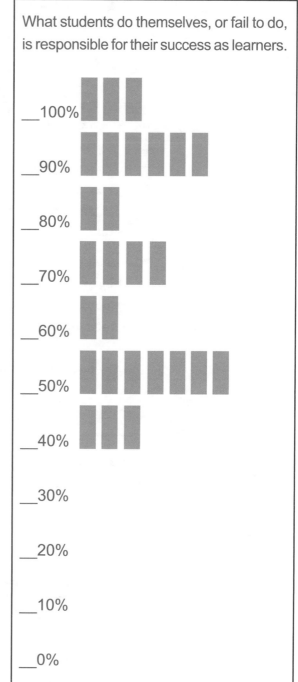

Color the Continuous Learner Caring, Collaborative, and Reflective

What traits or ways of being characterize teachers, students, and other members of a school community dedicated to continuously improving their learning and performance? What habits of mind drive those who strive to do the same thing a little bit better each day? This commitment to continuous, incremental improvement is called *kaizen* by the Japanese. *Kaizen* literally translates as "better way."[13] Whether a teacher seeking a better way to teach creative writing or a student striving to master a foreign language, individuals committed to *kaizen* exhibit the following kinds of habits of mind.

- **Caring**—This attribute relates to the extent to which we vest something of ourselves in others and in our work. Caring is a positive response that develops as we assign importance to someone or something outside of ourselves and, as a consequence, give of ourselves to that thing. Through caring, we demonstrate a willingness to become involved with, supportive of, and committed to some significant other. Caring transcends responsibility and involves a passionate desire as well as a dedication to duty.

- **Collaborative**—The collaborative approach springs from the belief that we learn with and from one another; that our work is enhanced when we engage with multiple and diverse perspectives. This embraces cooperation but extends beyond mutual support or assistance into the realm of shared responsibility, leadership, and ownership. Through the collaborative spirit we can enter into truly synergistic relationships with others.

- **Courageous**—The courageous exhibit a willingness to stand up for ideas, individuals, or innovations in which they believe—even in the midst of criticism or disapproval. This quality empowers an individual to be a lone voice in the wilderness, to break away from the conventional, the popular, the safe and secure position. This trait characterizes risk-takers as well as those with a quiet, but strong, will to stay a difficult and tedious course.

- **Creative**—The creative individual attempts to bring to life something new, to break new ground, to think outside of the box, to experiment, to blaze a new trail. This person is continually seeking ways to improve his own and others' performances and is willing to take risks in order to achieve this end. The creative impulse draws strongly from the imagination, from a vision of a better day and a more effective way.

- **Curious**—Inquiring, questioning, wondering. These are habits of the curious who are not content to accept passively what they experience, but actively engage in making meaning, extending understandings, posing the "why?" and "what if?" questions. The curious ask the "why?" question three times in order to get beneath the symptoms or surface issues into the core of a problem or issue.

- **Open**—A propensity to seek and consider diverse points of view, to withhold judgment, to remain vigilant to new possibilities—this is one side of the open individual. The other dimension of openness is the willingness to share of self with others, to put all cards on the table; to reveal one's agenda. Remaining open enables the bearer of this trait to continuously grow and develop.

- **Proactive**—Those who possess this quality do not "sit and wait" to be called upon; they do not habitually react to events. Rather, these "movers and shakers" look for opportunities to initiate new projects, promote new ideas, enlist others, and release creative energy.

- **Persistent**—Persevering, continued commitment and work in the face of obstacles, failures, disappointments—by these qualities you will recognize the persistent. Persistence is fueled by a deep and abiding belief in one's principles; a willingness to work hard, to stay the course, and to go against the popular tide when necessary.

- **Reflective**—The reflective trait is associated with thoughtfulness and with skill in looking back on one's experience in a self-critical manner. Through the exercise of this trait, the individual is able to integrate new learnings and experiences into existing structures or to modify these mental models. This approach also enables individuals to think about what they are doing and saying in the midst of activity, to practice reflection-in-action as well as reflection-on-action.

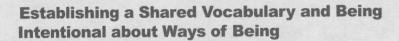

Establishing a Shared Vocabulary and Being Intentional about Ways of Being

The habits of mind just described are powerful when found as traits and qualities in individuals. How much more powerful if they are present and valued collectively within an organization! Several alternative strategies for bringing these ideas to a group for consideration and discussion are presented below.

A. Assign one trait to each of nine small groups. Ask each group to (1) read their brief description; (2) discuss the value of this "way of being" in a school community; and (3) prepare a skit, role play, or presentation to depict what this concept might look like in a school setting. Let the large group guess which trait is being depicted.

B. Allow participants to read the descriptions of all nine habits of mind, selecting the trait they personally value most highly. Ask them to reflect for a few minutes and write about why that characteristic is so important. Then direct them to meet with others in the room who selected the same trait, sharing their reasons for choosing it.

C. Use this as a warm-up activity at the beginning of a staff meeting or PTA meeting. As people enter the room, give them the one-page description of all nine traits and an index card. [On each index card is written one trait and a number (1-4).] Ask individuals to read through the description of their assigned trait and then reflect and write their responses to the questions that correspond to the number on their card.

1. Is this quality present among the staff of your school?
   On a scale of 1-10, with 10 being highest, how would you rate the staff at your school as to this quality or trait? Can you think of specific examples—or non-examples—of this trait being present (or absent) in your school?

2. How much is this quality present among students at your school?
   On a scale of 1-10, with 10 being highest, how would you rate the students at your school as to this quality or trait? In what ways are students rewarded or encouraged to exhibit this quality? In what ways is this trait discouraged, and why?

3. How prevalent is this quality in the community where I live?
   On a scale of 1-10, with 10 being highest, to what extent is this trait valued among the people in our community? Are there settings in which this trait is particularly encouraged or discouraged?

4. What would this trait look like in a school setting? Give examples of how you might recognize it. How essential is this trait in promoting, achieving, and maintaining school improvement?

Allow time for individual reflection, then group with others who were assigned the same trait. Discuss the following questions:

• How might this trait be intentionally cultivated within a school community?

• How might the culture of the school be affected if the quality were present to a higher degree?

Allow 10 to 15 minutes for volunteers to share with the total group any insights, questions, or new understandings they had as they thought about this trait. Suggest that, throughout the meeting, the group make an effort to encourage and model these traits and qualities.

Self-Assessment: Clarifying What I Believe

Following are 11 belief statements about conditions under which students are most likely to succeed as learners. Read each statement and answer the following two questions with your school in mind.

Do I believe this is essential?
(Rate from 1-5, with 5 = essential for learner success and 1 = not at all important)

Do I believe this is practiced in our school?
(Rate from 1-5, with 5 = clearly present in this school and 1 = not present at all)

Extent to which I believe this is **essential for learner success** (Circle one)	Statement of Belief	Extent to which this is **practiced in our school** (Circle one)
5 4 3 2 1	All students have at least one advocate in their lives.	5 4 3 2 1
5 4 3 2 1	Successful learners not only meet academic standards but also demonstrate qualities such as responsibility, respect, citizenship, caring, trustworthiness, and fairness.	5 4 3 2 1
5 4 3 2 1	Adults in the school believe all children can learn and set high standards and expectations for student learning.	5 4 3 2 1
5 4 3 2 1	Children feel safe and secure in school, at home, and in the community.	5 4 3 2 1
5 4 3 2 1	The school and classrooms have climates that cultivate curiosity through active participation and exploration in meaningful learning activities.	5 4 3 2 1
5 4 3 2 1	Teachers are committed and enthusiastic.	5 4 3 2 1
5 4 3 2 1	Teachers promote mutual respect and trust among all, in open and caring classroom environments.	5 4 3 2 1
5 4 3 2 1	A variety of teaching strategies is necessary to meet individual learning needs.	5 4 3 2 1
5 4 3 2 1	Parents are involved—directly helping students, staying informed, and providing support to students and the school.	5 4 3 2 1
5 4 3 2 1	Administrators support and assist teachers as they make decisions about what is best for students and their classrooms.	5 4 3 2 1
5 4 3 2 1	Ongoing professional development for teachers is focused and relevant, providing opportunities for reflection, connection, and restoration.	5 4 3 2 1

Celebrations and Rituals: Special Moments in Time

A school that has strong and powerful traditions is a school where leaders carefully cultivate and nourish rituals and celebrations. Like their counterparts in schools across the country, students at Alexander Elementary School and Natcher Elementary begin their days by reciting a creed that reflects their respective school's core values and beliefs. Each year students at Sewanee Elementary and Highland Elementary look forward to being assigned an older "buddy" with whom they will share special learning experiences. Other "procedures or routines that are infused with deeper meaning" include established class field trips, class performances, staff retreats, and student and staff induction activities.[14] Secondary schools are replete with rituals—many of which revolve around athletic events, including spirit days, pep rallies, special assemblies, and the like.

Rituals, traditions, and ceremonies make the routines of schools symbolize what is important, valued, and significant. They provide everyone with a chance to reflect on what is important, to connect as a community.

—Terrence Deal & Kent Peterson

While rituals are everyday-type interactions that are infused with meaning, ceremonies are "complex, culturally sanctioned ways that a school celebrates successes, communicates its values, and recognizes special contributions of staff and students."[15] Schools oftentimes celebrate individuals and teams—for their successes, good deeds to others, special events such as birthdays, marriages, and anniversaries, and for a host of other reasons. Likewise, they celebrate individual and community successes—including awards, victories, and promotions. Less frequently do we stop to acknowledge loss—of old procedures, curricula, buildings, and so forth. However, organizational specialists remind us that these kinds of ceremonies are of equal importance.[16]

In the stories that follow, we share some creative and effective rituals and ceremonies from schools that intentionally use these to build community, reinforce values and beliefs, and increase performance.

Celebrations of Learning: Morning Meeting

At the first meeting of the Quest Network for Elementary Schools, two schools were invited to share their stories. The purpose was twofold: (1) to model the use of storytelling as a way to prompt inquiry and learn together and (2) to hear the stories of two schools that had gone through the struggles and challenges of continuous improvement, with dramatic results for students.

We had learned of Dibert Elementary, a school in innercity New Orleans, from our colleague Shirley Hord at the Southwest Educational Development Laboratory in Austin, Texas. Hord had written much about this small school. It was one of the few schools that accomplished the successful formation of what Hord calls "professional learning community"—a place where professionals work together regularly and collegially for the benefit of improved student learning. Hord's videotape of Dibert pictured a school that, over the course of five school principals and many years, had indeed changed.[17]

When Dibert told its story at the Quest rally, two schools were especially moved by the "morning meeting" ritual that had been established by a previous Dibert principal. At the daily meetings, Dibert teachers and students (and parents, too) came together to celebrate student success, learn together, and celebrate birthdays and achievements. The principal used this as an opportunity to model good instructional practice. His main objective was to develop greater pride in accomplishments and to create a strong bond among all members of the school community. Being together in one place, sharing successes and celebrations, helped accomplish this sense of community. The stories that follow illustrate how two schools took this message home.

Nothing Is Ever as Easy as It Seems!

by Vickie Luchuck, Teacher and Parent, Lumberport Elementary School

The Quest leadership team from Lumberport Elementary School left the Nashville rally full of ideas and excitement. During the entire 11-hour drive home, we brainstormed. We wanted to share our experiences and excitement with the students and with our staff. To do this, we planned and worked together on a common goal.

Our first goal was to implement a Friday Morning Meeting for our students. We thought this would be a great time to share our experiences back at school with our students. We spent our first Friday Morning Meeting recounting the events of our trip to Nashville. One teacher cried as we told of taking food to the homeless. We dressed in cowboy hats and boots and line-danced with the students. Then we asked them to share things they did while we were gone. They jumped at the chance!

What made this sharing an important experience for the students? Sharing personal experiences with the students was a "first" for us! The kids saw us laughing and crying. They saw us as caring individuals. For months afterwards, the kids reminded us in the halls and on the playgrounds how much they liked having us talk to them. They thought we were "cool."

After our first success, we decided to host a morning meeting each Friday. The kids loved the opportunity to lead the school in the pledge, receive recognition on their birthdays, and be publicly acknowledged for their accomplishments. The teachers told stories, presented visitors like Santa, and often invited students to demonstrate their talents before their peers. Several brave souls danced or sang songs for the whole student body. Excitement showed on their faces as they braved the crowded gym and took the microphone. Friday Morning Meetings were a hit with the kids! Parents began to appear when their children's classes planned a special event. The gym overflowed, and we sometimes went past the tardy bell.

But even a great idea has a downside. Eventually, the meetings became a chore for the small group of teachers who led the programs. This was one more "extra" assignment that some of us had taken on willingly—with no support or assistance. As the Quest team talked among ourselves, we decided to ask the principal to encourage all the teachers to attend the Friday Morning Meetings and to take turns helping conduct the meetings. We thought it was time to share the leadership responsibilities. But other teachers were not happy with an additional assignment, and the principal was unwilling to insist.

Although the children loved the morning meetings, and parents thought it was great to engage their children before actual school hours, some of the staff rejected the idea. We had a split beginning to divide the staff. Those who thought the meetings were a good idea attended regularly; those who didn't like the idea avoided the gym on Friday mornings. Things finally reached the point where the principal told us to vote. As a full staff, we had to decide whether or not to continue the morning meetings. After discussion, we opted to hold once-a-month meetings and ask for help from everyone to lead them.

Last year, we held Friday Morning Meetings on the last Friday of each month. Grade-level teams planned and led the meetings. Few conflicts arose; and at some point during the year, every teacher attended a meeting. Although the meetings didn't turn out exactly as planned, we do still have them and everyone participates in some way. They have become an established part of our school culture. Parents line the gym walls when their youngsters participate in a skit, do a line dance, or read stories they have written. Morning meetings have evolved over the past two years. The teachers have also evolved as our expectations have changed.

Tennessee Style: Monday Morning Gatherings

by Ann Watkins, Principal, Sewanee Elementary School

The kickoff Quest rally sparked the beginning of a new venue to celebrate school success at Sewanee. We "borrowed" the idea for Monday Morning Gathering, making this time a focal point for student and faculty recognition at our school. We sing the birthday song to recognize student birthdays. We assign school jobs for the week. We publicize upcoming events. In short, we let our students know they are special! In the student-led programs, we recognize special achievement for things such as art and music awards, perfect attendance, academic excellence, class projects, and just about anything we can find to brag on.

Initiating the Monday Morning Gathering did not at first achieve unanimous support from our faculty. As time has passed, however, we see more and more teachers being drawn into the activities. Monday Morning Gathering is now recognized as being an integral means of unifying the school family. Celebration has become a weekly, expected activity.

Celebrations with a "Punch"

It's easy to celebrate with elementary students. Most of them don't mind standing up in front of a group of their peers and talking proudly about their accomplishments. They think it's "cool." Motivating high school students is another matter. The South Harrison High School Quest team came up with a unique idea to encourage and motivate higher performance on the annual state-mandated standardized tests. This story of SHOlympics (for South Harrison Olympics) is told by teacher Robin Anglin.

In an effort to motivate students to do their best on the SAT-9, we offered "SHOlympics" as a reward. When our school's scores improved, we held our first SHOylmpics on October 30, 1998. Presented as a game competition between classes and teachers, SHOlympics teams represented each group and competed in events such as the Firemen's Relay, A Dozen Eggzactly, Kitchen Medley, Blind Man's Obstacle Course, Shoe Relay, and a Three-legged Race. What fun we had when the captain of the last-place team took his place on stage to be "slimed," or egged, or to receive some other appropriate award!

Creating a Welcoming Environment: The Realization That Culture Is Everywhere

Even before Natcher Elementary School was built, the design team was thinking about using the environment—the actual physical building—to broaden the learning community and enhance the learning culture. They wanted a school that would be easily accessible, used by the community, and inviting to children and parents the minute they walked in the door. As a result of this planning, Natcher Elementary School has some very special "extra" square footage. An open, inviting lobby area was carefully designed—and even more carefully furnished and decorated to match a monthly theme—to meet these purposes. The lobby gives folks their first impression of Natcher. It communicates "welcome," "comfort," and "home."

The principal, Connie Allen, intentionally selected furniture that would be warm and inviting, yet safe. The fountain, the first thing to catch your eye upon entry, provides the soothing background noise of splashing water. The fountain also provides adequate humidity (and ample resting space) for plants; Allen is a believer in the importance of having living, green things in the environment. A 100(+)-year-old church pew, refinished by parents in the school, is a living history lesson. Hand-hewn from poplar, the sturdy furniture is from a church in a nearby Kentucky county. The area rug is surrounded by comfortable chairs, purchased when a local motel was refurbishing its rooms; dolls, stuffed animals, and other appealing objects; soft lighting; an antique card catalog, which often displays thematic decorations; and a coffee table, which is special because it was made for this area by one of the school's bus drivers.

The crowning touch is a very large piece of artwork created by Natcher students with help from one of the school's artists-in-residence. The 6' x 8' display looks something like a quilt, but it is made from clay that was dug throughout the state of Kentucky. (What a prime spot for math, science, geography, art, and geology lessons!) The only colors of the piece are the natural colors of the clay: from grey and pale yellow to the deep orange clay that was dug on the grounds of Natcher. This patchwork heightens Natcher's awareness of the importance of collaborative work.

Another wall displays trophies and plaques won by teachers and students. The trophies convey a sense of communal celebrations for both joint and individual achievements. A television monitor projects events of the day, the lunch menu, pictures of students, notices of upcoming events, and congratulatory messages for students and faculty. Parents are welcome to come to lunch at the school every day. It is a truly welcoming environment.

But it is clear the environment is beautiful and inviting to serve a specific purpose: the focus is on learning! Natcher has adopted the "SMART Learner" concept from its involvement with the Quest network. This SMART Learner idea permeates the school culture. Outside, the school marquee proclaims, "Welcome SMART Learners." The lobby banner reverberates, "Welcome, SMART Learners." "SMART Learners" leaps from the cafeteria wall. Throughout the school, bulletin boards prepared by teachers and students remind both residents and visitors that "SMART Learners" occupy this space at Natcher Elementary.

Everyday activities reinforce the message. Principal Allen boards the school buses before children disembark, asking, "What kind of learners ride this bus?" The unanimous response, "SMART Learners!" reverberates loudly. Every school day begins with the national anthem, the student-led Pledge of Allegiance, and the affirmation of the Natcher Student Resolution.

If you were a student at Natcher, wouldn't you be glad to come to school in this welcoming and nurturing environment? Wouldn't the first step into the school be a refreshing and relaxing one? If you were the parent of a student at this school, wouldn't you feel cared about? Wouldn't you feel special—almost pampered? Wouldn't you relish sitting in this lobby area, watching SMART learners and "feeling the pulse of the school" while working on a homeroom party or planning a Girl Scout meeting?

Walkabouts: Assuring Schoolwide Norms in All Classroom Environments

by Pam Brown, Former Principal, Woodbridge Senior High School

With the adoption of the Virginia Standards of Learning (SOLs) for the core content areas and a revised curriculum for Prince William County, a myriad of issues needed to be addressed simultaneously: Who would provide staff development? What would it look like? How would staff be assisted in planning for the new curriculum and requirements of the SOLs? How could administrators assess and assist, that is, assure that the classroom environments promoted good teaching and learning with so many changes occurring at one time? All staff faced a huge challenge.

We adopted the district-developed Walkabout for each of the core content areas—math, science, language arts, and social studies. This instrument allows administrators, department chairs, or other staff members to complete a walk-through of a department, noting the presence or absence of predetermined characteristics related to teacher characteristics, instructional strategies, classroom management, and the learning environment. The results are summarized and reported for the department as a whole.

At Woodbridge, one of our first activities was to introduce the Walkabout concept to staff and enlist their input in adapting district-developed instruments to meet our local school needs and expectations. Second, in an effort to include other content areas, each department developed its own instrument. As with anything new, there was some resistance. However, within a week, each department had collaboratively developed a Walkabout for its area.

The results of their work, which was sometimes very tedious and controversial, represented traits associated with strengthening the learning culture—collaboration, caring, courage, creativity, curiosity, openness, proactivity, persistence, and reflection.

Walkabout proved to be very valuable in strengthening the learning environment of our large comprehensive high school. At first, some staff were very concerned; the instrument and process were unlike anything they had experienced. After one of the first Walkabouts, our instructional assistant principal had many questions and reservations. This was not the usual 30-minute formal observation. It was not even a 10-minute informal observation. How accurate was the information collected? Would her feedback to the department be reflective of what was actually taking place? Would it be helpful in strengthening the learning environment? How could she convince staff this was not part of the evaluative process but rather a method for improving instruction and learning?

Staff who were observed shared these concerns; many were apprehensive. Some teachers spent their time trying to identify the teachers who were represented on the Walkabout form. Intentionally, no individual names appeared. Other faculty members stated that a walk-through of the department could not possibly present an accurate account of what was taking place.

Despite the early qualms, the Walkabouts became more frequent. Written feedback with "glows" and "grows" was provided immediately to departments. Many discussions on Walkabout results took place in formal settings such as department and staff meetings. Informal settings were soon abuzz with these discussions as well. The fact that instruction was being discussed by so many, so frequently, was a healthy improvement in the learning environment. Many staff members began to look on the Walkabouts as a nonthreatening means of assisting them in strengthening performance.

Others remained negative, as some employees began to refer to the Walkabouts as "drive-bys."

We didn't give up. By the end of the first year, some departments felt totally comfortable with the process and began to conduct their own Walkabouts. During the second year, each department revised its Walkabout form. Most departments have now come to value the feedback provided. Most teachers work together to share effective practices and support each other where performance needs strengthening.

Note: Two sample Walkabout forms are included here—one for mathematics and one for social studies. The observer visits all classrooms in a given department on a particular day. The numbered columns (1-10) represent individual classrooms. While in classroom 1, the observer places a check mark beside each item observed, e.g., teacher communicating learning expectations, in the column beneath "1." When observing in the second classroom, check marks are placed beneath column 2 beside the items for which the observer sees evidence.

Mathematics Walkabout Reprinted by permission of Woodbridge Senior High School, Woodbridge, Virginia										
TIME: _____ AM _____ PM DATE:	**Classroom**									
TEACHER	1	2	3	4	5	6	7	8	9	10
Communicates learning expectations										
Monitors students' performances as they engage in learning activities										
Solicits responses or demonstrations from specific students for assessment purposes										
Reinforces correct responses										
Provides corrective feedback										
Uses different methods or techniques to explain/demonstrate the same content										
INSTRUCTIONAL STRATEGIES										
Appropriately varies activities										
Interacts with students in group formats as appropriate										
Solicits student participation										
Extends students' responses/contributions										
Provides ample time for students to respond to teacher questions/solicitations and to consider content as it is presented										
CLASSROOM MANAGEMENT										
Secures student attention, or students are attending to task										
Uses administrative procedures and routines that facilitate instruction										
Has materials, aids, modern technology, and facilities ready for use										
Maintains seating arrangement/grouping appropriate for the activity and the environment										
LEARNING ENVIRONMENT										
Relates content to student interests/experiences										
Emphasizes the value/importance of the activity or content										
Reinforces learning efforts of students										
Establishes climate of courtesy and respect										
Establishes and maintains positive rapport with students										
Challenges students										

Social Studies Walkabout

Reprinted by permission of Woodbridge Senior High School, Woodbridge, Virginia

TIME: ____AM ____PM DATE:	Classroom									
TEACHER IS:	1	2	3	4	5	6	7	8	9	10
• Questioning students by name										
• Using strategies that promote integration of strands										
• Modeling techniques aimed at teaching students to formulate questions										
• Reading aloud excerpts from historically relevant text										
• Modeling strategies for gathering, organizing, and rethinking information—Information Management Process (IMP)										
• Modeling rubrics for gathering, organizing, and rethinking information										
• Providing ongoing assessments of student achievement in information processing and data analysis										
SMALL GROUPS ENGAGED IN:										
• Specific skill instruction in information processing and data and document analysis										
• Practicing strategies for gathering, organizing, and rethinking information										
• Examining data										
• Presenting graphic representations of data analyzed										
LARGE GROUP ENGAGED IN:										
• Interacting with video										
• Reading and responding to a variety of sources										
• Examining types of evidence provided in primary and secondary sources										
• Applying, monitoring, and assessing the use of the IMP										
• Individual presentations with graphic representations of data analyzed										
CLASS ENVIRONMENT:										
• Student work displayed										
• Rubrics are displayed										
• Students are purposefully grouped and regrouped for skill instruction and application										
• Consistent monitoring of individual student progress										
• A variety of reference materials are available										
• Sample models of the earth displayed										
• Teacher establishes a climate of courtesy and respect										
MISCELLANEOUS:										

Stories and Storytellers: Capturing, Celebrating, and Learning from the Past

Students of organizational culture emphasize the power of stories.[18] Likewise, teacher educators and staff developers point out the potential of personal stories as tools for reflection and learning.[19] What is the magic of storytelling? How can stories fuel the culture of schools?

Inside School Improvement is itself a compilation and celebration of educators' stories. Throughout this volume are sprinkled narratives written by teachers, principals, parents, and students. These stories feature heroes and heroines who have walked the talk of school improvement; individuals who have worked to create high-performing learning communities within their own schools. One of our visions for this book is that it will inspire you to craft your own stories; reflect upon, record, and share your own experiences; and celebrate together as a learning community.

Stories engage us more wholly and completely than a linear presentation of facts. Stories breathe life into our learning; they require us to bring our spirits, our souls, our emotions, our imagination, our reason, our analysis, our creative juices.

—Diane Cory & Paul Underwood, "Stories for Learning"

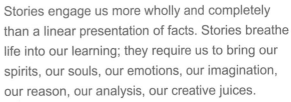

Storytelling: A Way of Learning Together

The power of the story often provides the light, the clarity of vision, the focus needed to move a school forward in its quest for improvement. It offers educators, who seldom grab a moment for reflective practice, an opportunity to see things as they might be.[20]

Stories enable us to share our individual and collective experiences in an open, honest, engaging, and complete manner. They require their tellers first to reflect on where they have been, what they have done, how they reacted to events and to individuals, and what they learned along the way. Such reflection is the springboard for weaving a story that will, by definition, have a beginning, a middle, and an end. Further, the good story will have a setting, characters, mood and

movement, conflict, climax and resolution, meaning, and perspective. All of these things—and more—make a story a story: a vehicle for communication that engages the storytellers' and the listeners' "minds and bodies completely, rather than just [their] intellect."[21]

Linear presentations tend to focus on the objective and quantifiable. They are typically used to promote or defend a position or convey the particulars of a narrowly construed project. These modes of communicating rely upon the analytical, logical left brain. Stories, on the other hand, incorporate the subjective, emotional, and spiritual aspects of human experience as well as the logical and analytical. Thus, they have the capacity to integrate various aspects of experience; to provide a holistic view. Because stories are multidimensional and capture the whole of experience, they enable learning in a manner that a strictly didactic approach cannot. And it is this quality of stories that imbues them with an almost magical capacity: "the same story can and will release new learnings every time we hear it—matching the learnings to our emotional and mental status." It is for this reason that Cory and Underwood characterize stories as "capsules of time-released learning."[22]

In order to optimize the power of a story as a learning tool, the story must meet certain standards. Cory and Underwood offer the following four requisites for a good, potentially moving story:[23]

1. **Completeness.** A good story must be complete—with a beginning, a middle, and an end, but also with the potential for future possibilities, for a sequel. Recall one of your favorite childhood stories; chances are it invited you to use your imagination, to think beyond "the end" to what might unfold for the characters on another day. The most engaging of these stories actually invited you into the story: you were in the action, with the characters, sharing their struggles and victories.

2. **Wonder.** Good stories leave space for their listeners (and the storytellers themselves) to reflect, question, and dream. The gift of a true learning story is this space in which to think and ideas about which to think. The space provides the physical room for the listeners to enter into the story with its teller.

3. **Touching.** A good learning story has the capacity to move us at a deeper level; to awaken our broader senses; to engage our inner senses as well as our five physical senses. How do storytellers accomplish this? By revealing their own passions, fears, hopes, disappointments, and courage as well as those of their characters. By inviting the listener to share in human feelings. By relinquishing control and revealing their own inadequacies, questions, and doubts. Stories that touch do not seek to provide answers so much as to invite questions. They do not attempt to instruct so much as to open up dialogue.

4. **Silence.** Effective storytellers know the value of pausing at critical junctions in their stories, or being silent and honoring silence among their listeners. Silence provides the space for thought, for absorption, for reflection. It enables dialogue for all who would become so engaged. And it allows time for the touching to occur within and across listeners, for a bond to develop between the storytellers and their audience.

Storytelling is a community art form. Stories are best told or read aloud, so that listeners can connect with and learn from the storyteller and one another. In their book, *Teachers' Stories: From Personal Narrative to Professional Insight*, Mary Renck Jalongo and Joan Isenberg argue that "a good and useful story of practice has at least four characteristics":

1. It is genuine and rings true.
2. It invites reflection and discourse.
3. It is interpreted and reinterpreted.
4. It is powerful and evocative.[24]

Sharing stories offers a means for professionals to inquire together into ways and means of continuously improving their practice.

Teachers' Stories: From Personal Narrative to Professional Insight by Mary Renck Jalongo and Joan Isenberg (San Francisco: Jossey-Bass, 1995).

The authors share their experiences in using stories as vehicles for reflection and learning with preservice and in-service teachers. From the authors' perspectives, stories serve both as mirrors for viewing one's own practice as well as windows for developing understanding and insights into the practice of others. Hence, benefits accrue to both the individuals who craft stories and their colleagues who read and listen to them. This book is a compendium of true stories written by the authors and their students over time. The examples are rich, and the shared stories have merit in and of themselves. However, it is the authors' descriptions of how these stories were used and the impact of their use that makes the case for using stories as vehicles for professional growth and community building.

Out of their experience with stories, the authors offer specific suggestions and strategies to practitioners who are interested in this type of growth experience. As described by the authors, story sharing nurtures the norms of collaboration, curiosity, trust, and respect. It also taps the creativity of teachers and provides products around which community celebrations can occur.

Tell Your Own Story

As individual preparation, think of a student you have known and about whom you can tell a short story. Think particularly of a student who never really reached his or her potential. (This may be a story about yourself, your own child, a student, or a child's friend.) This may be a student who had great ability but was not "turned on" to school; it may be a student with limited ability who, regardless of how hard he tried, nearly failed, or at any rate progressed through school feeling like a failure; it may be a student who faced so many personal problems that school seemed trivial by comparison.

A. Write down some notes about this student in preparation to telling this student's story to others.

B. In a small group (pair or triad), with one group member serving as recorder, share your stories. (2-3 minutes each)

D. In your group, discuss the following:

- Did the stories have anything in common?
- What did the school do—or fail to do—that may have contributed to that student's problems?
- In what kind of school environment might this student have thrived—or at least come closer to reaching his or her potential?

Professional Development to Enrich the Learning Culture

School leaders committed to the development of a strong learning culture adopt new ways of thinking about professional development. They realize that traditional approaches to in-service education do not nurture continuous learning and improvement. Usually a one-time event occurring outside of the regular school day, traditional in-service has been neither long-term and ongoing nor embedded in the realities of the classroom and student learning. Typically, an outside expert makes key decisions regarding the content of staff development. Even when teachers are afforded opportunities to provide input, the ultimate experience almost inevitably adopts a "one size fits all" approach to instruction. And, finally, staff development tends to be "done to" teachers as they assume the passive role of listeners.

Lieberman and Miller are among those who make a strong argument for rethinking professional development.[25] They suggest embedding teacher learning in the natural rhythms of work with colleagues and students in school and viewing professional growth as an integral part of teachers' work to promote student learning and achievement. They question the value of traditional "sit-and-get" in-service that asks teachers to listen to new ideas about school, rather than engaging them as learners to continually question established practices and test new approaches with peers and students. They observe that research, reflection, and systematic inquiry are at the core of teachers' work in schools that are restructuring themselves. Like their students, teachers are engaged in a process of continual learning. They are researchers, meaning makers, and scholars studying the question "How do students learn?" The inquiry is genuine, for it is based on real-life concerns that are raised in designing and promoting learning for real students. As this culture develops and teachers inquire more into their practice, they learn to find time and opportunities to talk together about their discoveries.[26]

Teachers in schools that are transforming themselves see teacher work mainly as helping students construct their own knowledge rather than as only transmitting knowledge to students.

—Ann Lieberman & Lynne Miller, *Transforming Their World and Their Work*

Little concurs with this view, arguing that "the main idea . . . is to mobilize the school's resources to place inquiry into student learning at the heart of teachers' professional development."[27]

Schools committed to "growing a stronger learning culture" incorporate research, reflection, and inquiry into their *modus operandi*. They are intentional as they seek and adapt processes that provide scaffolding to support individuals learning how to develop the skills and habits of mind associated with continuous learning and improvement. Included among these processes are action research, critical inquiry and dialogue, peer teaching and peer coaching, collegial examination of student work, and other strategies that put teachers in charge of their own learning and provide structures to support their learning in nonconventional ways.

In order to inquire, especially into one's own practice, professionals must cultivate dispositions as well as technical and intellectual knowledge and skills. . . . They have to unlearn the politeness norm that dominates most current teacher discourse.

—Deborah Ball & David Cohen,
Teaching and the Learning Profession

The four pieces that follow describe very different structures for promoting ongoing teacher learning within the context of real work in schools. Each structure encourages the development of norms supportive of continuous learning and improvement. The first, *collegial investigation*, is a structure for engaging a school faculty in inquiry and research focused on a question or topic of high relevance and interest. This structure, which can be used to address almost any topic, requires that teachers form truly collaborative relationships and approach the question or issue with curious and open frames of mind. Further, teachers are encouraged to think in creative ways and are challenged to be courageous in their thinking, speaking, and behaviors. The second example is *participative assessment*, an approach to evaluating professional development that emphasizes teacher engagement in reflection, targeted on the intersection of new learning with past learning and experience. This framework can be adapted by a school as a routine way of seeking self-assessment of teacher learning. The third piece describes a full-blown professional development program, *Questioning and Understanding to Improve Learning and Thinking (QUILT),* which focuses upon improving teacher and student questioning. The process design for this multiyear program incorporates research findings on effective staff development and features reflection on practice and peer partnering. Participation in QUILT also nourishes multiple norms associated with a culture that values continuous learning and improvement, including those of openness, collaboration, and reflection. Finally, we offer a synthesis of current thinking regarding inquiry and its role in strengthening a school's learning culture. Inquiry—a norm in and of itself—is at the heart of all professional learning in community.

Each of the four processes can be viewed as a vehicle for connecting individual teacher growth and development to the broader life of the school—to a shared vision for student learning, to ongoing experiences with students in their classrooms, and to colleagues throughout the school community. This new vision for professional development rests on the belief that only when "teachers change some of their beliefs, practices, and ways of working with others" can meaningful school reform occur.[28] Teachers are the centerpiece of a school's learning culture and are the linchpins of any school improvement effort.

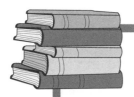

Teachers Who Learn, Kids Who Achieve: A Look at Schools with Model Professional Development by WestEd (San Francisco: WestEd, 2000).

This publication highlights the eight schools that won the U.S. Department of Education's National Awards Program for Model Professional Development during the first two years of competition (1996-97 and 1997-98). The vignette of each school overviews the signal features of its professional development—features such as coaching, action research, and parent engagement. The authors extrapolate from these cases principles of effective professional development, lessons learned, and implications for district and site leaders. Central to teaching and learning at all eight of these schools was the culture for learning. In the words of the authors, "The very nature of staff development [in these eight schools] shifted from isolated learning and the occasional workshop to focused, ongoing organizational learning built on collaborative reflection and joint action."

This engaging and easy-to-read book contains a host of resources for schools committed to ongoing renewal of their professional development programs. Furthermore, descriptions of the model schools are interesting, informative, and inspiring.

Learning Together through Action Research: The Collegial Investigation

Michael Fullan, one of the preeminent students of educational change and improvement, contends that "teacher as learner" is the impetus to both classroom and school improvement. Fullan's construct of "teacher as learner" contains four dimensions: mastery of technical skills, reflective practice, inquiry, and collaboration.[29]

Collaborative action research engages teachers in reflective practice, inquiry, and collaboration with the goal of improving classroom or schoolwide practice. This strategy, when adopted as a way of doing business in a school, can mitigate against powerful norms that deter teachers from sharing in the benefits of an enriched learning culture. These norms have to do with the ways in which teachers relate to one another, to knowledge, and to authority.[30] Traditionally, teachers have adhered to the notion that "what I do behind the closed doors of my own classroom is my own business and responsibility." Isolation and independence have been the underlying norms. Further, teachers have tended to view themselves as vessels for knowledge—receiving knowledge from outside experts and dispensing it to students; rarely have teachers seen themselves as knowledge producers. The norms of passivity and uniformity have supported this model. Finally, teachers have been subjected to external quality control, rather than having engaged in self-assessment and collegial support. Dependency and conformity are resulting norms.

Richard Sagor, a long-time advocate and mentor for teacher researchers, makes a case for action research as a transformational experience for both individual professionals and the school culture in which they work. He

suggests that when teachers engage in true discourse and inquiry centered on teaching and learning, they not only change their relationships to one another, but also the cultural norms of the entire school community.[31] Sagor reviewed 40 years of literature related to action research from which he identified the following six essential and sequential steps:

1. formulating a problem
2. planning for data collection
3. collecting data
4. analyzing data
5. reporting results
6. taking action[32]

Emily Calhoun advocates a similar cycle for action research, which she says is a "fancy way of saying, 'Let's study what's happening at our school, decide if we can make it a better place by changing what and how we teach and how we relate to students and the community; study the effects; and then begin again.'"[33]

The Collegial Investigation is a structure for conducting action research that embodies a framework for critical thinking as a part of the collaborative dialogue surrounding problem formulation and conclusion drawing. The process can be used by any group interested in studying and learning together—an entire school faculty; a small group of teachers within a school; or a diverse group of teachers, parents, and students. Through experiential learning, disciplined discussion, and guided reflection, participants learn to collectively define terms, question assumptions, examine issues from multiple points of view, and gather information with which to investigate the effectiveness of current ways of doing business in schools.[34]

Content. Collegial Investigations can be used to study almost any content area. The first task is to formulate a postulate—a statement that clearly and succinctly expresses a presupposition, hypothesis, or principle, and is worthy of study. The most compelling postulates relate to student learning and achievement. Collegial Investigations were first used by teachers to learn more about their own classroom questioning practices and how these helped or hindered student learning. The process of self-reflection and analysis of classroom behavior helped teachers see their own classrooms differently; assumptions under which teachers had always operated came into serious question after data collection and analyses.

The Process. Depending upon the complexity of the subject under study, a Collegial Investigation might be scheduled over a three-week or a three-month period. Whatever the time frame, the process involves four phases:

1. **Problem definition** occurs during the initial session as group members participate in skillful discussion about the postulate. This is no ordinary run-of-the-mill discussion; it is guided by an eight-component pattern for critical thinking, adopted from the work of Richard Paul.[35] Facilitators assure that participants don't just "share ignorance" as happens in some group discussions. Group members, committed to clarification and shared understanding, are pushed to be rigorous in their thinking. They are asked to adopt different lenses than their own as they think about the postulate from the points of view of high- and low-achieving students, parents, teachers, and other community members. Global generalizations are not accepted; specific terms are defined by the group; and assumptions are uncovered. The ultimate aim of the group is to identify

the evidence that would enable group members to reach an informed and reasoned conclusion regarding the postulate under study.

Elements of Reasoning

- Purpose
- Question at Issue
- Concepts
- Assumptions
- Point of View
- Evidence
- Inferences
- Consequences and Implications

---

2. **Information gathering**, or the collection of evidence, is the second step in the process. Action research teams collect data outside of the formal group meeting times and then meet to share findings. The following five investigative groups offer choices of data collection methods:

Philosophers identify, read, and critically discuss books or articles related to the question at issue.

Kid watchers gather evidence, over time, through the direct observation of one or more students.

Surveyors collect perceptual data from members of the school community through the creation, administration, and scoring of one of more surveys.

Analysts gather existing data from the school and community that, if analyzed differently, might shed new light on the issue under study. They may disaggregate test scores, analyze attendance patterns, study teacher-given grades, or look for patterns in course offerings.

Storytellers, through interviews with key members of the community, collect stories that shed light on the postulate.

The different investigative groups are suitable to different learning styles and working preferences; they collect a variety of hard and soft data that can help people look in new ways at familiar problems and issues.

3. **Information analysis** is initially undertaken by each action research team in the context of small-group deliberation. This leads to the drawing of inferences from the information gathered by the team.

4. **Conclusions** are reached during another meeting of the entire group as participants learn from one another's study and evaluate different evidentiary sources.

Benefits of such a process. Beyond the usefulness of learning to discuss a problem with colleagues, becoming more open to others' opinions, and thinking together in a disciplined way about an important issue, Collegial Investigation has many serendipitous benefits.

• When a faculty engages in serious study and reflection, students in that school see teachers modeling "lifelong learning." In this way, such a study promotes commitment to continuous inquiry and improvement.

• The model of "active learning" through shared research has been powerful enough to persuade some teachers to adapt the process for use with students. They have found it enriches the scope of study for topics such as environmental science, for example.

• The process provides a structure that facilitates self-directed learning. A facilitator might be needed for the first Collegial Investigation experience, but as the group gains comfort with the process, and learns to write a postulate for study, members assume ownership, planning their own learning experience. The process is adaptable and can be used to develop expertise in any content area or pedagogical technique subject to study.

• It is a group process in which teachers are not spoon-fed information; the learning—acknowledging the wisdom and expertise of participants—requires engagement of the learner. What and how much teachers learn is directly related to the amount of effort and time they put into the learning. Through the process, in the large group and small action research teams, there are multiple opportunities for collaborative work and for leadership by participants.

How to Use Action Research in the Self-Renewing School by Emily F. Calhoun (Alexandria, VA: ASCD, 1994).

This is a step-by-step primer on the why, the what, and the how of action research in a school setting. In the first two chapters, the author provides a rationale and framework for this collegial way of working together. Following are chapters on each of the five phases that she associates with an action research cycle: (1) selecting an area or focus, (2) collecting data, (3) organizing data, (4) analyzing and interpreting data, and (5) taking action. Each chapter contains specific strategies, resources, caveats, and suggestions for success. If you are looking for a user-friendly guide to implementing action research in your school, this is a "must-have"!

Action Research: Inquiry, Reflection, and Decision Making (Alexandria, VA: ASCD, 1994).

One in a series of Inquiry Kits designed for use by faculty study groups, this toolkit is an excellent resource for schools that may never have used action research, but are interested in adapting this process to their school setting. The toolkit contains four videotapes, a facilitator's guide, and a resource book. The videotape series includes (1) an introduction and overview of action research, (2) an illustration of how an elementary school used action research to focus on improving student writing, (3) the story of a school district's use of this process as a part of their commitment to implementing shared decision making, and (4) a look inside a junior high school in which faculty members are using action research to assess the effectiveness of a recently introduced advisory period. The case study schools bring the process to life and illustrate the flexibility of the strategy.

The facilitator's guide, packaged in a three-ring binder, provides both directions and resources for workshop leaders. The guide contains notes for facilitators, camera-ready copy for overhead transparencies, participant handouts, and discussion guides. Emily Calhoun's book, *How to Use Action Research in the Self-Renewing School*, is provided as an additional resource for facilitators.

Weaving Assessment into the Fabric of Professional Learning[36]

Emerging from the decade of the '90s is a new paradigm or vision for teacher learning characterized by the theme of connectedness: *Teachers are learning in community—not in isolation one from another. Teacher learning is embedded in the practice of teaching—not divorced from the dynamics of the classroom. Teacher learning is related to student learning—not a separate enterprise. Professional learning is interwoven with daily practice in a seamless fashion.* As education leaders embrace this vision, they require supportive frameworks for evaluation that can be woven into the culture for learning and the professional learning process itself.

Donald Kirkpatrick offers a four-level model for evaluating training programs. It calls for data collection regarding participants' (1) **reactions** to a learning event; (2) **knowledge** gains; (3) **use** of knowledge in classroom settings; and (4) program **impact** upon, for example, student achievement.[37] This framework is a useful tool in designing comprehensive evaluations geared to answering the all-important questions "How good was the learning experience?" and "What difference is it making?" Adoption of the Kirkpatrick model meets organizational needs; it does not, however, provide individual learners with the tools to gauge personal growth and development.

Participative assessment—a framework for promoting individual assessment in a learning community—offers four facets that serve as counterpoints to Kirkpatrick's four levels.[38] This model argues for the infusion of learner-driven assessment strategies into the very fabric of the learning experience by providing structures, time, and space for learner engagement in ongoing (1) **reflection** to grapple with new ideas and skills and to relate them to personal knowledge, beliefs, and practice; (2) demonstrations or performances of **understanding** that assist in transforming "inert" knowledge that can be memorized and recalled to "generative" knowledge that can be built upon and used;[39] (3) exercises that facilitate individual and community **commitment** to changed practice; and (4) recognitions of **renewal** where individuals publicly share and celebrate transformations.

The name *participative assessment* underscores the active participation of individuals in determining the meaning and value of any given learning experience to their development and for their practice. Participative assessment is a strong support to continuous professional learning that depends upon individual professional goal setting and monitoring; it affords individuals with a scaffolding to use as they develop skills in transforming learning. Whereas traditional evaluations assume a linear, cause-and-effect, outside-in approach to change, participative assessment views change as a dynamic, systemic, interactive, inside-out phenomenon.

Weaving assessment into the fabric of professional learning is a challenge to education leaders. Participative assessment and the Kirkpatrick model provide frameworks that can center conversations and guide efforts to intertwine assessment with learning throughout the organization.

Tenets of Participative Assessment

Participative assessment

- is about initiating processes, not about producing products
- is integrated into the learning design: assessment and learning are interdependent
- focuses on the whole system—not on discrete parts of individual components
- encourages divergent, not convergent, thinking
- seeks to be a vehicle for creative growth, not an instrument of control
- does not seek cause-and-effect relationships; rather, it honors diversity
- is not about making judgments, but rather about making meaning
- focuses on individual growth, not on implementation of program components; and empowers individual learners to make better decisions about their learning

Strategies for Participative Assessment

Reflection. Staff developers often stimulate reflection with simple prompts that give respondents a point of departure for thinking and writing. These questions or stems can be included in a participant journal to provide a physical reminder of the importance of inner journeying for learning and of the personal and confidential nature of the reflective act. More experienced learners initiate their own reflections.

Reflective questioning facilitates exchanges among peers through reflection-out-loud. An individual prepares and asks questions "designed to provide opportunities for the respondent to explore his or her knowledge, skills, experiences, attitudes, beliefs, and values."[40]

Understanding. Within a workshop, understanding might be solicited by a carefully crafted question-and-answer session; a small- or large-group dialogue where learners intentionally practice inquiry and advocacy as defined by Chris Argyris and Richard Ross and Charlotte Roberts; analysis of a case or scenario; or a role play.[41]

Job-embedded learning that enables understanding includes peer observations and feedback, cognitive coaching, individual practice of new skills with feedback via audio or videotape, teaching of concepts or skills to others, examination of student work, action research, and so forth.

Commitment. Structuring assessments of commitment is difficult work that involves weaving relatively simple techniques and strategies into a rich tapestry of opportunities for learners to align beliefs and practice. For example, commitment can be assessed by inviting learners to formulate personal vision statements that embody hoped-for behavior changes and to revisit these periodically, by facilitating use of a force-field technique that helps flesh out driving and restraining forces as they relate to a desired outcome, by structuring collegial discussions that allow for public discourse and encourage collegial support, and by installing a system of critical friends to support change efforts. All of these assessments are also structures that can support long-term behavior changes.

Renewal. Assessment of renewal is best done in community—through storytelling, sharing of personal anecdotes or success experiences, creation of new processes or products, or other individual expressions. An individual learner's demonstration of renewal will embody reflection, understanding and commitment.

Reflection at its best enables learners to relate concepts to self as demonstrated by these reflective comments written in response to the question, "What ideas are challenging your thinking?" About the content focus of a learning session, one participant wrote: "Concerning the idea of 'change,' I am beginning to feel that a change in 'mind-set' is the only step that we need to take. Once this is accomplished, specific changes will generate themselves." Regarding a process of collaborative learning, another observed: "The idea that the answers aren't already 'out there' for a facilitator to pass on to members of the workshop intrigues me. Most workshop participants have a mind-set that only allows them to feel that they've accomplished something if they come away with concrete information."

Evaluation as a Balancing Act: Inside-Out *and* Outside-In

Evaluation of professional development is not an either-or proposition. We do not have the luxury of focusing on program effectiveness to the exclusion of learner needs, nor can we ignore organizational needs for accountability. If the true purpose of professional development is to effect changes in the organization *and* for individual learners, a comprehensive assessment design will incorporate the four levels of Kirkpatrick's model as well as the four levels of the participative assessment framework. Within the educational context this would provide for evaluation of the impact of a program as well as assessment of the quality of the renewal experience for the individual adult learner.

QUILT: A Pathway to Increasing Shared Practice[42]

A school community with a strong learning culture finds both students and adults in learning situations. This norm for continuous improvement integrates ongoing professional development into school life. Teachers learn with and from one another, perhaps visiting classrooms, reviewing student work, sharing teaching dilemmas in small groups, and giving feedback to colleagues on questions under study.

This kind of culture does not evolve quickly; most schools find it requires intentional nurturing. A packaged program such as QUILT (Questioning and Understanding to Improve Learning and Thinking) may be adopted to begin moving the faculty toward this way of being together—and learning together—in school.

The QUILT professional development program focuses on improved student thinking and subsequent learning. Teachers learn about and practice ways of effectively posing classroom questions. Rather than continuing to ask the typical 40 to 50 questions per hour found in most classrooms, teachers are encouraged to construct a few "educative" questions that have the power to stimulate student thinking through discussion, as defined by James Dillon.[43] The ultimate goal is that students become effective questioners—but to accomplish this, classroom norms and behaviors must change.

At the school level, QUILT is led by a local team, who have been trained by QUILT staff. They lead their faculty through a yearlong process that includes teacher reflection; classroom application; collegial learning, with teachers working together across grade levels and subject areas; and partnering, in which teachers observe one another and give feedback on teacher behaviors. In addition, QUILT provides the opportunity for the entire faculty to have fun together. Some schools find the program is the first opportunity for teachers to share ideas and strategies across grade levels and departments. QUILT was intentionally designed to be interactive; active learning and reflection are major components.

For many schools, the biggest challenge in implementing QUILT is the piece that encourages classroom observations. Few schools have a norm of "shared practice," with teachers observing in others' classrooms regularly. Isolated occurrences, between teachers who team teach, for example, do not make observation a norm at a school. Over its 10-year history, QUILT has offered participating schools an expanded opportunity for shared learning in the following ways:

1. It is a schoolwide program that establishes a shared vocabulary and **common knowledge base** about teaching and learning.

2. It is a program to which the entire staff can commit—across disciplines and grade levels—because all teachers can see immediate applicability and a direct **benefit to students**.

3. It provides a **structure** for observing in one another's classrooms for the purpose of learning from one another and giving feedback.

4. It provides a basis for **collective learning and application**—for continual "sharpening of the saw." Most teachers, as they participate in QUILT, can see a need for improved skills in the area of classroom questioning and genuinely want to become better. As they apply what they learn in the classroom, QUILT provides an opportunity for teachers to share these experiences with others.

Inquiry: Questioning as a Way of Being Together

Collegial Investigations and other forms of action research assume that participants will adopt both the attitudes and the skills associated with inquiry. Through the practice of inquiry, individuals engage in "learningful" conversations in which they question their own and others' thinking; in which they do not casually accept ideas or assertions, but seek to understand these at a deep level. This requires a certain spirit as well as supporting habits of mind.

Individuals and groups dedicated to inquiry share core values and norms. Primary among these are intellectual curiosity, openness, and persistence as well as a commitment to collaboration. These qualities not only promote questioning and reflection, they also enable individuals to suspend judgment: to seek the right questions rather than the correct answers; to listen to points of view that may differ from their own; to expose their assumptions and beliefs; and to modify their thinking based upon new understandings and insights as well as new information.   This "focus on questions rather than answers" leads to "individual insight and collective discovery," the hallmarks of true inquiry. Inquiry, then, occurs in a "climate of discovery, questioning—even mystery and adventure";

Questioning to Stimulate Learning and Thinking, http://www/videojournal.com (Sandy, UT: The Video Journal of Education, 1999).

Questioning is a foundation of teaching and learning. Two video series—one for elementary teachers and the other for middle and high school teachers—feature a model for questioning developed by Jackie Walsh and Beth Sattes at AEL. The videos present both theory and classroom examples to enhance understanding, as they feature the QUILT (Questioning and Understanding to Improve Learning and Thinking) model. Teachers can see the power of questions, learn strategies to engage students in thinking, and explore ways to help students develop skills of inquiry in the classroom.

in a culture that encourages risk taking and fair-mindedness, honors diversity and independent thinking, tolerates uncertainty and ambiguity, and builds mutual trust and respect.[44]

Out of this spirit evolve companion habits of mind. These are dispositions and skills that enable individuals to remain true to the spirit of inquiry and to participate in learningful conversations. While these habits are interactive—that is to say, they work together to support true inquiry—we can separate them for the purposes of understanding. The following seven skills and attitudes, while not exhaustive, provide a beginning point for those who quest for deeper insight, greater understanding, and more authentic knowledge.

1. **Asking questions from a place of genuine not knowing.** Those who engage in true inquiry give up "the need to know for certain"; they look for the curious, the puzzling, and uncertain. They are willing to go into uncharted territory; to dig deeply into the dark unknown. They acknowledge the power of questions, and they become more conscious of their own questions and questioning processes. They seek to improve both.

2. **Suspending judgment and withholding evaluation.** Questions are not true or authentic when answers based upon personal values and assumptions are immediately forthcoming. Neither is conversation learningful if one is continually reacting with an evaluative statement. And yet most of us are conditioned to react immediately—to answer a question, resolve an issue, or correct a misguided point of view. How do we retrain ourselves to remain open?

3. **Reflecting on one's own experiences and assumptions.** The act of reflecting is a private and personal discipline that involves slowing down our thinking so that we can "make space to explore and question." True exploration can lead us to "change [our] inner landscape . . . the way we perceive the world, the way we think about cause and effect, the way we conceptualize the relationships among things, and the meaning we ascribe to events in [our] external world." To accomplish this, we must first be able to identify our own assumptions, those untested, often unconscious and unstated beliefs that we embrace as facts.[45]

Promoting Adult Growth in Schools by Sarah L. Levine
(Boston: Allyn & Bacon, 1989).

In this beautifully crafted and highly informative book, Levine makes a case for attending to the personal growth and development of all adults who work in schools. She argues that growing and changing are lifelong processes and that adults, like children, require learning experiences that are appropriate to their particular stage or phase of development. Honoring the individual needs and differences of adult learners enhances the well-being of the adults and the students whom they serve. Further, the author contends that the facilitation of adult growth in schools is compatible with and supportive of continuous school improvement.

Levine provides a balance of practice and theory as she develops the main theme of her book. She portrays four teachers and uses their voices as a vehicle to surface questions and issues important to school leaders committed to supporting the growth of their faculty and staff. Additionally, she provides a clear, concise, and highly understandable overview of stage and phase theories of human development and relates these to the school setting.

4. **Honoring silence, making the time and space to finish our thoughts and to explore our own and others' thinking.** Because inquiry involves thoughtfulness, the pace of conversation is best not hurried. A conscious attempt can be made to use wait times or pauses, a minimum of 3 to 5 seconds of silence, before responding to another's question or statement. Further, we can learn to be comfortable with longer periods of silence, resisting the temptation to speak just to fill the void.

5. **Listening deeply.** Silence typically does not occur in conversations because we do so often engage in a ping-pong game, preparing our return or response before receiving another's message. This habit prevents us from understanding and taking in another's meaning. Listening deeply involves active listening and more: It requires that we engage with the speaker intellectually and emotionally; that we listen from the speaker's point of view, not from an autobiographical stance.

6. **Seeking actively to understand another's point of view.** Sherrin Bennett and Juanita Brown maintain that "clear, bold and penetrat-

ing questions elicit a full range of dynamic responses and energy that open up the [possibilities] for learning." They proceed from the premise that all of us "have within [us] the wisdom and creativity to confront even the most difficult challenges . . . to access deeper knowledge about the underlying causes and leverage points for change." The potential of questioning provides a motivation for keeping the focus on questions; awareness and practice build this habit.[46]

The spirit of inquiry nurtures the habits of mind that promote this way of seeking and finding new knowledge. As we pursue this mode of thinking and learning together, we are promised "new discoveries that lead to new questions." These new questions, in turn, lead to new discoveries. Out of this, "a community of inquiry and commitment begins to form." Questioning and listening within this community enable us "to get to the 'aha' together." The source of the new questions and discoveries is, of course, the wisdom and creativity of each member of the community who comes willingly to share experiences and insights, curiosities and wonderings. The knowing that emerges from this community experience "reminds us of that which we have forgotten to remember."[47]

What might happen if your faculty adopted this approach to professional discourse? How difficult would it be to give up the position of certitude and move to those "what if" questions? In what ways would this affect the overall culture of the school? The cultures of individual classrooms? How might school leaders encourage colleagues to take a leap of faith toward use of inquiry? We believe that the best way to begin is to "just do it." Share this think piece on inquiry with colleagues. Talk about what it might mean in your school to begin to think together in this way. Experiment with this new behavior in a safe, controlled environment. Adopt group norms to govern your new way of being together. Be intentional in continuing the practice. Expect to have ups and downs along the way. Believe that inquiry will support a broader school vision of always seeking and finding ways to improve performance at all levels.

Putting Action Research to Work

Nancy Binder, Curriculum Coordinator at Natcher Elementary School, shares a story about action research at her school.

Several faculty members at Natcher were fortunate to team with AEL and a Western Kentucky University math professor to investigate growth in our students' math computation scores on the CAT/5. Every fall we administer a complete battery and compare these results with the spring survey. We have noted a lack of progress the last several years in math computation, which has surprised us. When the team started, most of us believed it was sporadic occurrences, but when we investigated whole classes of students of all levels of achievement and tracked them over time, we were amazed to see this was a more constant phenomenon. Our action research approach led us to interview the students and, from the mouths of babes, practically each one said it was a lack of motivation at the end of the year that caused their scores to decline. None of the students were happy about this, and some were even shocked. When asked what they could do about it, all said they would try harder and try to forget summer vacation was just around the corner.

Debbie Dingess relates an amazing story of the power of action research in mobilizing the Atenville Elementary staff to make parents partners in decision making.

Perception, whether right or wrong, becomes reality for most people. What a shock we felt when we discovered that what we thought we were doing for students at Atenville Elementary was not what their parents thought we were doing! And, even greater was our disbelief when we discovered that what we thought parents *were not* doing for their children at home was exactly what they thought they *were* doing. Needless to say, what we had here was a failure to communicate!

The story began when we wrote a proposal for a parent involvement grant offered by the Boston-based Institute for Responsive Education. Initially, we saw the funding as a means to get parents to assume some of the tasks we regularly performed but that took teaching time from us. We had grown weary of decorating for the annual talent show and the prom, and we really wanted help with the fund-raisers. The grant, which we ultimately received, provided for employment of a parent coordinator who could take over these jobs.

As part of the application process, we were asked to conduct in-home surveys of parents. To ensure objectivity, we had the surveys administered by neutral surveyors. The results overwhelmed our faculty. We really thought we were great communicators. Parents thought differently. We also believed parents did little to help their children with homework and readiness to learn. They thought differently.

Our response to the survey results was to direct our action research team to address parents' perceptions and to formulate a plan to change those perceptions. We held a series of workshops to offer parents additional materials and skills to help them work with their children at home. We assigned the parent coordinator responsibility for much more than prom decorations and fund-raisers.

Initially, our staff viewed the parent coordinator as our advocate. She, on the other hand, saw herself as an advocate for parents. Sometimes we felt threatened when she reported parent concerns to our principal, and we wanted to know "who said that." She remained firm in her conviction that, if the perception existed, it must be dealt with. We learned, over time, that she was right.

Today, we see our parents as equal partners in decision making at Atenville, not as the people who perform the jobs no one else wants to do. Parents actively participate on our school improvement committee, our local school improvement council, and our faculty senate. The process did not emerge overnight. Rather, through our action research team, our parent involvement program evolved as needs surfaced.

We now have a Family Center where parents and faculty gather to plan, to communicate their needs, to develop rapport. We have eliminated our faculty lounge because our teachers prefer the Family Center. We have learned to depend on each other to make the right decisions for our students.

At the close of the three-year grant period, we conducted the same survey with a random sample of parents. The results showed parents thought we had improved communication and they had gained knowledge in how to help their children learn at home. The school received a $5,000 award as a result of our exemplary parent involvement program. We used that money to place a phone in each classroom to enable teachers to maintain daily contact with parents. Now parents know exactly what is going on in their children's classrooms, and they can offer support as we teach their children.

Parents are truly equal partners at Atenville Elementary School.

Do We Have a Strong Culture for Learning? Looking at the Learning Culture in Your School

A. Use Interview Design to encourage people to talk about the learning culture at your school. The following questions can guide the initial discussion in pairs.[48]

Question 1. Shared vision. (a) What is your vision for student learning in your school? (b) To what extent do you think others in your school community—teachers, students, parents, support staff, and administrators—share this vision?

Question 2. Trying new things; risk taking. (a) To what extent do members of your school community welcome new techniques, ideas, or ways of working to improve personal performance? (b) Describe a recent change at your school that was intended to improve student learning.

Question 3. Celebrations of achievement. In what ways does your school celebrate individual and schoolwide achievements? Think of both (a) types of achievements that are celebrated as well as (b) the forms that these celebrations take.

Question 4. Cooperation within the school community to achieve goals. To what extent do individuals in your school community cooperate to achieve shared goals or solve common problems, share strategies and techniques, or set aside time to reflect with one another and share learnings? Give examples.

Question 5. Excitement for learning. (a) To what extent do curiosity and excitement permeate your school's classrooms? (b) What contributes to (or stifles) a sense of excitement for learning in your school?

B. Use the Inside-Outside Fishbowl as a structure to promote group discussion on this topic with a diverse group of students. (Alternatively, use the fishbowl technique with the school faculty, with a parent group, or with a school governance committee.) With 10 to 12 students sitting in the inside fishbowl, and a mixed group of parents and teachers sitting around the edges, ask students to talk about one or more of the items above as the beginning of a group discussion.[49]

Read through the following items and reflect on your own school community.

- Curiosity and excitement permeate the school.

- Individuals continually look for ways to improve their performance.

- Faculty and staff set aside time to reflect and share their learnings.

- Students and parents expect competent and caring teachers.

- The school regularly celebrates individual and community accomplishments.

- Individuals across the school share a clear and compelling vision.

- All members of the school community frequently question established ways of doing things for the purpose of improving student learning.

In which of the above areas does your school community excel? Can you think of examples of how these qualities have made a difference in the lives of students?

Stimulate thinking and individual reflection

A. As you read through the items above, identify one or more that trigger a personal response. Reflect on the story behind that response. Write your story in a journal: how one or more issues related to school climate made a difference in your life—as a student, a parent, or a teacher.

B. Consider how your own school experiences bias your perceptions of school culture. What beliefs about schooling come to mind because of your personal and past experiences?

C. In what ways can you affect the culture of your school for the good? How can you build excitement and enthusiasm, establish and share in celebrations, and find ways to continually question and improve "the way we do things around here"?

Notes

1. See Deal and Kennedy, *Corporate Cultures*; and Deal and Peterson, *Shaping School Culture*.

2. See the story "MicroSociety as a Culture: Bringing the Real World Into the School" in chapter three for more information about the MicroSociety program at Atenville Elementary School. The MicroSociety program was selected for inclusion in the *Catalog of School Reform Models*, published by the Northwest Regional Educational Laboratory. For more about the program, visit MicroSociety, Inc. at http://www.microsociety.org.

3. See Wheatley, *A Simpler Way*.

4. Deal and Peterson, *Shaping School Culture*, 10.

5. Kline and Saunders, *Ten Steps to a Learning Organization*, 44-45.

6. Richardson, "School Culture: A Key to Improved Student Learning," 1.

7. Kofman and Senge, "Communities of Commitment," 21.

8. Handy, "Managing the Dream," 47.

9. New Era Media, 1987.

10. Directions for Snowflake are included elsewhere in this chapter.

11. The following description of the Snowflake activity was published in *Creating Energy for Continuous School Improvement*, produced by Quest staff at AEL, Charleston, WV, 1998. AEL first learned of the process from colleagues at the Northwest Regional Educational Laboratory, Portland, Oregon.

12. See Brown, *The Important Book*.

13. Robbins and Finley, *Why Change Doesn't Work*, 208.

14. Deal and Peterson, *Shaping School Culture*, 32.

15. Ibid, 35.

16. Kouzes and Posner, *Encouraging the Heart*, 122.

17. Shirley Hord is the author of *Professional Learning Communities: Communities of Continuous Inquiry and Improvement* (Austin, TX: SEDL, 1997). The story of Dibert Elementary School appears on a videotape, *Learning Together, Growing Together: John Dibert Elementary School,* 1995 (15 minutes), available from SEDL, 211 E. Seventh St., Austin, TX 78701-3281; 512-476-6861; http://www.sedl.org. More about the establishment of learning communities can be found in this book in the "School as Community" section of chapter one.

18. See Deal and Kennedy, *Corporate Cultures*; Deal and Peterson, *Shaping School Culture*; and Kouzes and Posner, *Encouraging the Heart*.

19. See Jalongo and Isenberg, *Teachers' Stories*.

20. "Stories for Learning," by Diane Cory and Paul Underwood, in *Learning Organizations*, was a major source and a primary inspiration for this essay. Readers are encouraged to read the article in its entirety.

21. Cory and Underwood, "Stories for Learning," 129.

22. Ibid.

23. Cory and Underwood, "Stories for Learning," 133-35.

24. Jalongo and Isenberg, *Teachers' Stories*, 10-11.

25. See Lieberman and Miller, *Teachers—Transforming Their World and Their Work*.

26. Ibid, 21.

27. Little, "Organizing Schools for Teacher Learning," 238.

28. Sykes, "Teacher and Student Learning," 153.

29. Fullan, "Staff Development, Innovation, and Institutional Development," 18-20.

30. See Sagor, "Collaborative Action Research for Educational Change."

31. Ibid, 188.

32. Sagor, *How to Conduct Collaborative Action Research*.

33. Calhoun, *How to Use Action Research in the Self-Renewing School*, 1.

34. See Walsh and Sattes, *QUILT Collegial Invesigations*.

35. See Paul, *Critical Thinking Handbook*.

36. This article by Jackie Walsh appeared in *Insights*, Winter 1999. It is reprinted here with the permission of the author and the Texas Association of School Administrators.

37. See Kirkpatrick, *Evaluating Training Programs*.

38. Participative assessment was first introduced by Walsh and Sattes at a National Staff Development Council (NSDC) preconference of the NSDC annual conference in Chicago, 1994.

39. See Perkins, *Smart Schools*.

40. See Lee and Barnett, "Using Reflective Questioning to Promote Collaborative Dialogue."

41. See Argyris, *Knowledge for Action*; and Senge, Kleiner, Roberts, Ross, and Smith, *The Fifth Discipline Fieldbook*.

42. See information on the QUILT program in the "School as Community" section of chapter one, or visit QUILT's Web page at http://www.ael.org/rel/quilt.

43. See Dillon, *Questioning and Teaching*.

44. Bennett and Brown, "Mindshift," 173-74.

45. Brown, "Dialogue," 156-57.

46. Bennett and Brown, "Mindshift," 174, 167.

47. Bennett and Brown, "Mindshift," 183, 180; and Brown, "Dialogue," 155.

48. Directions for Interview Design can be found in chapter four.

49. Directions for the "Inside-Outside Fishbowl" can be found under "Processes that Build Community" in chapter one.

Enabling SMART Learners

The teacher's responsibility is to create a social environment in
the classroom that promotes active engagement and risk taking
on the part of students, as well as a high level of interaction
among students around problems. Classrooms that represent
this view of learning are characterized, for instance, by
students interacting around difficult and interesting problems
that engage their interests, rather than by passive assimilation
of knowledge purveyed by a teacher standing in the front of the
room.

—Richard Elmore

*T*he primary focus of any school improvement effort is the
enhancement of educational offerings for all students. While
each school community must formulate its own vision for
students based upon core values, this vision—to be viable and exciting—
must take into consideration the social context in which this generation
of students is coming of age. Much has been written about the emerging
demands of life and work for the twenty-first century. It is clear that we
will have not only to "work smart," but also to "learn smart," in an
environment in which the only constant is change.

Questions for Reflection

Cognitive research and theory can inform school communities as they seek to translate their visions into specific learning goals and instructional practices. However, only individuals within the community can answer the following kinds of questions for their school:

- What if there were no grades or achievement test scores? How would we then measure student success in school?

- What kinds of classroom practices tend to extinguish intrinsic motivation? Are we willing to give up these "carrots and sticks"?

- To what extent do we assist students in making their own meaning out of the knowledge they acquire in school?

- In what ways, if any, does our school assess student understanding?

- What does it look and sound like in a classroom when teachers are trying to help their students develop self-initiative and responsibility?

- What are we doing to encourage student reflection and thoughtfulness?

Developing SMART Learners: What's It All About?

Embedded in the questions above is the concept of a SMART learner, one who is Successful, Motivated, Autonomous, Responsible, and Thoughtful. The authors developed the concept of SMART in an effort to focus on these qualities associated with continuous lifelong learning.

Student *success* is most frequently measured by standard yardsticks such as test grades, report cards, class rank, achievement test scores, and so forth. Rarely does assessment of student success involve the learner in thinking about his or her own competence. Even education reform efforts seem predicated on the notion that teachers can find a way to create "success for all students" (that is, guarantee high scores for all) through "reaching hard-to-teach students." Among the more notable instructional theories addressing this goal are mastery learning, learning styles, multiple intelligences, and accelerated learning.

Teachers cannot make students successful; students must achieve this for themselves. According to Daniel Goleman, the most critical variable in student performance is student self-efficacy, the belief that one has

mastery over the events of one's life and can meet challenges as they come up. Goleman cites the work of Albert Bandura, whose research confirms that "ability is not a fixed property; . . . people's beliefs about their abilities have a profound effect on those abilities."[1] The culture of schools and class-

There is a great difference between knowing and understanding: you can know a lot about something and not really understand it.

—Charles Kettering

rooms greatly affects student self-efficacy. In classrooms where curiosity reigns—where questions are valued as much as answers—students are enabled to take charge of their learning. Such classrooms encourage risk taking and experimentation, thereby allowing students to learn from failures as well as successes and thus to stretch their abilities.

Key to this notion of success is an assumption that students are intrinsically *motivated* to learn. As the research of David Perkins makes clear, however, many well-intentioned classroom practices have the effect of undermining intrinsic motivation. In particular, extrinsic rewards such as grades, candy, and excessive praise can have the effect of extinguishing intrinsic motivation: "If an activity is both interesting in itself and rewarded in extrinsic ways, children's intrinsic interest tends to wane."[2] Also related to intrinsic motivation is the student's belief that he or she can be successful at the learning task. This belief is affected not only by self-efficacy but also by teachers' effectiveness in structuring challenging learning tasks and holding high performance expectations for all students.

Intrinsic motivation is a powerful factor in developing skills that enable *autonomous* or independent learning, skills critical in an ever-changing social and work environment. Autonomous learning does not suggest learning in isolation from others; rather, it is highly compatible with cooperative learning. Autonomous learners, however, do *not* depend upon teacher direction and control, but are able to initiate, plan, and monitor their own learning. They are intentional learners "exercis[ing] control over their own learning, . . . making judgments about what types of knowledge are required to solve problems, and . . . construct[ing] explanations of their own and test[ing] those explanations against facts or against the explanations of other students."[3] Metacognitive skills are a hallmark of the autonomous learner: this learner knows how to think about thinking and learning, knows how to learn. When teachers encourage students to reflect on not only the what but also the how of their learning, they help their students become more autonomous and successful.

Central to the SMART concept is the notion of individual *responsibility* for learning. Students' responsibility for their own learning can be fostered through curricular and instructional practices—problem-based learning, inquiry approaches, student exhibits and portfolios, senior projects, service learning, and others. In schools where it is a valued goal, expectations for student responsibility are part of the larger fabric of the school, a vital part of the school's culture. For example, in some schools students assume responsibility for planning and conducting conferences in which they lead their parents in a discussion of what is going well for them and what needs improvement. During these conferences, teachers are primarily observers.[4] This is but one strategy for engaging students in the assessment of their learning. Self-assessment, like personal goal setting, is essential to continuous learning.

Opportunities to plan and assess one's learning promote *thoughtfulness* about the learning process. An advocate of "thinking-centered learning," David Perkins calls for educational settings where "students learn by thinking through what they are learning about." He provides this compelling summary of the research on the nature of human learning and thinking: "Learning is a consequence of thinking. Retention, understanding, and the active use of knowledge can be brought about only by learning experiences in which learners think about and think with what they are learning."[5] In *Smart Schools*, Perkins offers practical guidance for transforming our "knowledge-centered schools" into "thinking-centered schools"—schools that promote both student and teacher thoughtfulness. Learners are challenged to develop thoughtfulness when pushed "to search for meaning in complex, non-routine situations, [to be] adventurous with solutions or interpretations, and to be reasonable in [their] thinking choices and judgments."[6] Thoughtfulness has both cognitive and affective connotations, the latter relating to a learner's attitudes toward others and thus "integrates thinking and feeling, a union of heart and mind."[7]

Successful, Motivated, Autonomous, Responsible, Thoughtful—these goals for learners have important implications for instructional practice. Additionally, if we believe SMART learners to be effective citizens and knowledge workers, these attributes have equally important implications for school governance and culture. Teachers and other adults can be afforded appropriate opportunities to exercise SMART learning in a school community that has a strong learning culture and encourages all to assume leadership responsibilities.

Learning as a Way of Being: Strategies for Survival in a World of Permanent White Water by Peter B. Vaill (San Francisco: Jossey-Bass, 1996).

Drawing from his long-term research and work as an organization development specialist, Vaill presents a strong argument and useful strategies for learning as a day-to-day discipline and practice for individuals in all walks of life. He likens work in today's world to white water, which is characterized by rapids, changing currents, and continuous movement. Survival requires constant awareness and adjustment to environmental changes. Likewise, in the world of work, continuous change demands daily learning. Vaill contrasts the type of learning needed for high performance in organizational life to "institutional learning," the type that goes on in most schools. He discusses seven qualities of learning as a "way of being": self-directed, creative, expressive, feeling, on-line, continual, and reflexive.

Promoting Parent Understanding and Buy-In for SMART Learning

The Quest Network included parents on school leadership teams. Early on in our work together, parents and teachers alike saw the value of informing parents about the SMART learner concept—to get parents working in partnership with schools to support Success, Motivation, Autonomy, Responsibility, and Thoughtfulness. A series of six workshops, *Doing Your Part to Help Your Child Become SMART*, is available through AEL. The materials include a trainer's manual, announcements, overheads, and handouts needed to conduct successful sessions with parents of K-12 students.[8]

Natcher Elementary School took the notion a step further and included a series on SMART parenting in its monthly parent newsletter, *Jaguar Tracks,* written by parent Shannon Gottke. Excerpts from this series are included in Appendix D.

A Renaissance of Learning

by Anne Yost, Teacher, South Harrison High School

Last year my honors English class spearheaded a **successful** effort to establish a schoolwide Renaissance/Shakespeare Fair. The students accepted **responsibility** for their own learning by organizing the fair. Some researched customs, foods, games, and dress. Others memorized parts of Shakespearean plays and reenacted them, dressed in period costume. On their own initiative, they demonstrated **autonomy** by inviting eighth graders from the middle school as their audience. They felt less self-conscious and more at ease with this audience than with their own peer group. In addition, they made a conscious, **thoughtful** decision to pique the interest of the middle schoolers so that, as ninth graders, they would be **motivated** to become involved in the fair.

This year, we are expanding the fair to involve other departments. I can just imagine plants and herbs from that time period, grown by students in the agricultural classes; costumes sewn by the home economics department; time lines constructed by the history classes; and stained glass windows from our art classes. The possibilities are endless and exciting.

Empowering Students to Achieve SUCCESS

SMART
uccessful

Teachers cannot make students successful. Students must achieve this for themselves. But how? The teacher's task is to empower students; to provide them with tools and skills they can use to produce work in which they can take pride. Valerie Harvey, fourth-grade teacher at Alexander Elementary School, believes that teachers also empower boys and girls "by expecting more of them, and when you expect more, they achieve more; when they achieve more, the self-esteem is built, and then you have success." Harvey empowers her students by teaching them strategies they can use to become more effective questioners. Her colleague, Pamela Dunigan, teaches her fourth-grade students how to use the Structured Reflection Protocol process to improve their writing. Catherine Ralston, a teacher at Highland County High School, uses the senior research project to facilitate her students' creation of products that will become testimonies to their success as learners. Sheila Leach, fifth-grade teacher at Our Lady of Fatima, teaches her students how to harness technology for the purposes of their learning in history. Larry Livingston, a special education teacher at Woodbridge Senior High School, provides his students with tools that enable them to monitor their own learning. These are but a sampling of strategies that creative teachers employ to provide students with tools that enhance their feelings of self-efficacy in the classroom—their belief that they can meet the challenges presented to them in and out of the classroom and that they do have control over their destiny.

Harvey draws from her own learnings in the QUILT staff development program as she teaches her students to become more effective questioners and respondents.[9] She relates the story of an impulsive, spontaneous fourth-grade boy who had difficulty staying on task academically. After learning how to formulate questions and pose them to his classmates using wait times and related questioning strategies, he demonstrated measurable improvement in both self-discipline and oral and written communications. When this young learner is "up front" and in charge of posing his questions to his peers, he will often admonish

175

them to "put your hands down; you haven't waited five seconds yet."

In the same school, Darrell, also in the fourth grade, began the school year "very reluctant to write." His teacher, Pamela Dunigan, knew that she would have to find some way to cajole him and like-minded students not only to write, but also to become self-critical about their writing. In Tennessee, all fourth graders must engage in the high-stakes, statewide writing assessment. Darrell had "low self-esteem and almost no self-confidence." Mrs. Dunigan taught Darrell and his peers how to analyze their own writing and how to give and receive both "warm" and "cool" feedback using the principles of Structured Reflection Protocol.[10] Over the course of his five-month experience with this process, Darrell became more motivated; he wanted to do well. He basked in the warm feedback of his classmates. Darrell, who had experienced real difficulty in writing a one-paragraph story in September, scored a 6 (the highest level of proficiency) on the writing assessment that he completed in February. Ms. Dunigan smiles and says, "At Alexander we are creating student success."

All students can learn, at high levels, the forms of knowledge, skills, attitudes, and habits of mind that are judged by relevant adults to be both important to the happiness and welfare of the students and socially and culturally significant. Furthermore, it is the obligation of schools, and those who work therein, to provide students with engaging work that ensures that students learn what they are expected to learn.

—Phil Schlechty

Catherine Ralston remembers Gary Anderson, a senior who had learned to hate school and to look forward to the day when he could leave it behind forever to become a logger in the only industry in his home county. As she made an impassioned introduction to senior projects in her English 12 class, she watched Gary's smiling face turn to a sullen scowl. When she approached his desk, he said, "I ain't doin' it. I'm not working on one stupid thing for eight or nine months just for school." Ralston tried to engage him in conversation about the project, but he was too angry to listen. She left him to sulk alone, but when class was over, sought out the agriculture and carpentry teachers to brainstorm ideas for dealing with Gary's reluctance. They told her of his interest in anything mechanical, and she began to gather materials for Gary to search for ideas.

As the days passed, this young man became less sullen and even ventured some tentative ideas. "I might build a car!" or "Could I build a farm machine that somebody else invented?" Getting him to do the research and writing necessary in the preliminary stages of the project continued to be difficult, but with the help of his other teachers and his family, Gary decided to build a gas-powered log splitter. Once his decision was made, it became a little easier to get assignments from him, but he never really enjoyed anything connected with his project except the hands-on building of the splitter. That is, not until the day he actually fired the thing up and split his first log! Then there was no stopping Gary. He told everyone about the "neat" project that Ms. Ralston had "made" him do and would drag them to the shop for a demonstration. When Ralston asked him to help her choose the committee for his presentation, she had to make massive cuts from the list he gave her. Gary's culminating activity of his senior year was one in which he achieved and felt success!

In Sheila Leach's fifth-grade class, all students learn how to create products using all of the technical tools available to their teachers. Leach takes the time to instruct students in the use of PowerPoint, the school's digital camera, and other technology as it becomes available in this small, parochial school. Leach shares stories of previously underperforming students whose excitement about creating their own presentations spilled over into other areas of academic performance. These students, who cooperate with others on their work team, are learning and practicing behaviors that will transfer into success in future academic settings as well as in other arenas.

> If he didn't learn it in the first place, he can't apply it now.
> —Larry Livingston, Special Education Teacher, Woodbridge High School

Special education students can benefit tremendously from acquisition of tools that help them become more aware of how they learn. Larry Livingston helps his students develop skills in self-assessment by drawing them into the planning process. He begins by conducting an assessment for each student to find out what each one wants to get out of his class, what goals each student has set for himself. Mr. Livingston states, "Then I attempt to work these goals into what I do in the classroom. If a student wants to become an engineer, I develop lessons that will lead him down that path. If he merely wants to be able to balance his checkbook, I work on more vocational skills, all the while adhering to the state standards for instruction." After instruction, Mr. Livingston asks the students if he is teaching them what they asked him to teach them, if he tested them on what he taught, and why they made the grade they made. Following the student assessments, he modifies his lessons to bring them in line with the students' goals.

Jason's Story

by Jackie McCann, Teacher, Atenville Elementary School

I first met Jason when he entered my third-grade learning disabilities class at Atenville. Jason experienced many of the difficulties common to LD students—his reading level was low, math concepts eluded him, and, in general, he simply found school a stressful experience. I continued to work with Jason over a three-year period, often becoming frustrated that he encountered so many problems in succeeding as a student. Little did I know that the introduction of the MicroSociety to Atenville would change Jason's life.[11] When Atenville became a Micro school, we reorganized into a community complete with businesses, a justice system, social services, and all that the name MicroSociety implies. Students chose their areas of interest.

Jason asked to become a business owner! Here was this child who read poorly, had trouble with numbers, and seldom succeeded in the school arena demanding a leadership position! What were we to do? After agonizing discussion with several teachers, the decision was made to allow Jason to begin his own business. We all knew it was simply a matter of time before he failed miserably, but we did not have the heart to tell him so.

Jason hired his staff. The business thrived. The business became the most successful in the school. We sat back in utter amazement. One day I sat with Jason and discussed his success. "Jason, I know you always have trouble with numbers, and I really am curious about how you have managed to keep the best set of books in the school." "Oh, that's easy, Ms. McCann. I simply hired the best math student in school to keep them for me. You know, I'm not very good in math, so I knew I needed somebody to help me. I just looked around and found the best person I knew to keep the books."

Another time we discussed a personnel problem Jason faced after hiring his best friend to work for him. It seemed that Jason needed to take care of some business matters, so he left his friend to watch the "office." When Jason returned, he discovered his friend had left the money on the table and disappeared. "Well, Jason, what did you do?" I queried. "Ms. McCann, I just told him this was his one warning; that if he ever left the business unattended again, I would fire him!"

If MicroSociety had not become reality at Atenville, Jason might never have realized his talent for business. He might have continued through school, and life, never succeeding and becoming more and more convinced that he had nothing to offer his community. He might never have learned about choosing the best people, supporting their efforts, and sharing success with them. MicroSociety unleashed the unrealized potential in that child and gave him a vision that will impact the remainder of his life.

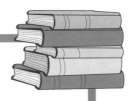

The Skillful Teacher: Building Your Teaching Skills by Jon Saphier and Robert Gower, 5th ed. (Carlisle, MA: Research for Better Teaching, 1997).

This is a comprehensive resource for teacher learning and learning about teaching. The authors bring us clarifying insights into the skills of teaching as a highly complex undertaking. They examine management, instruction, motivation, and curriculum in depth, with current research informing their work throughout. Saphier and Gower examine momentum in class, routines and disciplinary issues, clarity of instruction, principles of learning, curriculum design, objectives, assessment, teacher beliefs, and more. This is a resource that teachers will find at once practical, inspirational, and affirming.

Review written by Alice Phillips, teacher at Sewanee Elementary School.

Celebrating Successes: Our Schoolwide Multicultural Unit

by Alice Phillips, Teacher, discussing her former school in Massachusetts

Every year, in the heart of winter, our students all gather together to "kick off" the annual schoolwide unit of study. Originally designed by a committee of teachers to be a five-year project, we are now in our seventh year, and each year the enthusiasm and sense of accomplishment among our students grow stronger. The kickoff program involves singing, poetry recitation, a read-aloud, marching flag bearers, and much more. Teachers, students, and administrators all contribute and participate in the celebration.

For six weeks following the kickoff ceremony, each grade level focuses on a specific world region: first grade studies Africa, second focuses on Japan, third learns about Europe, fourth studies South and Central America, and fifth grade explores the Middle East. Thus, during their journey through the elementary school, our students will gain a full view and better understanding of their world. Individual teachers are free to incorporate the study in ways that best suit their teaching styles. Our specialists who teach music, art, library, and physical education work closely with the classroom teachers to enhance and teach to the theme.

Students learn regional dances and songs, explore artists from their region, and do related library research, games, and activities. Maps, artwork, and projects begin to fill the halls. As the final week approaches, each grade level plans a culminating activity, usually involving the parents. For example, the fourth grades have a fiesta, with students bringing in tortillas, salsa, and other South American foods. The third grades put on an international dinner for parents in the evening, bringing dishes from France, Italy, Spain, Portugal, Ireland, and Scotland.

A schoolwide celebration of learning is the final event, also open to parents as audience. Our most successful event has been a staging of "The Culture Is Right!" In a game show format based on the popular TV show, teams of three students from individual classes are called up to answer a question provided by their classroom teacher and the specialists. All students are challenged with at least one chance to answer a question. The principal stands nearby with a large sign in hand. If the answer is correct, she shows the happy face, and the audience is prompted to clap politely. If the answer is incorrect, the sad face is shown, and the audience says, "awwww." Audience responses are taught and practiced before the show. The class with the most points in the end has their teacher crowned King or Queen of Culture. The other teachers are dubbed princes, princesses, dukes, duchesses, so all classes are recognized, and learning is celebrated for all.

A Different View of Success

In SMART learning, a successful learner is not defined by her test scores or report card grades. Rather, a successful learner is one who takes charge of her learning and uses brain-based learning principles to increase her performance. A successful learner

- believes that she has control over her own learning

- knows that nutrition, exercise, and emotional well-being support successful learning

- understands how her brain learns and uses brain-compatible learning strategies

Brain-based learning uses what research has discovered about how the brain functions. The 1990s is called "the decade of the brain" because during this time period scientists found out a great deal about how the brain processes and stores information—and about what improves the brain's functioning.

Belief in Oneself as a Learner

Brain-based learning is a different way of thinking about working with our children. Much of what we do to "help" our children achieve success in school comes from a traditional approach to learning called "behaviorism." This approach is based upon a belief that adults can control and direct student learning: that through the use of rewards and punishments we can encourage—perhaps even force—our children to do their best in school. Basically, we have come to learn that no one can control another's learning. Only the individual learner has control over what and how she learns. Research on how the brain learns provides learners with knowledge that can help them be more successful.

A successful learner believes that he has control over his own learning and believes that he can learn at high levels. While we have long

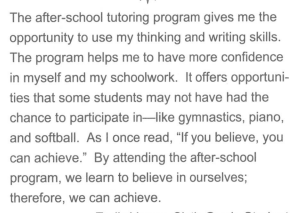

The after-school tutoring program gives me the opportunity to use my thinking and writing skills. The program helps me to have more confidence in myself and my schoolwork. It offers opportunities that some students may not have had the chance to participate in—like gymnastics, piano, and softball. As I once read, "If you believe, you can achieve." By attending the after-school program, we learn to believe in ourselves; therefore, we can achieve.

—Emily Vance, Sixth-Grade Student,
Atenville Elementary School

181

known the power of expectations—that is, when teachers and parents expect students to perform well, they are much more likely to do so—brain-based learning helps us understand why this is true. Put quite simply, we have learned that emotions are critical to learning. Renate Nummela Caine and Geoffrey Caine, two experts in this area, put it this way: "We do not simply learn things. What we learn is influenced and organized by emotions and mindsets based on expectancy, personal biases and prejudices, degree of self-esteem, and the need for social interaction."[12]

Teaching with the Brain in Mind by Eric Jensen (Alexandria, VA: Association for Supervision and Curriculum Development, 1998).

This is an interesting and easy-to-read book in which the author translates findings of neuroscientists into the context of classroom practice. The book contains a wide range of relevant topics and issues—from learning readiness to movement and learning; from the effects of stress and threats on learning to the brain as a meaning maker. For each topic, Jensen provides helpful visuals and specific classroom applications. We highly recommend *Teaching with the Brain in Mind* as a primer for the interested individual or as a resource for a study group exploring ways and means to incorporate research findings in this area into practice.

Learning Involves the Entire Physiology

Research on how the brain works has confirmed what many have long suspected: learning is strongly affected and supported by proper nutrition, adequate exercise, stress management, and student-held attitudes and beliefs. As you read through this section, think about the ways in which schools, parents, and students could act differently to support improved learning.

Nutrition. Research clearly demonstrates that proper nutrition can definitely boost thinking and learning. Ingredients in protein promote alertness, quick thinking, and fast reactions. They can help the brain perform calculations, increase attention span, and increase conscious awareness. Experts suggest that it is much better to begin the day with protein than with carbohydrates—which tend to give a temporary boost followed by a tremendous letdown in energy. Dairy products and leafy green vegetables keep the connections in the brain clean and sharp. Fruits and complex carbohydrates round out a brain-compatible diet. Nibbling of nutritious snacks throughout the day is beneficial. Too much time without eating can cause loss of concentration and decreased alertness. Good candidates for nutritious snacks include yogurt, fruits, nuts, and raw vegetables.

Dehydration is a problem that is linked to poor learning. Because the brain is made up of a higher percentage of water than any other organ in the body, it is quickly affected by a lack of water—children become inattentive, and lethargy sets in. Experts suggest that we all need between 8 and 12 glasses (64 and 90 fluid ounces) daily. Soft drinks, juices, tea, coffee, and other flavored beverages don't count.

Exercise. We've all heard the expression "thinking on one's feet." Research tells us that we do, indeed, think better while on our feet. According to Dr. Max Vercruyssen, a researcher at the University of Southern California, standing (compared to sitting) speeds up information processing 5 to 20 percent because of increased heart rate and subsequent increased blood flow to the brain.[13]

Aerobic exercise can improve learning and thinking. Researchers have repeatedly found that aerobic exercisers outscore nonaerobic exercisers in tests of short-term memory, reaction times, reasoning, and creative memory. A brisk 20-minute walk daily is adequate to yield these benefits. When safety and other circumstances permit a child's walking or bicycling to school, this is a great way to begin a day of learning.

Stress can interfere with learning. While individuals differ with regard to their perception of events, each of us has a point at which we feel threatened—stress is sufficient to cause a less-than-rational reaction. Neuroscientists call this particular phenomenon "downshifting." Essentially, what occurs in a time of threat is that we use our "old brain," which is designed to protect us. We operate from an emotional, not a rational, frame.

When threatened or overly stressed by school assignments, children can automatically downshift. This is not a conscious or intentional reaction—it is completely natural. It's important that we be aware of this phenomenon so that we can better assist our children in facing potentially stressful situations. This physiological reaction can help us understand some of the unfortunate reactions to stress. For example, completely blanking out on a test that a student has studied for—test anxiety—is a form of downshifting. Screaming or using disrespectful language can be another example of a student's reaction to feeling challenged.

Understanding and Using Brain-Compatible Learning Strategies

The human brain learns through making connections between what it already knows or has experienced and a new fact or experience. Helping students make connections between learning and their own lives supports learning. Rote memorization is not the brain's favored way of learning. Rather, we are better able to recall those facts that we have used in solving a practical problem. Again, students will learn better if they make connections between what they're studying and what they already know about in the world outside of schoolbooks.

Brain-Based Learning *a la* Eric Jensen

by Debbie Dingess, Teacher, Atenville Elementary School

A conference in San Francisco offered Atenville teachers an array of choices for studying student learning styles. Among these was a workshop on brain-based learning presented by author and speaker Eric Jensen. Jensen "translates" medical jargon into educator jargon, making the information he provides more useful to the teacher who is serious about increasing academic performance in the classroom.

Jensen changed our perceptions about many of the things we had routinely done in our classrooms. He also validated some things we did every day without ever taking the time to think about why we did them. One brain-based finding he shared with us was the fact that children need to change seats in their classroom from time to time. According to Jensen, we remember things by our location at the time we learn them. He used the example of staff development sessions for teachers, which he said should be held in different settings if teachers are to remember

more; as opposed to sitting in the same room month after month, year
after year. Applying this theory to the classroom, teachers should then
make every effort to change that environment as much and as often as
possible, so children feel they enter a fresh learning experience every day.
This theory can be further implemented by providing out-of-the-
classroom learning opportunities as often as possible.

As a result of the Jensen workshop, we embraced brain-based learning. We made changes in our approach to both teaching and learning.
We even purchased Mozart tapes for every classroom because research
suggests that students who listen to Mozart in D Major perform better
on tests. We told the students Mozart would make them smarter! They
believed us! Performance increased!

We also attacked the problem of test anxiety through the implementation of skills groups. At Atenville, we normally attempt to keep the
stress level of our students as low as possible. But when we learned that
students need to know how to perform under stress, we used the skills
groups to help us work on test anxiety. In the skills groups, formed
around individual student weaknesses reported on the Stanford test,
students attacked their deficiencies. Since research reports that the brain
shuts down when under stress, we provided some "practice stress"
situations, such as timed tests, to give the students experience in producing under stress.

Because of our growing interest in brain-based learning, three staff
members attended a six-day Eric Jensen workshop in Boston. Back at
school, we conducted a workshop with our teachers offering them tips
on little, inexpensive things they could do in their classrooms to stimulate learning—changing student seats, using color, burning incense to
create a calming effect (we think vanilla and cinnamon work best!),
allowing students to drink water frequently. Today, all our teachers allow
students to bring their bottles of water into the classroom. We know and
act on the fact that frequent water breaks rehydrate the brain and increase student receptivity to learning.

What has happened at Atenville as a result of our encounters with
Eric Jensen? We are happy to report that our student test scores have
improved. Through our fascination with brain-based learning, our
faculty also has enjoyed a little *lagniappe*. We decided as a group to
purchase Jensen's *Brain-Based Learning and Teaching* and form a faculty
study group that we named Literacy Circles. We studied the book one

chapter at a time, and then we came together to discuss how we could do the things he talked about in the book in our classrooms. We are now in the process of meeting to choose another book to use for our Literacy Circles. Clearly, Jensen's teachings have impacted Atenville teachers and students.

The Music of Gary Lamb

by Connie Allen, Principal, Natcher Elementary School

The music of Gary Lamb can be heard in classrooms, the library, and the office at our school.[14] Sometimes it plays throughout the school via the intercom as the children arrive in the morning. His original music contains 60 beats per minute, which matches the rate of the human heartbeat. His music is designed to soothe, inspire, enhance creativity, spur imagination, and generally provide an ambience supporting the learning environment.

One morning, two little boys asked the librarian if she could please start the music because they knew they could concentrate better if the music was playing when their special reading group met in the library. Another student who copes with many learning challenges informed us that he performed better on tests with the music playing softly in the background. Perhaps this is so because Lamb's music is wonderfully soothing.

Teachers use the music when children write, draw, or read silently in the classroom. It is also great after a long day as a means of untying the mental and physical knots we all accumulate. With the connections between music and brain functioning, it is no wonder that music makes a difference.

"Tooty Ta"

by Kim McCord, Teacher, Lumberport Elementary School

The "Tooty Ta" is a song/dance shown to me by Dr. Jean Feldman of Atlanta, an early education "guru."[15] During her presentation at the West Virginia Early Childhood Conference, we were exposed to numerous activities that teach children skills through song and games. It is my opinion that too many times we forget that five-year-olds are children first and students second. Many of the behavior concerns of our classrooms stem from the fact that, as educators, we expect children, especially the young ones, to pay direct attention to instruction much beyond their attention span limit. In my classroom, we are constantly on the move, singing and dancing, yet continuously learning.

The "Tooty Ta" is a repetitive song that teaches the following: one- and two-step directions, listening skills, sequencing, predicting, body parts, position words, rhythm and auditory patterning, and keeps the child moving all the while. Activities and songs like the "Tooty Ta" not only teach skills but also enhance mental alertness by aiding oxygen flow through movement or simply by standing rather than passively sitting. We have known for years that students learn more by doing than by hearing. Not only have I used the "Tooty Ta" in our classroom and at Quest events, we have used it in schoolwide assemblies, parent meetings, and presentations in the community.

My students love the "Tooty Ta." It isn't unusual for our class to see other students walking down the hallways singing and repeating the motions. The kindergarten children take great pride in the fact that they are singing our song. Children, parents, and our fellow educators need to realize that learning can be both fun and effective. There are many roads to our final destination; mine is just a bit more lively!

Who Wants to Be a Millionaire?

by Vickie Luchuck, Teacher, Lumberport Elementary School

This morning, Kathy DeMarco and her group of fifth-grade health students conducted our monthly morning meeting. I wish you could have seen the incredibly innovative project that these SMART kids have worked on for the past several weeks! Kathy is our Healthy Schools coordinator, physical education instructor, and health teacher. Using the popular "Who Wants to Be a Millionaire?" concept, her students presented "Who Wants to Eat Nutritiously?" to our entire student body. It was great!

Her fifth graders began by researching their questions and ranking them according to difficulty. They made the set of the program, complete with lights (flashlights and spotlight), lifelines (phone a teacher with a walkie-talkie, poll the students, and a 50/50). It's evident the kids took a lot of pride in their work, as it was a huge success. My first graders talked about it for the longest time when we came to our room. Many of them said they were answering the questions to themselves as the game was playing. Yea!!

Bryant Way Learning Center

by Connie Allen, Natcher Elementary School

The Bryant Way Learning Center is a cooperative project between our school and the Housing Authority of Bowling Green. It is our mutual response for after-school support with homework, skill development, and constructive leisure-time activities.

The Housing Authority converted one of the housing units into a school-like setting. They obtained computers, library books, and other resources. We provide two teachers for after-school homework and tutoring two days per week. Other staff have been hired through grants to provide recreation and counseling. The coordinator, with permission from the parents, comes to school regularly to check with the teachers on individual student progress. Quarterly awards are presented at the Center based on school successes. Being a visible presence in the area where the children reside has built strong bonds between school and home. Our students are the winners in this unique school-community partnership.

Robert's Story

by Robert McFall, Student, Class of 2001, Cave Spring High School

I have had a lot of teachers who have presented a lot of different styles of learning, but there is one who stands out in my mind the best. Peter Lustig is a United States history teacher for eleventh-grade students at Cave Spring. This man is no ordinary teacher. He goes out of his way to make sure that his class is going to be fun, entertaining, and informative. One thing that his class is famous for is the after-school trials. Throughout the year, whenever we got to a topic that was controversial, Mr. Lustig created a trial on the topic. These topics ranged from convicting Columbus of murder, to whether or not the atom bomb should have been dropped. Mr. Lustig asked for volunteers and then assigned sides for each issue. Some students would be key witnesses and some lawyers, but all had to do research on their side of the issue. When debate day rolled around, everyone from all the history classes came to see the trial. Sometimes the trials got a little heated but, in the end, everyone walked away knowing something about the subject they had not known before. Peter Lustig was just one of the many good teachers I had in school, but he truly made it clear to me that learning is not always a drag. You can do something fun and still have a learning experience.

We Hired a Momma

told by Earl Wiman, Principal, Alexander Elementary School

For many children who come to school from impoverished homes and neighborhoods, reading is not something that they do at home. Neither do they see people reading; their parents, siblings, and neighbors likely don't spend much time reading. So it is not surprising that these children—in whose homes books and magazines are not found—are slow to read in school. It is not surprising, either, that when I listened to my primary teachers talk they despaired of being able to overcome these lost experiences. "Their mommas don't read to them. They need their mommas to hold them on their lap, to read to them, to listen to them read!" So it was that I hired a "momma" with our Title I dollars: a warm, caring person to read to children, to spend one-on-one time connecting with them, listening to them read, and helping them with tough words and passages. "Ms. Hudson taught me to read," can be heard from many of the children in this school. It's hard to tell who feels more pride in their accomplishments—Ms. Hudson or the children.

Different Perspectives on Student Success: Sampling Opinion in Your School Community

"Success" means different things to different people, depending on previous experiences and perspectives. In order to gather the points of view from diverse stakeholder groups, the following sets of questions are suggested as stimuli—either for focus groups or one-on-one interviews. When you select respondents, try to include some diversity in your response group—in ethnicity, gender, content/grade level, experience, and so forth. The interview will probably require 10 minutes or so. You can decide when and where to conduct each interview. Just be certain to record what each respondent says to you, and don't attempt to "lead" them to right answers. The purpose is to find out what a variety of teachers (parents/administrators/students) think about school success and what supports or interferes with their helping students achieve success.

Ideally, students will interview students; teachers, teachers; and parents interview parents. When all bring their responses back, an "inside-outside" fishbowl discussion could facilitate the listening that will be important to truly understand the different points of view.[16]

Questions for Teachers

1. How do you define a successful learner?

2. What percentage of students that you teach do you consider to be successful? What do these students do that helps them achieve success as learners? What might they (and others) do to be more successful as learners?

3. What do you do as a teacher to help students achieve success as learners? What else might you do to help more students achieve such success?

4. What do parents do to help their children be successful learners? What else might they do?

5. What characteristics of the school-at-large seem to help students become successful learners? What policies, practices, and structures seem to interfere with student success as learners?

6. Do you have other comments related to this topic?

Questions for Parents

1. How do you define a successful learner?

2. Do you consider your child(ren) to be a successful learner? What does your child do that makes her a successful learner? What else could your child do to be more successful as a learner?

3. What do you do to support your child's becoming a successful learner? What else might you do to support your child in this area?

4. What do your child's teachers do to help him become a successful learner? What else do you think they could do to help him be more successful?

5. What characteristics of the school-at-large seem to contribute to students becoming successful learners? What policies, practices, and structures seem to interfere with this?

6. Do you have other comments related to this topic?

Questions for Principals/Administrators

1. How do you define a successful learner?

2. What do students whom you know do to become successful learners? What might they do to become more successful learners?

3. What do you personally do (in your role as administrator) to help students become successful learners? What else might you do?

4. What do parents do to support their children in becoming successful learners? What else might they do?

5. What characteristics of the school-at-large support successful learners? What policies, practices, and structures interfere with this?

6. What other comments do you have regarding this topic?

Questions for Students

1. How do you define a successful learner?

2. Do you consider yourself a successful learner? What do you do that contributes to your being a successful learner? What might you do to be more successful as a learner?

3. What do teachers do to help you achieve success as a learner? What do teachers do that makes it difficult for you to become more successful?

4. What do your parents do that seems to help you become a successful learner? What else do you think they could do to help you be more successful?

5. What characteristics of the school-at-large contribute to your being a successful learner? What characteristics interfere with your being as successful as you might be?

6. Do you have any other comments relative to this topic?

"Mapping" the Way to Success: A Districtwide Initiative to Improve and Align Curriculum, Instruction, and Assessment

by Becky Burns, Research & Development Specialist, AEL

In August 1999, Lunenburg County, Virginia, began implementation of AEL's Teaching/Learning Mapping Strategy (TLMS), a two-year curriculum alignment and professional development program. TLMS assists districts with systemic standards-based reform through a K-12 cross-curricular approach that promotes alignment of curriculum, instruction, and assessment with state standards; extends instructional repertoire so that teachers are better able to meet the needs of diverse learners; and emphasizes connection and reinforcement of learning between and across grades. TLMS has its roots in Interdisciplinary Teamed Instruction, a research-based strategy developed at AEL for building learning communities in schools by dissolving boundaries between disciplines.[17]

TLMS has five primary goals:

1. to align curriculum, instruction, and assessment with state standards

2. to enrich instructional practice

3. to increase understanding of results-oriented teaching

4. to improve communication and collaboration between teachers across and between grade levels

5. to improve student achievement

Four TLMS components support attainment of these goals: (1) a Web-based curriculum mapping and design tool that enables teachers to design learning activities and instructional units, link them to standards, and cluster them into monthly maps; (2) weekly meetings of teachers by grade level, department, interdisciplinary team, or by preparation period that promote reflection on student learning and collaboration among teachers; (3) capacity building, provided through both face-to-face and electronic meetings with district and school site leaders who are responsible for TLMS leadership in the schools; (4) professional development activities that address needs identified by teachers and administrators as they review curriculum maps and student performance data.

Lunenburg has made significant progress toward attainment of all five TLMS goals.

Goal 1: To align curriculum, instruction, and assessment with state standards. Teachers in all content areas K-12 completed, analyzed, and revised their curriculum maps to improve alignment with the Virginia Standards of Learning (SOLs). They are now developing exit outcomes that clarify the concepts and skills needed to master SOLs for each content and grade and are designing classroom assessments to measure student progress toward mastery of SOLs. One teacher described mapping as "a way to see where you've been and where you are going." Another said, "It's very important in improving the knowledge of our students and ourselves."

Goal 2: To enrich instructional practice. Lunenburg teachers have found many ways to enrich instruction. For example, at the February 1999 Quest Rally, Central High teachers described their infusion of Howard Gardner's Multiple Intelligences Theory into their instructional practice. Teachers discussed how they have each student complete an intelligences inventory and then use the information to differentiate teaching. For example, one Central teacher explained that she was capitalizing on the strong interpersonal intelligence of many of her students by restructuring the classroom environment to include more cooperative activities. She reported that student engagement has increased as a result of these activities. Other teachers shared how they work with colleagues to design a repertoire of activities for each of Gardner's eight intelligences. One teacher reported that using multiple intelligences in the classroom had led to a winning science fair entry for a special education student. Lunenburg teachers also use Bloom's Cognitive Taxonomy as a guide for promoting higher-order thinking skills. In team meetings, teachers analyze their activities to determine cognitive level, then discuss ways to alter activities to raise the bar on thinking skills. At Central High, teachers are also identifying more opportunities for collaboration and interdisciplinary teaching. For example, the history and English departments are working together on an oral history project.

Goal 3: To increase understanding of results-oriented teaching. A component of TLMS is using student performance data for instructional decision making. When Lunenburg initiated TLMS, their first step was to review 1999 SOL test data and to identify two areas for improvement. Teachers decided that math and writing would be emphasized across grades and courses during the 1999-2000 school year. When the 2000 SOL scores were published, there was noticeable positive impact on student math and writing scores at elementary, middle, and senior high levels. Also, led by Central High teachers, all schools developed a rubric for written work to be used districtwide. Increased focus on result-oriented teaching occurred as teachers began using Structured Reflection Protocol during some of their team meetings. Teachers have begun to abandon ineffective strategies through review of student performance data, critical reflection on their practice, and learning from colleagues.

Goal 4: To improve communication and collaboration between teachers across and between grade levels. Lunenburg site leaders are not only leading weekly team meetings in their schools, but are also working collaboratively across schools to design and deliver in-service workshops. Administrators support the collaborative efforts by providing time during the school day for team meetings, releasing site leaders once or twice a month for planning meetings, and earmarking all in-service days for TLMS-related professional development activities. One site leader recently remarked: "The time for teachers to meet has been a great forum for teachers to discuss instructional concerns." Another said, "We think collaboration and communication among teachers have changed. All grade level teachers are meeting and planning together." Teachers report that they are communicating with others more frequently and about deeper pedagogical issues. Teachers also are working together on more cross-curricular efforts. Site leaders have done a wonderful job of facilitating and nurturing the growth of these learning communities. In fall 2000, site leaders planned and conducted professional development activities for two in-service days.

Goal 5: To improve student achievement. Lunenburg students' scores on the state SOL test improved in 2000. At all grade levels, scores increased in three out of four tested areas and were at or above the state accreditation benchmark score for several grades and content. For example, Central High students' SOL test pass rates in English and science both surpassed the accreditation benchmark. In addition, pass rates nearly doubled between 1999 and 2000 scores in World History to 1000 A.D., going from 27 percent to 47 percent.

Lunenburg's journey is a true success story. Although they have struggled with the change process, teachers and administrators are beginning to see positive results. One teacher leader observed that as teachers were working together on a schoolwide interdisciplinary unit on Election 2000 they had very positive attitudes about collaboration. She stated, "People want to work together!" Another teacher leader from Central High explained that her staff had set five goals for the 2000-2001 school year: (1) develop a rubric for written work; (2) create a style sheet for research for districtwide use; (3) develop a "technology use map" to give everyone equal access to the computer labs when working on projects; (4) develop, and use consistently, vocabulary that is matched to SOL tests in all content areas; and (5) design more interdisciplinary projects. She went on to say, "Everything is finally coming together—school improvement plan, High Schools that Work, TLMS . . ."

Teachers are becoming the architects and the gatekeepers of curriculum in Lunenburg as they begin to own what and how they teach and to share responsibility for student achievement and success. The process of continuous school improvement is well on its way to being institutionalized, largely due to strong teacher leadership for change in the schools. In August 2000, when teachers and students returned to school, they found some changes. Three out of four principals were new, the teacher leader at Central High had left, and there was a new superintendent. However, other school leaders have stepped right into the vacant shoes and are wearing them well. They continue the strong internal facilitation that is essential to implementing and sustaining change.

What MOTIVATES Students to Learn—Extra Credit or Increased Connectedness?

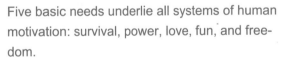

S**M**ART
otivated

Ask students what motivates them to learn in school, and they will tell you straight up. The themes that resonate through their responses are the same, whether they come from Virginia or Oregon, Kentucky or Arizona, Tennessee or Texas, West Virginia or Alabama. Likewise, the themes are constant from elementary to middle to high school. Over the course of three years, Quest staff conducted dozens of focus groups with students in all of the above settings. One of the most striking conclusions emerging from our analysis of student responses is the high correlation between student insights and research findings. Students *know* what motivates them and their peers; they know what classroom practices lead to true learning. If you want to know, just ask them.

In February 2000, 11 students from three high schools across three states participated in such a focus group. The high schools were diverse—ranging in size from 300 to 3,000 students in grades 9-12, and from very rural and isolated to urban. We asked, "How does SMART learning occur in school?" The students were very forthcoming and definite in their responses. Among the more salient were the following:

- I like to be active, conversing with my fellow students.
- I really like hands-on activities.

> Five basic needs underlie all systems of human motivation: survival, power, love, fun, and freedom.
>
> —William Glasser

- It is important for me to have a good relationship with my teacher before I really want to pay attention and to learn.
- Students need to be clear about what is expected of them.
- Everyone needs to slow down—instead of just rushing through the material.
- Kids are motivated by teachers who find clever ways to get the word out and make teaching and learning fun!
- When teachers mix up their teaching styles and techniques, they reach more kids.
- If I could change one thing about my learning environment, it would be for teachers and students to have more respect for one another. Some teachers don't show respect for students, and some students don't show respect for teachers. Either way—this interferes with other students' learning.
- When teachers help relate an assignment to real life, I am more motivated.
- When teachers get to know students rather than judging them, students are more inclined to want to learn. Teachers and students need to become more connected.

The theme of connectedness runs through these responses: with content, with one's peer group, and between teacher and learner. What kinds of instructional practice promote connectedness—and thereby provide internal motivation to students?

The Oral History Project at Central High

Ask Susan Lenhart's students at Central High and they will probably talk about their oral history project. Inspired by the *Foxfire* project,[18] Lenhart realized the power of this approach for students in her small, rural community. She sees oral history as an avenue that "gives voice to her [students'] expression" and believes that central to the success of this project is her encouragement of students "to pick a topic they can *connect* to." She takes obvious pride in the transformation of Sarah, a junior who selected her father as the subject of her project. Sarah found out things that she never knew about her father—most poignantly his experiences during the Vietnam War. In her reflection about the work she did over time on this project, Sarah concluded: "My father now shapes and molds who I am by the way he acts. I watch him and try to act with the same passion for life as he does. My father is a role model for any person, and he is the person I look to for guidance and encouragement." Not only was this learning experience inherently motivating for Sarah and her peers, its residual value was also potent. These students have a new appreciation for the relationship between "book learning" and real life.

On the last day of school, students at Natcher Elementary School are actively engaged in learning. However, they are not sitting in their desks straight-in-a-row; rather, they are circled on the floor. Some are stretched out on their sleeping bags; others are sitting cross-legged in front of actual tents. These students are participating in Camp Learned-A-Lot, an annual event celebrating (and reviewing!) the learnings of the school year. This somewhat unorthodox approach ("a new way to do an old thing") succeeds in engaging and motivating these kids until the last bell of the year rings.

> Making subject matter understandable to students requires an understanding of the cultural and community contexts that shape their experiences, so that representations of content can connect to those experiences and can take into account the ways these contexts shape students' ways of knowing and modes of learning.
>
> —Linda Darling-Hammond
> & Milbrey McLaughlin

MicroSociety provides Atenville Elementary students a week-in-and-week-out opportunity for hands-on, cooperative learning in a real-life context.[19] This program provides an umbrella for learning, enabling teachers and students to make connections to real-life situations even when engaged in traditional learning settings.

Short-term learning simulations can also be motivating. Caroline Botkin, fourth-grade teacher at Highland Elementary, integrates these kinds of experiences into social studies instruction. To teach about taxes imposed on the colonists, she organizes "an unannounced tax day" and charges the children money for the things they want to do most. The principal, cafeteria workers, custodian, faculty, and staff are aware of what's going on and go along with it. Botkin "keeps it going until [the students] are good and angry," and says that this never fails to "give the children a good sense of how the colonists felt." She also engages parents and community members in an annual "Pioneer Day," which is a culminating activity for a history unit. Adults demonstrate craft skills and join students in cooking a meal over an open fire. Students and adults alike find this day to be an exciting learning experience.

In an effort to increase student motivation for learning in the sciences, the South Harrison High faculty organized a summer science enrichment activity. Participating students traveled to a North Carolina beach where they experienced interdisciplinary learning in a variety of science, math, and language arts activities—by studying marine life, the tides, local geography and history, and so forth. Students were also responsible for personal budgeting and journal writing.

Although different strategies and techniques motivate each individual learner, the common denominator is the heightened potential for individuals to make some type of personal connection during the learning experience. Effective teachers have always recognized this truism; creative teachers are continually challenged to find clever ways to make teaching and learning fun!

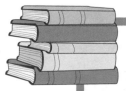

Punished by Rewards: The Trouble with Gold Stars, Incentive Plans, A's, Praise, and Other Bribes by Alfie Kohn (New York: Houghton-Mifflin, 1993).

In this book, Kohn provides a compelling argument for examining conventional beliefs and behaviors regarding motivation and behavior management. The author maintains that "carrots and sticks"—tangible rewards and punishments—are not effective in promoting long-term change. Rather, Kohn provides evidence that external motivators can extinguish the learner's interest in what they're being "bribed" to do.

In effect, Kohn calls into question B. F. Skinner's behaviorism. Kohn offers multiple alternative strategies for motivating and directing student behaviors. His book, which has ignited debates regarding the effectiveness of smiley-face stickers, gold stars, and reward candy, is provocative and can serve to promote constructive dialogue within a school community.

Building Excitement for Learning: Getting Everyone in the Act

The "good old days" when Dad was the bread winner and Mom was Mom, smiling at the back door with a plate of freshly baked cookies in her hand, are no more. Today, Dad goes in one direction, Mom in another, and the kids go all over the place. With traditional routines disrupted, parents struggle to make the time to encourage and motivate their children to be SMART learners. Finding the time and the energy to be visible and supportive in their children's educational process can take on a life all its own. Sewanee Elementary, realizing how difficult it is to keep parents involved, developed a creative approach to getting parents into the school with their children *and* offering them ideas to help reinforce the school curriculum.

Family Math Night

by Alice Phillips, Teacher, Sewanee Elementary School

Open house in the fall used to be a time when I talked nonstop for two or more hours. Most parents wanted to know how their children were doing (of course!), even though the school always stressed that this was not a time for conferencing. When we changed the focus to "Family Night," that changed. The first year we tried this we had purchased a new supply of wonderful math manipulatives. At the suggestion of the principal, the faculty decided to showcase these learning materials by presenting Family Math Night instead of the traditional open house. Teachers were given the freedom to set up their classrooms in any way they wished, as long as they included activities with math manipulatives.

I arranged my fifth-grade classroom in several stations, with a different activity at each. One station featured pattern blocks. Alongside the tub of colorful, geometrically shaped blocks, I placed a stack of picture outlines that could be filled with various blocks. Both children and parents could take a picture and design a way to fill it. Next they filled in a chart describing the number of blocks of each shape and color they had used. Last, there were a few critical thinking questions to respond to, such as "How could you change your design so that you use the *least* number of blocks possible? The *most*?" This data sheet was left in the classroom, and various teachers used it with follow-up activities. Other Family Math Night stations featured activities with Base 10 blocks and calculators.

In addition to the manipulatives stations, various charts, graphs, and challenges were posted on the walls around the room. There was a tally chart that asked people to record whether their first name was longer, shorter, or the same length as their last name. There was a graph displaying visitors' choices for the most important quality in a friend (good listener, loyal, honest, smart, funny, cheerful, generous). There was a chart for recording which part of the newspaper was one's favorite part and how often the paper was read each week. After Family Night was over, my class used the data collected to extend learning, develop new questions, conduct follow-up surveys, and connect to other areas of the curriculum.

Family Math Night was a huge success. Parents not only got to see what their children were working with every day, but they got a better idea of just how challenging and different education is these days! Family Nights became annual events, with a different focus each year: science, technology, and language arts have all had their chance to shine.

Family Science Night

by Alice Phillips, Teacher, Sewanee Elementary School

What a great time everyone had at Family Science Night in October, during the traditional open house time. Weeks before the event, I began to gather ideas and materials for activities and experiments that parents, grandparents, and others could do with their children. Our class's fall theme was "Water, Water, Everywhere!" so that was my focus. On the afternoon of the event, I set up the stations. On one table, I set up three identical gallon containers labeled A, B, and C, along with a stack of small paper cups. A laminated card on the table explained that this was clean, safe drinking water from three different sources, and would visitors please "taste test" each one. They then were to rank them from best to worst, describing what they liked or didn't like about each. The next day, students learned where the samples had come from: bottled spring water from the grocery store, well water from an approved private well, and treated city water from a city school. This activity became the springboard for learning about the issues of ecology, city water systems, the water cycle, our town's water supply, and so much more!

Another station had a sink-or-float activity. With a supply of foil squares and a jar full of pennies, visitors were challenged to construct a boat that would hold the most pennies possible. A chart was posted nearby for recording the capacity of each vessel. Another station used pennies and water in a different way. Using eyedroppers, guests tried to see how many drops of water a single penny would hold before spilling onto the paper towel. These fun and interesting activities led the class into explorations of water density, surface tension, and other properties of water.

The parents loved it. There was an immediate clamor for information on the results of the experiments. Where did the water come from? How many pennies did the best boat hold? What did the boat look like? How many drops of water can a penny hold? So the students got into the computers to write the explanations, which were then published in our classroom newsletter. Family Science Night had blossomed into something that had reached across the curriculum, incorporating science, math, social studies, and language arts. It also brought home and school together and provided a common ground for conversation and learning.

A Family Night Postscript

by Alice Phillips, Teacher, Sewanee Elementary School

This past fall, I used math activities around my room during open house. Since we had just finished an addition to the school and I am in one of the new rooms, I was expecting quite a crowd of visitors unrelated to my kids. Though I didn't have many manipulatives to highlight, I did put up several charts and graphs for data collecting (see Family Math Night story for examples).

One intriguing activity involved a jar of rice. This activity solicited estimates of the number of rice grains in the jar. I tied a string across the corner of the room. Visitors put their estimates on precut pieces of paper, then folded and hung them on the line in order from least (on the left) to greatest (on the right). This challenge got a lively reaction! Visitors argued with each other, studied the estimates already up, and examined the jar closely before deciding on their own estimates.

We left the string of estimates up and analyzed them the next day in class: What's the greatest? Least? Can we find the mode, median, range?

Then I piled some rice from the jar on each student's desk, and they started counting. At first, some students just piled them up and said they had 23 or 57, or whatever. I asked, "How do I know you're right? Can you show me groups that I can count up and check easily? Show me the evidence that you've counted correctly!" Soon they discovered it was easiest to count out the rice in groups of 10. Ten groups of 10 were then scooped into paper cups and lined up on the whiteboard ledge. When ten cups were collected up front, they were poured into a colored cup labeled 1,000. In less than 50 minutes, my class of 18 students triumphantly reached a total of just over 11,000 grains of rice! We located the closest estimate, and discovered that it was a student in our own class who had made that guess. Then I wrote up a quick announcement of the total and the name of the best estimate winner to be published in the next PTO newsletter. It was none too soon! I had people stopping me on the street and in the store to ask how many grains of rice were in that jar!

Successful? Clearly! Will I do it again? Absolutely!

More on Motivation

In their book, *Emotionally Intelligent Parenting*, authors Maurice Elias, Steven Tobias, and Brian Friedlander describe different kinds of motivation by using a simple-to-understand graphic. Think of the target as a "Motivated Learner." The bull's-eye is a self-motivated student who is eager to learn. The outer rings are increasingly external to the learner; they are effective to varying degrees, but do not constitute a motivated learner as we define it in the SMART construct.

The outermost ring is **material motivation**; students perform, do their assignments, and follow the rules because of some material reward they expect to earn. The reward may be candy, stickers, a new toy, money, dinner out, or other special privileges; it may be provided by the parents or the teacher. This kind of motivation is temporary and fleeting. Material motivation may help a student get over a hurdle when other motivation is missing, but if we want students to develop internal controls and motivations, providing material "bribes" is least effective in helping develop a truly SMART learner.

Social motivation constitutes the middle ring. Examples of social motivation include praise, good grades, and congratulations from others. Students who are socially motivated get positive feedback from teachers; they aim to please the important adults in their lives and those adults who value adequate and high performance in school. As students become more and more interested in the opinions of their peer group, the social motivation from adults fades. Again, social motivation is nearer the center target and helps students move from material rewards and reinforcements, but it is not the same as being internally motivated.

The innermost circle or bull's-eye is **intrinsic motivation.** This is the winning target, in which students do something because it makes them feel proud and good about themselves. Schools rely so heavily on grades, which are material or social motivators, that it is hard for most students to associate their school experiences with the phrase "love of learning." Giving students choices in what they study and learn; assigning interesting and meaningful work; challenging students, yet providing adequate support for the work to be accomplished successfully; creating activities and projects that fully engage students; using a variety of teaching styles; presenting content that students understand will be useful and relevant in their lives; and providing opportunities to celebrate true learning— these are the conditions that foster intrinsic motivation in schools.

What Do You Think?

- How much does our school community use material motivation with our students to promote responsible behavior and good grades? What are some other options?

- What can our school community do to create an environment where learning is joyful and fun, where students and teachers alike are curious to learn new things, try out new ideas, and take risks? How much do we intentionally try to develop internally motivated students?

The AUTONOMOUS Learner: Competent and Self-Directed

According to Malcolm Knowles, the guru of adult learning theory, a hallmark of adult learners is their self-directedness: "Adults have a self-concept of being responsible for their own decision, for their own lives. Once they have arrived at that self-concept, they develop a deep psychological need to be seen by others and treated by others as being capable of self-direction."[20] Hence, writes Knowles, a goal of all education should be to help learners become increasingly self-directed. Our concept of a SMART learner is one who is setting her own learning goals, learning where to go for information, monitoring her progress toward goals, and assessing learning outcomes. This ability is becoming ever more important in the emerging information age. However, students today are no less accustomed to being "spoon-fed" information than their counterparts in generations past. This "sit and get" type of instruction breeds passive, not active, learners who wait for the teacher to give them information for later regurgitation.

Consider the story shared by Mickey Hickman about his 12th-grade government class in Pulaski, Virginia.

We were using a strategy of cooperative problem solving to help our senior government students better understand gerrymandering.[21] For this purpose we had formed groups of four students. One group consisted of two cheerleaders, a football player, and a relatively unengaged student named Sam. Sam was an average student who usually earned Cs or Ds; the other three group members were A students. The activity design required that all group members participate in order to solve the problem—each student possessing a vital piece of information. After the activity was under way, some of the students began to complain. This was not the type of activity they usually encountered in school; they wanted to be told what they had to know so that they could "learn" it and give it back. As the teacher-facilitators, we stood back and watched the dynamics at work. We soon realized that Sam was interested in this activity. He started to speak up but was ignored by his team members. Sam rarely participated in class, and his group didn't consider him to be "smart." However, from listening to what Sam had to say, I knew that he had a plan to attack the problem. The others did not demonstrate these attack skills. After a couple of attempts to interject, Sam succeeded in getting the group's attention. The other group members began to connect with his idea, and the group was able to unravel the problem. We invited Sam to coach a couple of other groups who were experiencing difficulty. In the debriefing sessions, we asked Sam to explain the steps he used in problem solving. Sam's status and self-esteem grew on this day. Another highlight of the day was feedback given to us by one of our highest achievers. "Thank you, my brain needed this," he said as he left the class.

This story clarifies a misunderstanding some have of "autonomous" or "independent" learners—that they work alone and apart from their classmates. To the contrary, as Hickman's story reveals, autonomous learning can be developed in the context of a cooperative or group setting. The key is that students be facilitated in developing and practicing skills that undergird continuous, lifelong learning.

Peter Vaill, a respected scholar and consultant in the area of organizational development, conceives of "learning as a way of being." In a book by the same title, Vaill addresses the conundrum of self-directed learning that oftentimes prevents teachers from adopting strategies such as the one described above by Hickman.

> How can we know enough to direct our own learning? Isn't self-directed learning just a polite phrase for blundering, floundering, and thrashing around in some unfamiliar territory of new material? Is this what learning as a way of being is advocating? The answer is no. Learning as a way of being admits the problem: there can certainly be periods in a self-directed learning process when we are blundering, when we are frustrated, losing motivation and getting demoralized, and beginning to look around for a quick fix or a magic bullet to dispel the confusion. At this critical moment, two things can occur: first, we can proceed to turn over substantial control of our learning's purpose, content, form, pace, and evaluation to someone else. This amounts . . . to adopting a passive, dependent mentality that says, "Okay, teach me."
>
> The second alternative also involves other people who know more, but when we are engaged in self-directed learning, our attitude toward these others . . . is completely different. We seek help not from a position of dependency but on our own terms, and we are conscious of our self-directed state. We have questions to ask experts, questions that grow out of our experience to date with material, frustrating as it has been. We have reasons, which remain conscious and clear, for wanting to continue to struggle with our learning.[22]

How many times have you in your role as teacher thought *Why should I waste valuable class time waiting for students to come up with an answer that I could easily provide them?* And, how many times in your role as student have you asked *Why doesn't she just go ahead and give us the answer?* These widespread attitudes are the greatest barriers to the development of autonomous learners. Teachers and students who adopt the SMART concept have to really think and talk about what the individual constructs mean for them personally and for the class as a whole. SMART really is a different way of thinking about learning; autonomous learning affords a dramatic example of the kinds of paradigm shifts that must occur in a true quest for SMART learning.

You can't dig a hole in a new place by digging the same hole deeper.

—Edward de Bono

Fitting the Pieces Together

by Alice Phillips, Fifth-Grade Teacher, Sewanee Elementary School

One of my favorite learning strategies is a cooperative learning activity. All students are seated in "color teams" of three to four. They are asked to number themselves. Then each number is given a role. The Gopher from each group comes to get a set of clues and hands one clue to each member. Members take turns reading their clues—no one else can see the clues. They read as often as needed. Together they solve the puzzle. Puzzles may involve Base 10 blocks, pattern blocks, tangrams, etc. When solutions are found, students record their answers. They explain and defend solutions orally. Then they write in their math journals. Skills developed (besides math!): reading, listening, speaking, writing, critical thinking, problem solving, social skills, sense of interdependence, and appreciation for others' abilities.

Learning in Different Ways Means Teaching in Different Ways

In education, we used to accept the idea of IQ (intelligence quotient) as a definitive measure of someone's intellectual ability. We now know that an IQ is a very limited way of measuring human potential. IQ, as measured on standardized tests, often predicts how well someone will do in school. This correlation confirms only one thing: that schools teach and test to the same strengths that are measured by traditional tests of intellectual ability.

Howard Gardner proposed the concept of "multiple intelligences" to suggest that humans have many different ways of being intelligent.[23] His eight intelligences define very different talents. Schools have long rewarded high performance in just one or two of these ways of being smart. In most traditional schools, students who excel are those who also perform well on tests of intellectual ability. Gardner labels these traditional "book-learning" smarts as two of his eight intelligences: linguistic and logical-mathematical.

The challenge for schools today is to help students be *successful* by providing opportunities for learning that draw on their strengths as well as their weaknesses. Interestingly, most students do not learn best by sitting still, quietly listening to the teacher talk, doing "boring" worksheets without interacting with peers. And yet this is the style of teaching found in many schools across America.

Don't lecture for the whole hour, hour and a half. Because if you think we're listening for that whole time, you're crazy.

—High School Student, York, Tennessee

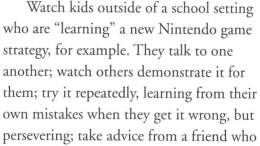

Watch kids outside of a school setting who are "learning" a new Nintendo game strategy, for example. They talk to one another; watch others demonstrate it for them; try it repeatedly, learning from their own mistakes when they get it wrong, but persevering; take advice from a friend who "coaches" them to do it correctly; and then become teachers themselves, demonstrating for friends who haven't yet mastered the skill. The result? They remember it for as long as they need it—long after the "test" of doing it successfully has come and gone. This kind of activity uses several different intelligences: interpersonal (working with others), bodily-kinesthetic (physical touching and moving), spatial (creating, building, designing), and logical-mathematical (looking for patterns and relationships).

When the staff at Central High used the multiple intelligences inventory with their students, they found that most students were strongest in "interpersonal" skills and interests. Doesn't it sound like teenagers to be wanting to relate to others? Teachers at Central are having success by building in opportunities for students to learn through cooperative learning activities, interviews, group discussions, and other "interpersonal" teaching strategies.

To me it's always been important to have a good relationship with my teacher before I want to pay attention and to learn. . . . It helps me focus on what the teacher is saying.

—High School Student, Roanoke, Virginia

Understanding Gardner's Multiple Intelligences

Gardner theorizes that none of the different intelligences is, by itself, a predictor of success in life. All of these intelligences—and there may be more than eight—will figure in the portfolio of student work. Gardner makes several presumptions about the various intelligences:

- each person possesses all eight intelligences
- most people can develop each intelligence to an adequate level of competency
- intelligences usually work together in complex and unique ways with each individual
- there are many ways to be intelligent within each category

According to Gardner, the identified intelligences include

1. **Linguistic Intelligence**—likes to read, write, and tell stories. Good at remembering names, places, dates, and detailed information. Learns best by saying, hearing, and seeing words.

2. **Logical/Mathematical Intelligence**—likes to do experiments, explore patterns and relationships, ask questions, work with numbers. Has strong problem-solving and reasoning skills. Excels in math. Learns best by categorizing, classifying, and working with abstract patterns and relationships.

3. **Musical Intelligence**—likes to sing, hum tunes, listen and respond to music, play an instrument. Remembers melodies, pitch, and rhythm. Is acutely aware of sounds, such as the ticking of a clock or the singing of a bird. Learns best through rhythm, melody, and music.

4. **Spatial Intelligence**—likes to draw, build, design, and create. Also enjoys watching movies, looking at pictures, and playing with machines. Often skilled at taking something apart and putting it together. Good at maps, charts, and diagrams. Uses a mental or physical picture in order to understand new information. Colors and pictures are used as learning tools.

5. **Bodily/Kinesthetic Intelligence**—is strong at physical activities requiring coordination, timing, and balance. Likes to move around and touch things while learning, and likes to gesture while communicating. Often excels at sports, dancing, acting, or crafts. Processes information by touching, moving, and interacting with space.

6. **Intrapersonal Intelligence**—prefers to work alone and pursue own interests. Has a strong sense of self. Likes to daydream. Creates original work. Learns best with individualized projects and self-paced instruction. Likes having "own space."

7. **Interpersonal Intelligence**—understands and works well with people. Has strong leadership skills and is good at negotiating, mediating, and communicating. Learns best when sharing, comparing, relating, and cooperating with others.

8. **Naturalistic Intelligence**—understands and enjoys everything in nature. Likes to collect and categorize plants; enjoys animals—even the unusual, such as lizards, snakes, and bugs; excels in outdoor activities such as camping and fishing. Learns best through outdoor activities and nature study, when possible outside in nature; when not, in an environment that includes things from nature.

Multiple Intelligences Inventory[24]

Directions: Read each item and choose a number that describes how much the statement is true for you. Put the number in the blank beside each item.

5 = Almost Always, 4 = Usually, 3 = Sometimes, 2 = Occasionally, 1 = Rarely

___ 1. I would rather draw a picture than tell a story.

___ 2. I enjoy playing a musical instrument.

___ 3. Ideas or answers to questions just seem to pop into my head.

___ 4. I feel happy and relaxed when I am in the woods.

___ 5. I see pictures in my mind.

___ 6. I like to work with computers and calculators.

___ 7. I like to work on projects with other people.

___ 8. I can understand how friends are feeling by looking at their faces.

___ 9. I enjoy listening to other people talking.

___ 10. I find my way around easily when I am in a new place.

___ 11. I need a quiet place to work or just be alone.

___ 12. I listen to music a lot.

___ 13. I like to take things apart and try to figure out how to put them back together.

___ 14. I collect things from nature like rocks, leaves, seashells.

___ 15. When my friends are in a bad mood, I usually understand why without having to ask.

___ 16. Riding a bike and skating are easy for me.

___ 17. It bothers me when people use improper English.(e.g., He don't know the answer.)

___ 18. Walking on a balance beam is easy for me.

___ 19. I like to make collections of things that have special meaning for me.

___ 20. I can look at an object and imagine how it would look if it were turned upside down.

___ 21. When I'm given a long list of numbers to add, I like to invent unusual ways to add them.

___ 22. I enjoy wildlife such as animals, birds, bugs, and fish.

___ 23. I use lots of hand gestures and body movement when I talk to my friends.

___ 24. I like to learn and use big words.

___ 25. I have lots of friends, not just one or two best friends.

___ 26. I find myself humming and singing a lot.

___ 27. Math is one of my favorite subjects in school.

___ 28. I like to pick out shapes (square, circle, triangle, etc.) when I look at buildings or clouds.

___ 29. I like to take care of a garden.

___ 30. When I am sad, I think of songs that will make me happy.

___ 31. I can run, swim, or exercise for a long time without getting tired.

___ 32. I am good at mental math.

___ 33. I enjoy writing stories.

___ 34. Listening to certain kinds of music can make me happy or sad.

___ 35. I like playing and working with others on a team.

___ 36. I remember my dreams.

___ 37. I enjoy outdoor activities such as hiking, camping, or fishing.

___ 38. When I give directions to my friends, they usually understand me the first time.

___ 39. I learn to play new sports quickly and easily.

___ 40. I really enjoy doing science experiments.

Multiple Intelligences Scoring Sheet

Directions: The numbers below correspond to numbered items on the Inventory. Beside each item number, record the number (1-5) you rated it for yourself. Add up the five numbers in each scale to get a score for your "intelligences."

Body/Kinesthetic	Interpersonal	Intrapersonal	Logical/Mathematical
16. ___	7. ___	3. ___	6. ___
18. ___	8. ___	5. ___	21. ___
23. ___	15. ___	11. ___	27. ___
31. ___	25. ___	19. ___	32. ___
39. ___	35. ___	36. ___	40. ___
Total _____	Total _____	Total _____	Total _____

Musical	Verbal/Linguistic	Visual/Spatial	Naturalistic
2. ___	9. ___	1. ___	4. ___
12. ___	17. ___	10. ___	14. ___
26. ___	24. ___	13. ___	22. ___
30. ___	33. ___	20. ___	29. ___
34. ___	38. ___	28. ___	37. ___
Total _____	Total _____	Total _____	Total _____

Now fill in your scores from highest to lowest and find the intelligences you are naturally good in.

A. ____ _____   E. ____ _____

B. ____ _____   F. ____ _____

C. ____ _____   G. ____ _____

D. ____ _____   H. ____ _____

Different Strokes for Different Folks: Thinking About Learning Styles

Read about the four students described below. For each, identify the strengths and weaknesses, *à la* Gardner's multiple intelligences. What teaching strategies might help each of these students learn optimally?

Matt is an avid conversationalist (his teachers say he "talks too much"). He knows a lot about historical and current events, and can fascinate adults and peers alike as he talks on a wide variety of subjects. He enjoys all kinds of music: rap, rock, classical, country, and spiritual. It's not uncommon for him to beat out a rhythm at the kitchen table or on his desk at school. He can draw an exact duplicate of nearly any picture—especially cartoons—and sometimes he gets in trouble for "doodling" at school. Facile with computers, he taught himself to make a home page on the Internet. At school, it is hard for Matt to be quiet and sit

still. He has never been able to retain simple math facts; can't seem to "get" grammar; often doesn't remember homework assignments; has difficulty getting organized to complete his work; has a hard time staying focused; and performs badly on most written tests. This "bright" child has already failed one grade and stays close to failing another.

Learning seems easy for **Jonathan**. He particularly loves math and even developed his own way of adding and subtracting, not using the teacher's prescribed methods. Jonathan has a very good memory; anything he hears, he remembers. This good "ear" translates into a real talent for language. As he has begun to learn Spanish in elementary school, Jonathan speaks with a perfect accent. But Jonathan is truly "all boy." Sitting still in school is not for him! He doesn't like to sit down to do homework or read a book. His comprehension is good—that is, he can understand really complicated plots

Answerable, Accountable, Trustworthy, Reliable, Dependable . . . RESPONSIBLE Means Much More than "Doing As I Say to Do"

SMA**R**T esponsible

Color the responsible student reliable, dependable, trustworthy, answerable, and accountable. At least, this is how we might define *responsible* using *Webster's Collegiate Dictionary*. What does this really mean for a first grader? Fourth grader? Eighth grader? High school junior? What would these students be saying, doing, and otherwise conveying to their teacher and their classmates? These are difficult questions to answer because responsibility means different things to

and difficult vocabulary—but his ability to read to himself is limited. Jonathan is a reliable classmate. He understands what is expected and complies with the rules; he completes assignments on time. Jonathan is a gifted athlete. In karate class, the combination of intense mental concentration and extreme physical energy seem to be a perfect match for this energetic and "smart" boy.

David is excellent with his hands. He can build almost anything—a robot, a tree house, wagons, and benches. He received a special award for the unique design of his brake system in the local soap box derby contest. Without the aid of a manual, he can take apart transmissions and engines; they fascinate him. David also has a knack for playing drums. Despite these obvious talents, most school-work is a struggle. When he brings home poor grades, his teachers report that he does not "apply himself." David—a starter on the football and baseball teams and a reserve on the basketball team—has to work hard to remain eligible for sports. But it seems that no

matter how hard he tries, he can't make good grades. The frustrations of school have trans-lated into social problems. His temper flares; he argues and gets into fights with other kids. This "smart" young man seems to be plagued with the sense that he is not very smart.

Brian loves to be outside. Whether shoot-ing baskets, hiking, biking, or hunting, he has a smile on his face and excitement in his voice. He likes to be in motion and moves gracefully. He is at home in nature. He can identify bird-calls, animal tracks, and many different plants. Brian's participation in Boy Scouts has always been a highlight of his learning. Brian, a natural athlete, made the all-star teams in baseball, basketball, and football. But Brian has trouble staying focused in school. He is a slow reader, and most of his high school assignments depend heavily on reading. He finds it difficult to stay on task doing written work. In fact, there is little about the academics of school that he enjoys; his favorite part of school is the social side. A popular young man, he has a wide network of friends throughout the school.

different individuals in different contexts. But if we value *responsible* learners, we must grapple with the meaning of this term for teacher, student—and even parent or guardian. We must seek a shared under-standing of responsibility.

One high school senior defined responsibility as "preparedness"—as being accountable "for your end of the bargain." In her mind, teachers and students alike have responsibilities in this area. Students, she said, should be responsible for coming to class with assignments completed, with books and other tools required for the day's work; respecting the teacher and fellow classmates—showing them basic courtesies. Teachers, too, have responsibilities to their students. Responsibilities such as coming with an interesting lesson that meets each student where he is and getting to know each student as an individual who has his own unique learning style and sets of interests.[25]

213

"Like Now"

told by Ruby Vaulx, Teacher, Alexander Elementary School

David, a student in Ruby Vaulx's second-grade class, apparently had a different view of responsibility. According to Ms. Vaulx, David began the school year with a real "attitude," oftentimes conveyed through a "smirky smile." He refused to complete assignments or to bring in his homework. In spite of Ms. Vaulx's repeated trips to his grandmother's house, where he stayed before and after school, he continued to exhibit unacceptable behavior—both academically and socially—until the night of the first student-led conference.

As Ms. Vaulx tells the story, David arrived with his mother and grandmother at 6:00 p.m. for his conference. Like his classmates, David guided his mother through each of the four centers Ms. Vaulx had set up in the classroom. He also sat across from her sharing the papers he had selected for his portfolio. As David talked, his mother realized how few of his assignments he had completed. She began to understand why he had earned an F in reading, a D in spelling, and a D in math. Further, she saw behind the "needs improvement" that he had received in every conduct area. David was, in fact, very honest in his communications with his mother. As they neared the end of their 45-minute conference, the mother said, "We're going to have a contract. I will always have time for you." To which David responded: "Like now?" His mother smiled and said, "Like now."

Enabling SMART learners is at the heart of education because it emphasizes growth rather than compliance—it's active rather than passive and honors both equity and individuality.

—Connie Allen, Principal, Natcher Elementary School

Following this conference, David's approach to school changed. He completed all assignments, brought in all of his homework, and even began to help Ms. Vaulx motivate other students. By the end of the next grading period, David had all As and Bs and all Ss in conduct; he was an honor roll student!

What does David's story have to say about developing responsible learners? First, a teacher can't make a student be responsible. In spite of all Ms. Vaulx's extra efforts, she was unable to change David's behavior.

The behavior change required a shared understanding between David, his mother, and his teacher. Second, putting a student in charge—making him answerable and accountable for his performance to those who matter—seems a powerful strategy. The student-led conference makes students feel important; it also causes them to reflect on their own work and work habits. In David's case, having the opportunity to answer directly to his mother in the conference setting was a catalyst for change. Having his mother on "his turf," his classroom, seemed to be an important part of the mix that led to their new commitments to one another and to themselves. Finally, when a student is empowered to account for his own behavior, he is more likely to become reliable and dependable in the completion of assigned tasks. Responsibility, then, is not passive compliance; it involves much more than following someone else's directive. Responsibility involves an active choice by an individual to take ownership of his own work and behavior.

Mara's Story

by Alice Phillips, Teacher, Sewanee Elementary School

Mara's body language said it all. The other three members of her cooperative team were huddled in close, heads together, talking. And, there was Mara, chair shoved back from the table, slumped down in her seat with arms folded tightly across her chest. She was a smart girl, good at schoolwork, always getting As on her papers. She liked being the one to get the answer. She liked raising her hand and telling everyone else what the right answer was. No one else was going to see her work either, no sir! When she worked, she made sure her arm was wrapped secretively around her paper so no one else could see what she did.

Now, here she was, with a single clue in her hand, and the rest of the information she needed to solve the puzzle in the hands of the other team members. This made her very unhappy, and she didn't want to "play"! The rules of the activity required students to read their clues aloud to the rest of the team, and she wouldn't do that. So her team got very upset at her as she stubbornly looked away and refused to cooperate. They got so frustrated that they started shouting, "Mrs. Phillips,

215

Mara won't cooperate! Make her read her clue!" It was difficult not to take over and tell this child that she had to cooperate. But I stayed calm and reminded them that she was part of their team, and they needed to figure out for themselves what to do. Other teams cheered as they solved the puzzle while Mara glowered. Students shared their solutions, and we celebrated the successes while Mara's team sat in steamy silence.

After starting the other teams on a second puzzle, I went to that team and asked them to talk about their experience for a few minutes before starting their new task. They talked angrily about how it felt to depend on a team member who didn't cooperate, and Mara shot back about how she didn't care and just wanted to work alone. I offered a compromise: Mara would be allowed to watch the team solve their puzzles today if she agreed to participate with at least one cooperative activity tomorrow. She shrugged. I said I would take that as a yes, and I walked away. Her team started working on their problem, with one member doing two roles. They were enthusiastic and engaged and cheered wildly when they succeeded. Meanwhile, I unobtrusively kept an eye on Mara. First, her eyes began to follow the action, and then I saw her chair inching forward a little. She sat up a little straighter. But she stayed out of the dialogue. The next day she read her clue to the team, and reread it when asked, but that was all. She didn't help find the solution, and she sat passively in her role of Task Master.

Nevertheless, Mara had turned a corner in her life as a student. From then on, each time we tackled a cooperative team puzzle activity, she participated a little bit more. By the end of the year, Mara was up on her knees, leaning into the team huddle, as enthusiastically engaged and cooperative as any other student in the class. She had discovered that work is both easier and more fun when you collaborate with others. She had grown to respect the talents and abilities of her peers and was able to celebrate team success with them. She had learned a valuable life skill that she will, hopefully, carry with her forever!

SMART learning is meaningful and challenging. . . . It begins at the learner's level of understanding and grows in a climate of curiosity, active participation, and exploration. SMART learning thrives in the presence of high standards and expectations.

—Jackie Walsh & Beth Sattes

Making Stories Personal

by Sheila B. Leach, Teacher, Our Lady of Fatima School

As an effort to promote values and inclusion, the sixth grade class participated in an interdisciplinary study of disabilities and acceptance using the life of Helen Keller as a basis. The project was language arts based and used an excerpt from Helen Keller's autobiography as a springboard to activities, research, and study.

The entire project covered a four-week period and really increased knowledge and sensitivity among the students of disabilities of all kinds and the unlimited potential of those who have one or more disabilities. There was a student in my class who had a facial deformity at the time.

The first unit in the sixth-grade basal reader is centered on the themes of hero/heroines and personal courage. These themes were expanded during the project with activities, guest speakers, field trips, and a multimedia slide presentation. The project was funded with a grant from Macmillan-McGraw Hill Publishers.

The Buddies: Another Thrust in Peer Teaching

by Alice Phillips, Teacher, Sewanee Elementary School

One of the most exciting projects I am working on this year involves our Buddies. This is part of Sewanee's Mentoring Program, which is a classroom-to-classroom relationship between grades. My fourth-grade students partner with the kindergarten students in Jennifer Raulston's class. Each Friday our classes get together for about half an hour for a variety of activities. We have done lots of reading together and have included elements such as discussion of plot, characterization, and main idea. We have interviewed each other and created a "Buddy Book" that travels home with a different student each night. We have also explored fractions, with older students explaining halves, thirds, and fourths to the younger students, and then assisting in the division of tortillas into fractional parts (and then eating them, of course!).

But, my favorite activity in this year's ongoing project is the creation and writing of an Alphabet Book about our town. We began by having the Buddies choose a letter and brainstorm everything important in our town that started with that letter. We came up with many great ideas, such as "B is for the bluffs," and "F is for the fog," for example. Next, we shared our ideas and added to the list. Then we evaluated the ideas, trying to decide on one for each letter. We had so much difficulty eliminating ideas that we eventually decided we would just keep multiple ideas as needed!

The older students are now in the process of researching. For this step, we must use interview skills quite frequently. Students look for primary sources of information, asking questions, calling organizations, and seeking out the older members of our community for their thoughts, memories, and information. We recently used part of our buddy time to have the fourth-grade authors read their work aloud to their kindergarten friends, in a whole group presentation format. It was a wonderful opportunity for them to use speaking and listening skills!

Jennifer and I hope to find a way to actually publish the finished book by the end of the year. Each letter will have photos, a quote from a kindergarten student, and a researched paragraph on the history and importance of the chosen places or attributes of our very special town. We believe that this will be a book that appeals to all ages, from preschoolers just learning the alphabet to long-time residents reading about their town's history.

Critical, Reflective, Considerate, Creative— The Many Faces of THOUGHTFULNESS

SMAR**T**houghtful

The information age is bringing increased attention to the long-standing instructional goal of developing high-level thinking skills within all students. Phil Schlechty, for example, advocates that schools consider how to produce knowledge workers, those individuals "who put to use facts, ideas, theories, beliefs, and supposed forms of knowledge to produce a product." In Schlechty's view, "knowledge work requires thought, analysis, articulation, insight, brainpower, and reasoning." Among his arguments for a focus on preparing knowledge workers is the contention that new technologies will require all citizens "to handle more information each day than was available to the average citizen in a lifetime only a century ago."[26]

Milbrey McLaughlin and Joan Talbert are among those who propose "teaching for understanding" as a means toward producing thoughtful citizens who can themselves thrive in this new millennium and who can also contribute to the vitality of our democratic republic. With other education reformers, they "envision classrooms where students and teachers acquire knowledge collaboratively, where orthodoxies of pedagogy and 'facts' are continually challenged in classroom discourse, and where conceptual (versus rote) understanding of subject matter is the goal." Implicit in their writing is a notion advanced by other reformers: that students not only need to "learn to think," but more important, perhaps, they must "think in order to learn." Thinking to learn is at the heart of what Schlechty has in mind when he proposes the model of "student as worker" and argues that one of the most important tasks facing teachers is to design meaningful work.[27]

"Teacher as designer" is a metaphor used by Grant Wiggins and Jay McTighe, who suggest that a key design task for teachers is formulating questions that serve as organizers for the curriculum. They propose the use of "provocative and multilayered questions that reveal the richness and complexities of a subject" as vehicles for getting to "matters of deep and enduring understanding." They refer to these questions as *essential questions*.[28] Alice Phillips, third-grade teacher at Sewanee Elementary, adapted Wiggins and McTighe's framework. In Alice's words:

> I have a permanent display in my classroom on a small bulletin board featuring four "global" essential questions, which I adapted from Wiggins and McTighe's book. I labeled these as "Questions for SMART Learners," and I refer to them frequently. The one I reference most is: "How do I know I'm right? What's the evidence?" In the simplest daily lesson, posing that question elevates the discussion to a higher-order thinking level. For example, a geography worksheet asks which continents are all or partly north of the equator. When a child answers, I say: "Prove it; show me your evidence." The child then goes to the map, identifies the continents and the equator, locates the compass rose, and demonstrates that she is correct.

Through this procedure, children in Alice's room are practicing skills of critical thinking.

Thoughtful students also reflect on their learning and thinking.

219

They are metacognitive in the sense that they think about their thinking. David Perkins makes a strong case for metacognition in his book, *Outsmarting IQ,* in which he offers compelling evidence that when teachers coach students in metacognitive skills IQ scores increase.[29] Teachers can assist students in developing metacognitive skills by encouraging them to reflect on the conditions under which they best learn, the procedures and cues that support their learning, and related issues.

While higher-level thinking, metacognition, and reflection are important dimensions of thoughtfulness, respect for and consideration of others are equally important. The affective dimension of thoughtfulness is at play when students (and adults) listen with respect to one another. In fact, we argue that listening is the hallmark of a thoughtful learner. One extension of listening with respect is being open to divergent points of view; another is listening without interrupting or cutting off other speakers. These aspects of thoughtfulness can be encouraged by classroom norms that are embraced by teacher and students alike.

Another aspect of thoughtfulness that can be cultivated by teachers is that of creativity. Interestingly enough, the digital age has brought about a renewal of interest in artistic expression, which can nurture creativity. One author submits that "it seems inevitable that citizens of the internationally networked world would move away from text-centric communication and toward pictures, diagrams, sound, movement, and other more universal forms of communication." This same author holds that when students are provided opportunities to develop their own creativity and artistic vision, they improve their expression, develop both cognitive and affective skills, and engage in both multicultural awareness and personal growth.[30]

The "T" in SMART touches upon all parts of the school curriculum and evokes questions and issues that get at the heart of teaching and learning. As schools strive to create high-performing learning communities, thoughtfulness becomes a vision for both students and adults alike, within and outside the school.

Thoughtfulness combines two aspect of our lives: intellectual or cognitive operations plus feelings, attitudes, and dispositions.

—John Barell

Last Friday one of our six-year-old students asked his teacher, who had been battling allergies and sinus problems, "What's wrong with your voice?" A very grown up seven year-old replied, "Oh, she just has a frog in her throat." The next question from the six-year-old? "Why did she swallow a frog?"

—Connie Allen, Natcher Elementary School

Teaching for Thoughtfulness: Classroom Strategies to Enhance Educational Development by John Barell (White Plains, NY: Longman Publishers, 1995).

Barell explores two aspects of thoughtfulness: (1) the disposition toward thinking and metacognition, and (2) that toward consideration and courtesy. He maintains that the cognitive and affective dimensions are interrelated. When an individual demonstrates respect toward others, for example, by listening and honoring their ideas, this individual is concurrently expanding his own point of view and displaying qualities of the critical thinker. With this as a backdrop, Barell chronicles strategies of teachers who are successful in producing these student outcomes on a day-to-day basis. The chronicles include both classroom vignettes and stories and specific tools and strategies. *Teaching for Thoughtfulness* is a book for practitioners seeking both inspiration and hands-on techniques that can be used tomorrow.

The Writer and the Roller Coaster

by Nancy Binder, Curriculum Coordinator, Natcher Elementary School

Writing is an integral part of the curriculum for every grade in Kentucky. At the fourth-grade level, progress is assessed through review of a completed portfolio from each student, which includes examples of personal, literary, and transactive writing. The piece that supports and demonstrates a child's growth is the Letter to the Reviewer. It is here that a student reflects on what has been learned, what has been strengthened, and what can be improved.

Many times a student will use an analogy to show growth. I remember one student compared her portfolio experience to riding a roller coaster. In the beginning of the ride you wait for it to start, just like in writing "you sit there waiting for an idea to come to you." A piece needs to be developed through the use of thoughtshots, just like a roller coaster ride "would be boring if you never got scared or excited." A good piece has "a good lead to make people want to read your story, like a roller coaster starts out with a big hill and makes you want to ride the ride." Soon enough, "the roller coaster ride ends, just like my portfolio did."

The Implementation Dip

by Micky Hickman, Teacher, Pulaski High School, Virginia

It was my first day of attempting to incorporate the Socratic seminar into my instruction.[31] I had been impressed with its power as a learning activity, but was a bit skeptical; there was a voice inside telling me that it would not work with the caliber of students that I was instructing at the time. We used excerpts from the Law Code of Hammurabi as our text for discussion. We sat in a circle, and I posed the opening question. After about 20 seconds of silence, a student made a comment and then another. All around the circle I was getting contributions from the students. Great comments! They even asked each other questions. And, they piggybacked on one another's responses. The seminar went as it was supposed to go.

I was smiling inside; it was all I could do to keep from running into the hall to bring someone—anyone—in to hear my kids having a great discussion. I was amazed when I heard a comment from one student whom I had taught the previous year in another class. Her name was Brenda, and she was so, so shy. She would answer the roll call with just a smile and a nod if she could get by with that. But, here was Brenda with an opinion, and she supported it well.

The seminar gives you such a wonderful chance to see inside your students' heads. The period passed, and the next class came in. I was anticipating another great class. When it came time for the seminar, I introduced it the very same way. This seminar did not go as well. I had to pump questions into it to give it life, even direct questions to students, which you are not supposed to do in this format. I was brought down to earth a bit. But I had seen the technique work, so I would just have to work harder and be ready to try variations. Of course, it occurred to me that the same lesson plan does not always work with different students—student learning styles vary. I was just thankful that the sequence of the two classes was not reversed. I might well have bagged the activity if it had not gone as planned for me at first. It was sometime later that I heard about Michael Fullan's "implementation dip" and realized that I had lived it. He says that you might have to experience failure and setbacks at first when you make a change—until you learn how to thrive in that world of change and get things right.

Reflection: Developing Student Awareness and Skill

Context for Reflection

This idea—"We all need time to reflect on past experiences if we are to gain new understandings"—embodies a norm that can enhance teaching, learning, and thinking. This norm can serve as an important piece in the structuring of a learning community. *Webster's* defines a norm as "an ideal standard binding upon the members of a group and serving to bind, control, or regulate proper behavior." In a learning community, this ideal standard would be understood and shared by teachers and students alike. Ideally, members of the community would believe this statement to be true and would act upon this belief.

What can a facilitator of learning do to cultivate and nurture such a norm in the hearts and minds of students? First, provide a rationale for the idea by demonstrating why and how reflection promotes new understandings. Next, allocate time for students to question, think, and talk about the statement and the rationale that has been provided. Finally, model this norm in a variety of ways—by reflecting and sharing the results of your own thinking processes.

> Everyone is asked to venture into the realm of curiosity together. With this invitation comes the challenge to suspend certainty and the need for answers outside ourselves.
>
> —Stephanie Ryan, "Learning Communities"

- Talk about your own thinking processes.
- Provide time for group reflection at appropriate points in instruction.
- Use this time to reflect yourself, even while you expect students to be reflecting.
- Encourage students to talk about the connections they make during their private reflections.

What are the implications for instructional planning and practice? As previously suggested, the teacher or facilitator of learning must "walk the walk," not just "talk the talk" of reflection. This means not only allocating time for individual reflection, but providing tools that enable students to reflect—to observe their own thinking and behavior and to make connections.

Relationship to Learning and Thinking: A Rationale for Reflection

David Perkins makes a strong argument for "reflective intelligence," which he defines as "the contribution of knowledge, understanding, and attitudes about how to use our minds to intelligent behavior." Perkins submits that reflective intelligence is learnable and that it can increase our general intelligence. He writes that it can be thought of as "mindware," or "software for the mind"; that it is "whatever people can learn that helps them to solve problems, make decisions, understand difficult concepts, and perform other intellectually demanding tasks better."[32] In order to develop reflective intelligence, individuals must be afforded time for reflection and provided tools with which to develop this mindware. One important tool is that of question formulation. Perkins, Gardner, and other cognitive scientists and learning theorists offer approaches to developing skills in problem solving, decision making, conceptual thinking, and understanding. They suggest ways that reflection can be used to enhance thinking.[33]

Reflection also provides opportunities for students to retrieve past knowledge and experience from long-term memory so as to relate these to new learnings. More specifically, reflection enables students to tap into schemas—network structures that store our general knowledge about objects, events, or situations. As John Bruer discusses in *Schools of Thought*, these "associative structures do not simply provide ways to store information; they also influence what we notice, how we interpret it, and how we remember it." Bruer concludes, "school instruction that ignores the influence of preexisting knowledge on learning can be highly ineffective."[34] Because all individuals derive their own particular schemas from unique sets of experiences, time should be provided for private reflection to enable each student to call these forth at appropriate points in the learning process, thereby building upon past knowledge to develop new understandings.

Sample Procedures for Creating a Reflective Classroom

A. Introduce students to the following norm regarding reflection and learning by making a "truth sign" to post in the classroom:[35] "We all need time to reflect on past experiences if we are to gain new understandings."

B. Engage students in a discussion related to the rationale behind this idea. Pose pivotal questions such as (a) Why do you think this statement might be true? (b) Can you think of a time when you were able to understand a new concept quickly and easily because of knowledge and experience gained outside of the classroom? (c) How does quiet time assist your thinking?

C. After encouraging students to share their thoughts about this belief, share your rationale for introducing this belief to the classroom.

D. Provide a "Thinking Journal" for each student, and allow time for students to write in them routinely and at specified times in a unit of study. (See "Sample Prompts" below.) For example, as you introduce a new unit, set aside time and provide appropriate prompts for students to think about what they may already know about major concepts, related information, and so forth. As you progress through a unit, you may wish to periodically take time out for students to reflect and write about how their new learnings may be challenging or reinforcing old ideas—or how new learnings are helping them answer questions they may have had about their environment or a particular content area. Be sure to use a "Thinking Journal" yourself when you ask your students to reflect and write. Not only is this good modeling, it enables you to slow down your own thinking and become more reflective as you interact later with your students.

E. Provide students with routine reminders and with varied tools for practicing the art of reflection.

Sample Prompts from a Student "Thinking Journal"

Note: Following are an Introduction and prompts from a Thinking Journal designed by the authors. The prompts were followed by ample "white space" for student responses. Additionally, the journal contained blank pages for recording reflections on other topics. The "Thinking Journal" and prompts afford students an opportunity to reflect on their learning and thinking styles and habits.

About Your Reflections on Questioning, Thinking, and Learning

This year, our class will take time each week to think about how and why we question, think, and learn. Our purpose in doing this is for you and your classmates to reach better individual understandings of how you think and how you best learn. Usually, I will ask you to think silently and then write about a question or topic related to your own understanding, thinking, and learning in this class. Many times, we will follow these individual reflections with a time for sharing with one another. Always, I will read what you have written because, as your teacher, I want to understand you and your own individual learning and thinking styles.

Reflections: On Learning

1. Do you consider yourself a successful learner? In school? In what ways? Out of school? In what ways?

2. What does it mean to be a successful learner? How can you tell if someone is a successful learner?

Listening: The Hallmark of a Thoughtful Learner

Thoughtful learners listen to others with attention and respect. This encompasses two types of listening: active listening and empathic listening. Active listening can be simply defined as "tuning in" to the speaker who has the floor, processing the information that is being provided. The active listener "engages with the speaker at the intellectual level . . . not [by] asking the speaker questions—but by analyzing and asking questions of [himself]."[36] Empathic listening, on the other hand, involves "getting inside the speaker's head"—seeing the world the way the speaker sees it. Both active listening and empathic listening are skills that support thinking and learning; they are also critical to effective teaching. Further, they nurture and enhance good questioning.

3. How can you learn best? How do you know when you're learning?

4. What are your teachers and your school doing to help you learn?

5. What do you wish that your teachers and your school were doing to help you learn?

Reflections: On the Subject of _____ (e. g., math)

1. Write about your experiences with _____. Include your strengths and weaknesses, your successes and failures, your likes and dislikes.

2. What is _____? Why do we study it? How would you change how we study?

Reflections: On Thinking

1. Do you consider yourself a good thinker? In school? In what ways? Out of school? In what ways?

2. What does it mean to be a good thinker?

How can you tell if someone is a good thinker?

3. What do your teachers and your school do to help you become a better thinker?

4. What do you think your teachers and your school could do to help you become a better thinker?

5. What does thinking have to do with learning?

6. Recall a time when you tried to do your best thinking. Describe the situation that caused you to think deeply. How did you go about your thinking? Were you satisfied with your thinking? Why or why not?

Reflections: On_____ (a specific content focus, e.g., global warming)

1. What important or interesting questions do you have about_____? List each question and tell why the answer to each would be important or interesting to you. How would you go about answering each of these questions?

Listening and Questioning

Active listening promotes interactive questioning. Active listening involves "physically attending to what a person is saying, focusing upon the speaker, and attempting to create a mental picture of what the speaker is saying." It also involves keeping in check one's own feelings and point of view about the topic or issue being addressed.[37] Students learn to listen actively when teachers (1) help them understand what active listening involves—what it looks and feels like, (2) consistently model active listening themselves, (3) provide opportunities for practice with feedback, and (4) work toward making active listening a classroom norm. As students actively listen to their teacher and to one another, they ready themselves for interactive questioning.

Interactive questioning is a process whereby teacher and students alike can seek

Understanding . . . [is] the development of powers of discrimination and judgment. . . . Understanding is more stimulated than learned. It grows from questioning oneself and being questioned by others.

—Theodore Sizer

Reflections: On Questions	Reflections: On Answering Questions
1. How often do you think of questions that you would really like to answer or have answered? What seems to cause you to formulate questions? In school? Out of school? What seems to cause you to form questions? (Do not include questions that you ask to find out if something is right or wrong, allowable or not, etc. Think of the questions that you ask yourself or others when you are really curious or perplexed about something).	1. When someone asks you a question, how do you go about answering it?
	2. How do you feel when the person asking you a question doesn't give you time to think of your answer or interrupts you when you are trying to finish your answer?
2. When you have a question in school, what do you usually do? When you have a question outside of school, what do you do?	3. How do you feel when the person asking you a question gives you a lot of time to think of an answer before repeating the question or interrupting your thinking?
3. Do you think that you ask good questions? In school? Outside of school? Do you think other people think that your questions are important?	4. How do you feel about answering questions that your teacher asks in class? Do you almost always raise your hand when you think you know the answer to a teacher's question? Why, or why not?
4. Do your teachers encourage you to ask questions? When? Do your parents and others outside of school encourage you to ask questions? When?	5. What do you do when you are not sure of an answer to a teacher's question? Why?

clarification, ask for a rationale, request additional information, try to understand the relationship between facts and ideas, or otherwise seek to enhance their personal understanding of a speaker's statements. Research confirms that students infrequently engage in interactive questioning;

Strategies for Facilitating Reflection

1. Introduce students to Leila Christenberry's "Questioning Circle,"[38] and encourage them to use this as a framework for activating and organizing prior knowledge and experience related to a topic under study.

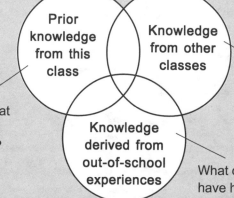

What have I already learned in this class that is related to the topics we are about to study?

Prior knowledge from this class

Knowledge from other classes

What have I learned in other classes or courses in school that relates to the topic we are about to study?

Knowledge derived from out-of-school experiences

What do I know from experiences I have had outside of school that relates to the topic we are about to study?

2. Encourage students to identify gaps in their knowledge about the topic under study and to formulate questions that are expressions of what they would like to know, understand, or ponder about the topic.

3. Help students search for meaning and understanding by offering them frameworks to assist in reflective problem solving. John Barell offers one such framework, "the Eight-R Strategy," in *Teaching for Thoughtfulness*.[39] This strategy, summarized below, is another way to stimulate student reflection.

- **Recognize:** What feelings do I have about the problem?

- **Research:** What information do I need to solve this?

- **Represent:** Can I draw a picture or make a diagram?

- **Relate:** How is this related to other problems? What ideas or concepts do I recall from other problems? What patterns are evident?

- **Reduce:** Can I reduce the problem to several parts? Can I identify reasons why the problem exists?

- **Reflect:** What assumptions/biases/definitions should I question? Have I identified all significant information?

- **Resources:** Are there persons and things that can help?

- **Reasons:** Are there causes to identify?

students' questions are rare occurrences in most classrooms.[40] If students are to engage in interactive questioning, they must be taught how and why to question interactively. The teacher should encourage students to pose questions when experiencing the following:

1. They are confused about a point of information, or a concept is not clear to them. Sample questions: "Can we go over that point again? It is not clear to me." "What did you mean when you said . . . ?"

Active listening involves capitalizing on your thought speed to process information. There's a band of available time between the rate at which people speak (about 100 to 150 words per minute) and the rate at which listeners can process information (500 to 600 words per minute). That difference is a window of opportunity for distractions and daydreaming, or for information processing and analysis.

—Gay Lumsden and Donald Lumsden, *Communicating in Groups and Teams*

Introducing the Art of Listening

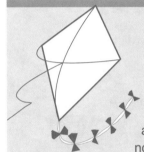

A. Introduce students to the following norm: "We learn best when we listen with attention and respect." Post this norm in a prominent place in your classroom.

B. Engage students in a discussion related to the rationale behind this idea. Pose pivotal questions such as (a) Why do you think this statement might be true?, (b) Can you think of a time when you were able to learn from a classmate by listening with attention and respect?, and (c) How does listening to others assist your thinking? After encouraging students to share their thoughts about this belief, share your rationale for introducing this belief to the classroom.

C. Describe, model, and provide students opportunities to practice behaviors associated with active listening. For example:

- "Get set physically for listening." Classroom arrangements that allow students

to see one another foster active listening. Encourage students to use nonverbal cues such as looking toward the speaker, maintaining eye contact, and nodding as appropriate.

- "Screen out distractions." Focus on the speaker and her words. If the mind begins to wander, jot down the speaker's key points for future reference.

- "Focus your listening to get main points and concepts." Don't get bogged down in the small details.

- "Organize and key the information while you're listening," using a technique such as mindmapping.[41]

- "Analyze the information mentally." Ask yourself questions about speaker's statements. Look for the speaker's evidence, assumptions, point of view, and values.

D. Provide students with routine reminders and with varied tools for practicing the art of listening.[42]

2. They sense that a statement is incomplete. Sample questions: "What else can you tell me about this?" "What else can we find out?"

3. They want to understand what is behind the speaker's thinking. Sample questions: "Why do you say that?" "What leads you to this conclusion?"

4. They are trying to relate a new learning to prior knowledge or experience. Sample questions: "How is this connected to. . .?"

Strategies That Facilitate Active Listening

Listen with interest to the speaker's statement or answer—not with your own answer or response in mind. Barell suggests using "self-talk" while listening to students. Such self-talk proceeds from the following kinds of questions: "What am I listen-ing to? Do I understand what she is saying? What can I picture in my mind? What is not quite clear yet? Where is her thinking going from here? If I don't understand, I can ask a clarifying question." He further suggests that teachers share this strategy with their students and encourage them to use it themselves.[43]

Piggybacking. Refer to comments made by students, and encourage students to refer to statements made by their peers. By encouraging students to build upon one another's answers, teachers promote active and respectful listening. All people enjoy "getting credit for" a statement and hearing their name spoken by a peer.

Ask students how they know when someone is listening. As Barell states, students are likely to respond: "They can repeat what you say and add on to that. They ask good questions. And they look you in the eye."[44]

Ask students what they do when attempting to figure out what someone else is saying. They will likely reply:

- "Try to visualize what the speaker is saying; identify and 'see' key ideas and relationships."
- "Ask myself if I agree or disagree."
- "Pretend I'm in the speaker's shoes, and see how I feel."
- "Predict what the speaker will say next."
- "Figure out what questions I want to ask when the other person is through."[45]

Try to use Wait Time II (3 to 5 seconds of silence following a student's answer) consistently, and encourage students also to honor the 3 to 5 seconds of silence after their peers finish talking.[46] Stress to students that they should refrain from raising and waving their hands while another student is speaking and during the 3 to 5 seconds after the student stops speaking. Encourage students to use this silence as a time to continue thinking about what the speaker has said and to formulate questions or responses to her statements.

Develop signals to help students form good listening habits. For example, place your hand on your ear while a student is speaking; remove it 3 to 5 seconds after the speaker stops talking. Then, open your hand to the class to signal that others may speak or raise their hands.

SMARTer Learning through Technology

As Barbara Jones introduced the concept of historical fiction to students in her 11th-grade English class, she incorporated technology—purposefully and effectively—to teach the concept. Students corresponded by e-mail with survivors of World War II and then wrote their own short stories based on their keypals' historical experiences. Technology enhanced students' understanding of the meaning of "historical fiction" as it could not have done before the advent of the Internet.

Many teachers are incorporating technology into their classrooms and lesson plans. What makes its use effective? The North Central Regional Educational Laboratory (NCREL) has been studying the effective and purposeful use of technology in teaching. Some of the resources are highlighted below.

Learning with Technology is an NCREL-developed course in which two overarching questions govern discussion and curriculum development:

- How does the lesson exemplify meaningful, engaged learning?
- How does the technology extend the lesson in ways that wouldn't be possible without it?

Tools from this course—including the Unit Analysis Worksheet to help teachers reflect and the Planning Framework—can be accessed at NCREL's Technology in Education Consortium Web site [http://www.ncrtec.org] that also offers tools for planning for hardware needs.

Plugging In: Choosing and Using Educational Technology provides a description of the eight indicators of engaged learning and can be found on the Web at http://www.ncrel.org/sdrs/engaged.htm.

In addition, teachers can access The Amazing Picture Machine (http://

www.ncretec.org/picture.htm), a database of pictures, maps, and other graphic resources on the Internet. This Web site includes sample lesson plans that give teachers ideas about how they can incorporate pictures in their own classrooms.

Captured Wisdom Library includes videotapes of K-12 teachers who are using technology to make instruction more meaningful. The library also contains CD-ROMs with questions and answers about how these teachers planned, managed, and organized instruction with technology to promote learning. If you like to "see it" to understand it, this set of materials is for you.

Another good "see it" package comes from the Northwest Educational Technology Consortium. Called *classrooms@work/tools@hand,* this professional development tool uses videos and Web-based multimedia to access classrooms where teachers are using technology successfully. Access to the Web site (http://www.netc.org/classrooms@work) and downloadable documents is free; related videos and a CD-ROM can be ordered on-line or by phone (800-211-9435).

Educators who want to explore topics in depth can consult The Knowledge Loom, an interactive Web site developed by the nation's regional educational laboratories (http://knowledgeloom.org). Each month the site "spotlights" an area and presents research summaries, how-to information, chat sessions led by expert panelists, links to additional resources, and more.

ParenTech is a project designed to help families learn about how technology makes a difference in the ways their children learn, work, and live. At the project's Web site (http://www.parentech.org), families and educators can share ideas, questions, and concerns. In addition, they can find links to dozens of interesting and educational sites.

Mindmapping

Mindmapping is a visual, nonlinear way to organize information and stimulate the thinking power of the mind. It allows the mind the freedom to explore new territory, to mix ideas up in new ways, to develop new patterns and channels of thought, and to go deeper into a subject while maintaining a broad view.

Mindmapping can be used for a multitude of purposes: writing projects, project management, meeting agendas and notes, presentations, brainstorming (individually or in groups), note taking, memory enhancement, personal growth—almost anyplace where information, problems, or people are involved.[47]

The technique is so simple that the only real challenge is to do it.

1. Put a word or symbol that represents what you want to think about in the center of a page.

2. Capture every thought that comes to mind *(no censoring)*.

3. Link thoughts to center focus by printing key words on lines extending out from the center.

4. Link ideas related to each other as "branches" off the original line from the center.

5. Use color as a way to organize thoughts, stimulate new thoughts, or just because it's fun!

6. Use symbols to create thought pictures.

Put on Your Thinking Hats: Edward de Bono's Six Hats

When teachers want their students to become better thinkers—or when faculties try to be more intentionally "thoughtful" in conversations—it is helpful to have a shared vocabulary as a cue for different ways of being thoughtful. Edward de Bono provides us with a framework for six different ways of thinking and uses graphic metaphors to help us remember.[48] De Bono's "six thinking hats" are each associated with a particular way of thinking. When you don the "white hat," for example, you think objectively about known facts; white hat thinkers try to avoid jumping to conclusions. The "red hat," though, is the opposite. This kind of thinking is emotional and intuitive; "hunches" are the norm. De Bono's book is easy to read. Read

more about de Bono's hats in Appendix E.

When a group is familiar with these different ways of thinking, members can ask each other to "put on the green hat" for some creative thinking, or to "take off the black hat" when they have heard enough from the critical thinker who anticipates potential problems. Joy Runyan, a middle school science teacher in east Tennessee, used the colors as a way for students to self-assess. Runyan used construction paper hands (rather than hats), giving each student the color that represented his or her predominant style of thinking. She used these colored hands in grouping students—making sure each group had multiple colors—and the "thinking styles" became yet another way for students to learn about and appreciate diversity.

Using Assessment to Promote SMART Learning: The Big Picture

The Two Faces of Assessment: Accountability and Learning

Fear, anxiety, mystery, aura. Assessment stimulates different thoughts and feelings in the minds and hearts of students and parents—and even teachers and other educators. Such feelings emerge from a lack of understanding of standards and a sense of helplessness when confronted with testing and test results. Walk into any school or classroom community, and ask students, teachers, parents, and administrators about their concerns regarding assessment. The following kinds of questions are likely to emerge: *What will be on the test? How will it be graded? What grade will appear on my child's report card? How will my students do on our state's high-stakes test? Will our students' performance on the state test reflect well on our school?* These feelings and concerns are common responses to the equation of assessment with accountability. This view sees assessment as something done *to* the learner by some outside authority for the purpose of judging the learner's performance—usually in comparison to the performance of his peers.

> Assessment should improve performance, not just audit it. Assessment done properly should begin conversations about performance, not end them.
>
> —Grant Wiggins

The accountability perspective also places emphasis upon the consequences of assessment results to the future of both individual learners and their school.

Security, clarity, focus, understanding. These feelings emerge from meaningful involvement of students, parents, teachers, and other stakeholders in conversations around such issues as (1) the purpose and focus of assessment, (2) criteria for acceptable performance, and (3) how results can be used to improve future performance. These conversations can be driven by the following kinds of questions: *What am I accountable for knowing and being able to do? What is my present level of proficiency? How can I improve my work—moving it to higher levels of performance? How can we align instruction with assessment? How can we use student work to improve instruction? How can I use feedback from assessments to improve teaching and learning across our school community?* This perspective recognizes the power of assessment to improve both teaching and learning and places emphasis upon assessment as feedback in the overall teaching and learning cycle.

Although the above two perspectives on assessment are not mutually exclusive, too often there is a dichotomy between the two in the real world of schools. The pressures of high-stakes testing can cause a school community to focus on test results as ends in and of themselves—and to "drop everything" during the days and weeks preceding the actual testing to get ready for this event. Likewise, students are inclined to think of learning in terms of "what will be on the test" and to view tests as terminal events in the learning process. The real challenge in many schools is to link these two sides of assessment in ways that enable all stakeholders to take more ownership for both assessment results and the use of these results in efforts to continuously improve student performance.

Schools committed to continuous improvement embrace Wiggins' view that "assessment should begin conversations about performance, not end them."[49] These schools seek tools and strategies that yield enriched data to fuel these conversations for *all* members of the community—beginning with the students themselves. They also look for tools that meaningfully engage students, teachers, parents, and members of the extended community in reflecting on the results of a variety of assessment measures and in using these to improve learning for all students. Leaders of these school communities are helping others ask and answer such questions as the following:

- To what extent are we using the results of current assessments to improve the performance of all students?
- What kinds of assessment information would be useful to teachers? To students? To parents?
- What would it look like if assessment were an integral part of learning for students and teachers?
- How can we engage students in assessment of their own learning?
- What do the results of standardized tests tell us about the effectiveness of our instructional program?

This complex, controversial subject lies at the heart of continuous school improvement. When assessment becomes a topic for conversation in schools, stakeholders at all levels are afforded opportunities to take ownership for improving student performance—and, as a result, test scores.

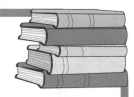

Understanding by Design by Grant Wiggins and Jay McTighe (Alexandria, VA: Association for Supervision and Curriculum Development, 1998).

Wiggins and McTighe bring their considerable knowledge of assessment and curriculum to this important model for instructional planning. Advocating a "backward design" process, the authors suggest that teachers begin with the ends in mind as they plan instructional units and follow a three-staged process that includes (1) identifying desired results, (2) determining acceptable evidence, and (3) planning learning experiences and instruction. The authors relate this process to the goal of teaching for understanding; that is, teaching in ways that enable students to make personal meaning of new knowledge and to construct connections to prior knowledge and experience. They identify six facets of understanding—explanation, interpretation, application, perspective, empathy, and self-knowledge—and provide clear examples that assist the reader in understanding what each facet looks like in practice.

The chapters dedicated to assessment are clear, comprehensive, and on target for those looking toward classroom application. The authors provide multiple examples of the kinds of evidence teachers might seek to assess and document each facet of student understanding. They advocate "uncoverage" of material as a goal of instruction; that is, depth of understanding as opposed to simple coverage of content. They use this as a theme in their chapters on curriculum and instruction. Finally, the authors provide a planning template for teachers to use with this design.

This well-written and well-organized manual provides both a rationale and how-to directions for teaching "understanding by design." It should be of interest to the individual practitioner seeking new ways of thinking about instructional planning as well as to groups of teachers exploring alternate instructional models. ASCD has also produced a videotape by the same name and provides electronic access to resources that can assist in this new way of lesson design. This can be accessed through http://www.ascd.org.

Students Talking and Listening: Fourth Graders Use Protocol to Improve Writing

Alyssa, a 10-year-old fourth grader, is on her way to Lexington, Kentucky, with three of her classmates, her teacher, and others from Alexander Elementary School. She and her classmates will "teach" a group of teachers, principals, and parents from schools across Tennessee, Kentucky, and West Virginia about Structured Reflection Protocol, a fun way of working with other students.[50]

In another month Alyssa and all other fourth graders at Alexander will be required to write an essay in response to a prompt provided on

Tennessee's statewide writing assessment. She knows that this writing test is important—that Mr. Wiman, her principal, is very hopeful that she and her classmates will score at least a "proficient" because this will affect what people think about Alexander Elementary. She also knows that she *will* score "proficient"—and probably a 6 out of 6—because she knows what a proficient essay looks and sounds like, thanks to Mrs. Dunigan and her classmates! And that's where Protocol comes in.

Since October, Alyssa has attended a special, after-school class taught by Mrs. Dunigan to help students improve their writing. The unusual thing about this class is that Mrs. Dunigan doesn't actually teach the students; they teach themselves—using the Protocol process that Mrs. Dunigan *did* teach them.

Protocol works this way. Each student brings an original story or essay. Mrs. Dunigan tells them the question that will focus their Protocol. For example, *Do descriptive words paint a picture for the reader? Is the opening interesting and attention-getting? Are the characters well described? Is my story organized and sequenced properly?* Students work in groups of four. Two, named as readers, read their stories and then explain to the group their assessment of their own writing, in response to the question of the day. As these two read their stories aloud and reflect, the other two listen carefully. After they finish, the job of the listening pair is to give feedback. Mrs. Dunigan helps them to give both "warm" feedback, in which the students identify positive characteristics of the writing sample, and "cool" feedback, in which the students suggest possible improvements. Finally, the readers reflect on what they would do differently, based on the feedback they hear about their writing.

When the pairs complete the first round of reading—giving and receiving feedback—the students exchange roles; the readers become listeners and vice versa. Alyssa remembers how much she has learned by listening to her classmates read their essays and giving them feedback. She's thought about what makes a good descriptive essay. She's heard some really good—and some not-so-good—examples. She knows that she's a much better writer now than she was five months ago!

Mr. Wiman, the principal of Alexander, also knows that Alyssa and

Protocol helped me
1. be able to speak well
2. have dignity in what I wrote
3. have creative ideas
4. calm my fears in the public . . . and that was a BIG FEAR!

—Alyssa Ozier, Fourth-Grade Student, Alexander Elementary School

her classmates have improved their writing through their experience with Protocol. This is why he's arranged for them to come to the meeting in Lexington. He photocopied essays that they wrote four months ago in October and essays that they just completed last week to show the other principals and teachers how much his students have improved. He wants to brag on them! Then he will ask the students to demonstrate their uses of Protocol to these adults—doing it just like they do back in their classroom.

The students are now in front of 35 educators whom they don't know. They've completed their demonstration. A teacher from another school asks the students how Protocol has helped them to become better writers. David says, "It makes you think about what you're trying to say." Alyssa adds, "Students have good ideas to give one another. You can learn a lot from your classmates." Another student adds, "Students talk in words that other students can understand."

Mr. Wiman and Mrs. Dunigan talk about how Protocol "empowers" students to take charge of their own learning, how it brings student voice into the assessment process, how it makes students take more pride in their work. The other educators are asking about other ways protocol might be used by students. Alyssa has tuned out. She's daydreaming about the day she'll get her writing scores back and see a perfect 6. She knows she can because she has confidence in herself as a writer.

P.S. And she did!

Last year when we did protocol, I learned from others and what they thought about my stories. First, we read our stories to each other. Next we gave the good points about the story, and the bad points. I really liked it a lot. Instead of asking the teacher was the story good or not, we asked our classmates. We also learned from others the right spelling and grammar. I liked learning from my classmates. . . . We could bring snacks to soothe our mind so we could write better. I really liked having the protocol.

—Kristyn Mayberry, Fourth-Grade Student, Alexander Elementary School

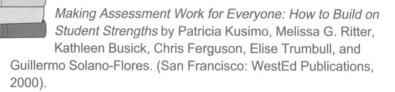

Making Assessment Work for Everyone: How to Build on Student Strengths by Patricia Kusimo, Melissa G. Ritter, Kathleen Busick, Chris Ferguson, Elise Trumbull, and Guillermo Solano-Flores. (San Francisco: WestEd Publications, 2000).

This publication provides information to help teachers modify assessments so they are more equitable, effective, and beneficial to students and teachers alike. Particular attention is paid to the needs of learners from diverse cultural backgrounds and strategies that eliminate the inequities of many traditional assessments.

Student-Led Conferences: A New Twist on a Familiar Strategy

Keeping parents informed of student progress is essential. Besides report cards, the most common strategy teachers use is the tried-and-true parent-teacher conference. Most schools, in recognition of the importance of this kind of communication, schedule conferences into the school calendar as a regular event once or twice a year.

These conferences often prove very unsatisfactory to both parties. Some schools have difficulty encouraging parents to come. It's common to hear teachers bemoan the obvious. "The parents who come are the parents I don't need to see!" When parents do come to typical teacher conferences, the experience can be frustrating. They can expect to wait in the hallway for 10 to 20 minutes, see the teacher for a brief 10 minutes, leave with very little new information, and go home to an anxious student. ("What did she say about me?") For the most part, a traditional conference serves as an opportunity for parents and teachers to touch bases and for parents to communicate, "I care about how my child is doing; please let me know if problems arise."

Because of the short time that is usually scheduled for traditional conferences—during which parents and teachers have to get to know one another as well as get down to business about the student work they have come to discuss—they rarely serve the purposes for which they were established: meaningful discussion of student progress, assessing student work, sharing information about student strengths, identifying areas of concern, and planning for needed assistance.

The student-led conference is one solution to the problem of time because multiple conferences can occur simultaneously. Students with one or more adults—meeting all around the classroom—can have up to 30 minutes to look at and discuss actual student work samples. Appropriately enough, students are the focus of these conferences. They are responsible to assess their own performance—and to explain that assessment to their parents.

Taking a Risk That Paid Off: Student-Led Conferences in Kindergarten

by Kim McCord, Teacher, Lumberport Elementary School

I stepped out on a limb and decided to try student-led conferences with my kindergartners. I had my doubts that they would remember what the papers in their portfolios were about or if they would actually take the time to explain each piece to their parents. Wow! I was amazed at what they could do.

The benefits of the student-led conferences are unbelievable. They clearly build pride and responsibility among students. In addition, we saw parents we hadn't seen in years. The children literally pulled them in.

The schedule. In a three-hour period, we had 14 thirty-minute conferences. Each student began with introductions. Then, at computer stations with their parents, they demonstrated a lesson from our computer network. Many of the parents were amazed that the children could access the network and pull up their own lesson. The students followed directions so well. I had explained that since their parents didn't have headphones and couldn't hear the computer, the students would have to tell their parents what they were doing on the computer. One little boy repeated every single word that the computer said, "This is the letter L. L, L, L. That is the sound for L. Now you try." What a character!

> I realized that my child had learned many things. The student-led conference gave me a chance to learn about my child's routine and become part of what she does on a daily basis. I think it made my child feel very important to play the part of the teacher.
>
> —Parent of Kindergarten Student, Lumberport Elementary School

Next, students rotated through two centers with activities and learning games on them—one for math and the other for beginning reading. Finally, students presented their portfolios. They took such pride in explaining their work to their parents. They were extremely careful to discuss each and every page in great detail. After a successful conference, students and siblings headed off for refreshments while the parents completed an evaluation.

Modifications. A few parents couldn't attend due to conflicting work schedules. We scheduled dates for these makeup conferences. One couple couldn't find a time that they could come to the school. One of our teachers has agreed to "play Mom" and attend the conference in place of the parents. Every child will have had the opportunity to talk to an interested adult about his or her progress in kindergarten before the year's end.

Parent reactions. All of the parents were very positive about this way of conducting conferences; they all agreed they would like to do it again. Listen to some of their comments concerning what they liked best about the student-led conference: "It helped my child feel important and proud." "I see now that he can be a leader." "Sharing time with my son and having him tell me what he has learned." "Doing the activities together." "Everything!!!" "My child was able to show me what he could do. He was full of pride because he was involved in this conference." "That my child showed me his work instead of the teacher." "He got to show me what he could do on his own."

Spreading the word to the rest of our professional community. As it happened, our faculty senate met the very next day. Our principal, Mr. Van Meter, had asked our Quest team to present on SMART learners. In talking about promoting student responsibility, I told of my experience from the night before and shared my evaluation data and a short video. I believe many other teachers at Lumberport will be conducting student-led conferences in the future.

From Portfolios to Student-Led Conferences: Making a Successful Transition

by Alice Phillips, Teacher, Sewanee Elementary School

I have worked with student portfolios for about six years. Although each year I do something a little different, I feel pretty comfortable with them. This year, students organized their portfolios by subject in a three-ring binder. Although notebooks don't accommodate actual projects and performances, there's always a written component to such things that can be included.

Each notebook begins with a baseline section in which students include their "firsts"—math problem solving, cursive writing, geography challenge, Reading Response Journal entry, and so on. Then every week when papers go home, students select papers to keep. My only rule is that on each paper, students must write a statement that explains *why* they selected it and what knowledge or skills are demonstrated in the chosen paper. This is still a big struggle—for students to engage in the metacognitive task of analyzing their own learning and to articulate that learning in writing. As I write this story in March of the school year, some students still have to rewrite vague or unclear statements of learning.

At a Quest symposium in the summer, I attended a session on student-led conferences and was determined to use it as a method for students to share their portfolios with their parents. By fall conference time, however, I didn't feel ready. Instead I took a step in that direction: student-participant conferences. In conferences that included students, parents, and myself, I modeled for students what I hoped they would do in the spring. I used the student portfolios to talk to parents about their children's learning and progress. Afterward, I asked parents to share their perceptions of how it went. The response was generally enthusiastic, with lots of appreciation for the portfolios and what they showed about the children and their learning. I told the children then and there that *they* would be leading the parent conferences in the spring.

I gave myself just over three weeks to help prepare students to lead the conferences. Students reviewed their entire portfolio collection, selecting three pieces from "literacy" and two from all other subject areas. Working with students, I helped them create a full-page entry slip for each selected work. We struggled to find a strategy for discussion and decided on four categories: best work, hardest work, most improved work, and something I want to work on. On each page, students had to write (1) what they had learned, (2) what they were proud of, and (3) what they wanted to set as goals.

Final preparations involved readying the room. Our student desks were arranged in groups of four for cooperative learning teams. This arrangement allowed adequate space for each conference. We covered each grouping of desks with bright-colored bulletin board paper, put a little flower in the center, and we were ready!

In my introductory letter to parents, I had explained what would happen during the course of this "new" way of conferencing. I asked each to sign up for one of three blocks of time: 3:00, 4:00, or 5:00. What a difference from the standard 10-minute slot! The day of conferences arrived, and I found I was a bit nervous. It couldn't have gone any better! Some parents stayed for 45 minutes; others were done in about 15. I greeted each family, ushered them to a table, and assured them I would come back to answer any questions they had before they left. I was able to talk to every parent who attended. No one had to wait, bored, with nothing to do. Everyone seemed pleased about the strategy; the energy level was high.

The children wrote thank-you notes to their parents the next day. Most wrote about how proud they were of themselves and how proud their parents were of them! We had 100 percent attendance, including the two families who, because they couldn't attend the day of the conferences, came in the very next day.

My opinion? I'll never do it the old way again!

Assessment in the Learning Organization: Shifting the Paradigm by Arthur L. Costa and Bena Kallick (Alexandria, VA: ASCD, 1995).

Costa and Kallick consider how schools must change their approach to both organizational and individual assessment if they are to become learning communities. A primary theme running through this book is the importance of feedback for improved performance. The authors illustrate the extent to which feedback needs to flow through organizations in a spiral; they also provide practical strategies for introducing this concept to schools. They further espouse authentic assessment, especially portfolio assessment. The content of the book is wide-ranging—moving from classroom instruction to professional development to whole-school reform. This is a potentially valuable resource for any school rethinking its approach to assessment.

Are We Creating SMART Learners: Interview Design[51]

Interview Design is a process in which all participants ask questions, answer questions, and analyze responses.

Purposes
- to quickly generate and analyze data from a large group of participants on a number of questions
- to balance and increase participant involvement in (1) collecting information, (2) analyzing data, and (3) reporting conclusions

Time Required
The process can be completed in 1 to 2 hours, depending on the size of the group and the number of questions used.

Group Size
Interview Design has been used effectively with groups ranging in size from 10 to 500 members.

Room Arrangements
For the interview, chairs should be arranged in lines facing one another. The length of the lines should match the number of questions to be posed. (For example, when using four questions, make each line four chairs long.)

For the analysis, chairs should be arranged around tables (one for each question) to accommodate the size of each analysis group.

Materials Needed
For the interview, each participant needs a pen or pencil, a copy of the appropriate question, and a surface upon which to write (e.g., a conference folder or pad of paper).

For the analysis, each group needs easel paper and markers.

Rationale
Interview Design is a powerful way for a group to generate and analyze information on a limited number of key questions. Interview Design promotes the following:
- **Active involvement.** No one can simply sit back and listen.
- **Participant equality.** All answers are recorded anonymously so each person's opinions are given equal consideration regardless of his or her role or position in the organization.
- **Candor.** When people talk in pairs, they tend to be more open and honest.
- **Informality.** The process helps people to get to know one another around a substantive exchange.
- **Objectivity.** Interviewers do not argue or give their own opinions; they ask questions only for clarification.
- **Involvement in analysis.** Instead of outside experts analyzing data, participants experience the difficulty of consolidating the data to a few key points. Participants learn about diversity and similarity of viewpoints in the large group.
- **Excitement and energy.** As the interview phase progresses, the noise level increases.

Description of the Process
Develop the questions. Questions must be developed beforehand, once the specific content is identified. Good interview design questions require careful crafting. It is helpful to ask respondents for a specific number of ideas. Questions can also direct them to organize their responses into useful categories.

Prepare 4 to 10 questions, depending on the number of participants and the time available for this activity. Have extra questions prepared in case the size of the group changes. (See sample questions at the end of these directions.)

Prepare interview sheets. Label each question A, B, C, D, etc., and type each question on a separate sheet of paper. Include these directions to the interviewer and duplicate as many sets of questions as there will be interview lines.

Directions: Using this question, interview the person across from you. Record the responses in the space under the question and on the back of the page. You will have 3 minutes to conduct each interview. You will interview several people one at a time. Record each individual's response even if it is the same as someone's else's. Record each respondent's ideas, not your interpretation. Reread the question to the person you're interviewing as needed.

Arrange the room. Before participants arrive, arrange chairs in facing rows so that participants will face one another in pairs. Rows should be arranged according to the numbers of questions and people. For example, 16 participants might be arranged in 4 lines of 4 (4 questions) or 2 lines of 8 (8 questions). Diagram possible arrangements prior to the workshop.

There are several options if the group size does not conveniently match the number of questions.

a. Have an extra question in one set of rows. This pair will have only two members in their analysis group.

b. Pull a chair up at the end of the nonmoving lines. (See Figure 1.) Now two people work as a team to ask and answer questions. This works especially well as a technique to incorporate latecomers.

c. Use different questions in the rows. For example, suppose there were seven questions (none of which could be deleted without hurting the data collection) and 40 participants. Set up 4 sets of rows, 5 chairs long. In one set of rows, use questions 1-5; in another set, use questions 2-6; in a third, use 3-7; and in a fourth, use 1, 2, 3, 6, and 7. One analysis group will have 8 members; some will have 6 members; all will have at least 4.

It is important to have the full group there on time. You might begin with some other short activity—such as workshop goal-setting—to wait until all arrive. This is a powerful technique because once under way, people cannot duck out without leaving a visible gap in the interview chain.

To conserve time and eliminate confusion, distribute the questions after the chairs are arranged but before the participants move into the chairs. Remind people to leave the questions in the chair in which they are found until they receive further directions.

Conduct the interview phase. After people have moved into their chairs, allow time for them to read the directions and their assigned question. Repeat the instructions at the top of each question, stressing that their role—while interviewing—is to listen for

Room Arrangement for Interview Design: 25 participants; 6 questions, A-F

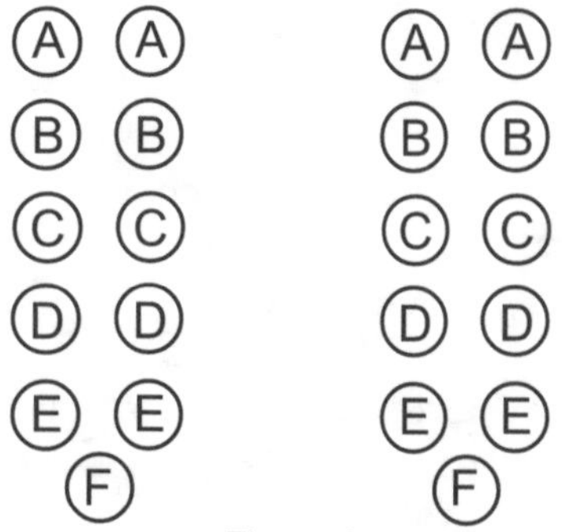

Figure 1

comprehension. They should record everything that is said to them and not ask questions except for clarification. Remind them to record everything that is said even if remarks duplicate something said earlier.

People are now ready to begin interviewing. The diagram and following description give an idea of the progression of the interview process:

1. Select one row in each set of rows and ask people in these selected rows to begin by posing their question to the person they are facing. Remind them to record the responses carefully. After 3-5 minutes, call time. Announce that it is now time for the respondents to become interviewers. Note that the interviewer and respondent have the same question, which means the interviewer will now respond to the same question he just asked. This allows each to get comfortable with their question and with the interview process. (Allow somewhat more time during this first round of interviewing.)

2. Designate one of the rows the "movers" and the facing row the "sitters." (It is helpful if the movers have plenty of space to move; sitters can have their backs against the wall, but movers need room to get in and out of chairs.) In the movers' row, everyone should move one seat to the left, and the person at the far left of the movers' row should walk around to the other end of the row. (See Figure 2.) After both people facing each other have asked and answered their questions, it is again time to move. Continue in this manner until everyone has responded to all the questions.

Conduct the analysis phase. After the interviewing, all those individuals who were asking the same question assemble and compare their responses. Without overly emphasizing their own views, they should try to identify the major themes. If the question asks for 3 or 4 ideas, they should strive to identify the top 6 rather than listing all responses. This keeps the reports brief. The worksheets can be collected for further analysis by workshop staff for those ideas that are insightful but were not mentioned by others. After the analysis, each group should write its question on the top of a flip chart and the responses below. This phase takes from 10 to 20 minutes, depending on the size of the groups.

An alternate method of summarizing data: Ask people to move one last time—to meet with their original questioning partner. As a pair, they review the responses they obtained and prepare a summary that captures the most frequent responses. After 5 to 10 minutes, ask these pairs to meet with other pairs who had the same question. As a group, they compare their summaries and make a consolidated list of frequent responses. In the interest of time, the facilitator may want to limit the number they will report out to the entire group. Each question-analysis group should summarize its responses on a flip chart or overhead transparency.

Conduct the reporting phase. Each group should report briefly, perhaps 2 or 3

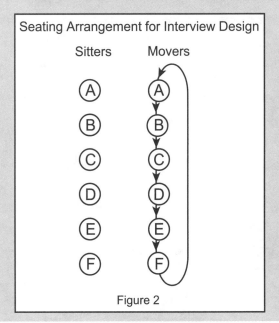

Seating Arrangement for Interview Design

Figure 2

minutes. Questions can be held until the end or taken after each report. The charts can be typed and distributed as a quick record of the key points.

Sample Interview Design Questions

1. What if there were no grades or achievement test scores? How would we then measure and report student success in school? What criteria would we use?

2. What kinds of classroom practices tend to extinguish intrinsic motivation? What kinds of problems might you encounter if you tried to eliminate such practices?

3. In what ways are students allowed and encouraged to become independent learners? What specific skills and attitudes does your school attempt to develop in students to facilitate their becoming continuous, lifelong learners?

4. What does it look and sound like in a classroom where teachers are trying to help their students develop initiative and responsibility?

5. What kinds of practices encourage student reflection and thoughtfulness during the course of a school day? How prevalent are these in your school?

Questions for Reflection

- Do teachers in this school create classroom environments that promote active engagement and risk-taking on the part of students?

- Do teachers hold high performance expectations for all students and provide academic support to help students meet these standards?

- Does the instrinsic motivation of students increase as they move through this school? Are policies and practices designed to nurture and develop intrinsic motivation?

- Do adults in this school hold a common expectation regarding student responsibility for learning behavior?

- Do teachers value student questions? Are they intentional in nurturing and supporting student questioning?

- Are our students learning how to learn—developing the skills and habits required for lifelong learning?

- Do teachers engage in problem-based learning and use other strategies designed to help students link academic learnings to real-world situations?

Notes

1. Goleman, *Emotional Intelligence,* 89-90.

2. Perkins, *Smart Schools,* 65.

3. Elmore, Peterson, and McCarthy, *Restructuring in the Classroom,* 4.

4. Fried, *The Passionate Teacher,* 182-83. For a description of student-led conferences, see "Student-Led Conferences: A New Twist on a Familiar Strategy" near the end of this chapter.

5. Perkins, *Smart Schools,* 7-8.

6. See Perkins, *Smart Schools.*

7. Barell, *Teaching for Thoughtfulness,* 6.

8. For a more complete description of these materials, see "Workshop Series: Doing Your Part to Help Your Child Become SMART" in chapter one. See also Walsh, Sattes, and Hickman.

9. QUILT is an acronym for Questioning and Understanding to Improve Learning and Thinking. Stories about QUILT can be found in "School as Community" in chapter one and "Professional Development to Enrich the Learning Culture" in chapter three, or see the QUILT Web page at http://www.ael.org/rel/quilt.

10. Structured Reflection Protocol is one of four strategies presented in the *Self-Study Toolkit* produced by the Regional Educational Laboratory Network Program. Stories about the use of this process can be found throughout this book. The protocol process was originally introduced to us in *Horace* (November 1996, Vol. 13, No. 2), a document produced by the Coalition of Essential Schools in Providence, RI. It promotes collaborative reflection and analysis. It is more fully described in "The Pot of Gold at the End of the Rainbow" in chapter two.

11. See the story "MicroSociety as a Culture: Bringing the Real World Into the School" in chapter one. For more information about the program, visit the MicroSociety Web site at http://www.microsociety.org.

12. See Caine and Caine, *Teaching and the Human Brain,* 128.

13. Reported in *Brain-Based Learning* by Eric Jensen, 150.

14. Gary Lamb can be reached at http://www.garylamb.com or by e-mail at music@garylamb.com.

15. "Tooty Ta" is an energizer included in the CD *Dr. Jean and Friends,* copyright 1998, by Jean Feldman. For more information, contact 770-396-9249, 360 Aldenshire Place, Atlanta, GA 30350.

16. The Inside-Outside Fishbowl is more fully described in chapter one.

17. For more information about the Teaching/Learning Mapping Strategy, its Web-based Curriculum Mapping and Design Tool, or Interdisciplinary Teamed Instruction, contact Becky Burns at AEL. Phone 800-624-9120, send e-mail to burnsb@ael.org, or visit the Web site at http://www.ael.org.

18. See information on the legendary *Foxfire* story in "School Within Community" in chapter one.

19. See the story "MicroSociety as a Culture: Bringing the Real World Into the School" in chapter one for more information about the MicroSociety program. Visit the MicroSociety Web site at http://www.microsociety.org.

20. Knowles, *The Adult Learner: A Neglected Species,* 58.

21. See Hickman and Wigginton, *Catch Them Thinking in Social Studies.*

22. See Vaill, *Learning as a Way of Being.*

23. See Gardner, *Frames of Mind.* Others have translated Gardner's ideas of multiple intelligences into classroom applications.

24. Adapted with permission from the work of J. Hazel and H. Oeschner, Tempe, AZ, National Education Association Learning Lab, 1994; revised by AEL, 2000.

25. Comments made during a student focus group at a rally of the Quest High School Network, Roanoke, VA, February 2000.

26. Schlechty, *Inventing Better Schools,* 37-39.

27. McLaughlin and Talbert, "Introduction: New Visions of Teaching," 1.

28. Wiggins and McTighe, *Understanding by Design,* 28.

29. See Perkins, *Outsmarting IQ.*

30. Ohler, "Art Becomes the Fourth R", 17.

31. The Socratic Seminar is described as a form of structured discourse about ideas and moral dilemmas. Socratic Seminars contribute to the development of vocabulary, listening skills, interpretive and comparative reading, textual analysis, synthesis, and evaluation—predominantly higher level thinking skills. Perhaps the greatest advantage of the Socratic Seminar is that it reinforces the formation of the classroom as a learning community. See the following Web sites for more information:
http://sitebuilder.liveuniverse.com/seminars/whatisSS.html
http://sitebuilder.liveuniverse.com/seminars/research/benchmarks.html
http://sitebuilder.liveuniverse.com/seminars/whatsay.html

32. Perkins, *Outsmarting IQ,* 12-15.

33. Researchers at Harvard School of Education's Project Zero have focused on connections between neuroscience and learning. Several cognitive scientists have published books on the topic: D. Perkins, *Outsmarting IQ: The Emerging Science of Learnable Intelligence* (San Francisco: Jossey-Bass, 1995); H. Gardner, *Frames of Mind: The Theory of Multiple Intelligences* (New York: Basic Books, 1983); J. Healy, *Failure to Connect: How Computers Affect Our Children's Minds for Better and Worse* (New York: Simon and Schuster, 1998).

34. Bruer, *Schools for Thought,* 27-28.

35. We learned about "truth signs" from the book, *Inspiring Active Learning: A Handbook for Teachers,* by Merrill Harmin, Alexandria, VA: ASCD, (1994).

36. Lumsden, *Communicating in Groups and Teams,* 244.

37. Barell, *Teaching for Thoughtfulness,* 51.

38. Francis P. Hunkins describes Christenberry's "Questioning Circle" in *Teaching Thinking Through Effective Questioning,* Boston: Christopher-Gordon Publishers, Inc., 1989.

39. See Barell, *Teaching for Thoughtfulness.*

40. See Barell, *Teaching for Thoughtfulness.*

41. Mindmapping strategies are outlined in Joyce Wycoff's book, *Mindmapping,* New York: Berkeley Publishing Group, 1991.

42. Lumsden, *Communicating in Groups and Teams,* 244.

43. Barell, *Teaching for Thoughtfulness,* 82.

44. Ibid, 83.

45. Ibid.

46. *Wait Time* is a term coined by Mary Budd Rowe. She identified two points in classroom questioning where a teacher's intentional pausing, or silence, can stimulate student thinking. Wait Time I is a pause after posing the question—before a student responds. Rowe recommends 3 to 5 seconds as optimal. Wait Time II is the pause after a student answers a question—before the teacher speaks. In most classrooms, Wait Time II is nonexistent; Rowe found 3 to 5 seconds to be optimum for benefits to student learning. See article by Mary Budd Rowe, "Wait Time: Slowing Down May Be A Way of Speeding UP!" in *Journal of Teacher Education,* January-February 1986, vol. 37, no. 1, 43-50.

47. Interesting links about mindmapping with examples:
http://www.thinksmart.com/productmindmapexcerpt.html
http://artfolio.com/pete/MindMaps/Uses.html
http://www.buzan.co.uk/cgi-bin/nav.pl?doc=Welcome.nav&uid=521057
http://www.thinksmart.com/bookpages/creativityskills.html
http://mindman.com/
http://www.inspiration.com/

48. See de Bono, *Six Thinking Hats.*

49. Wiggins, *Educative Assessment,* 13.

50. Stories about Structured Reflection Protocol as professional development can be found throughout this book. The process is fully described in chapter two.

51. The Interview Design Process was introduced to us by Oralie McAfee, from Colorado Northern State University, presently in private consulting from Evergreen, CO. She learned of it from The Wharton School, Management and Behavioral Science Center.

Appendixes

Descriptions of Schools in the Quest Elementary and Secondary Networks

Alexander Elementary School

Earl Wiman, Principal
900 North Highland Avenue
Jackson, TN 38301
901-422-1841
Fax: 901-424-4801

Principal Earl Wiman knows every child by name, and he meets each one with an armload of love and high expectations every day. Wiman and his staff pride themselves on meeting the needs of each child while teaching the value of hard work and good behavior. Located in the heart of inner-city Jackson, Tennessee, the school, with an enrollment of 530 students (73 percent African American and 27 percent White), serves its immediate neighborhood and an extended attendance area approximately five miles away. Sixty-three percent of the students receive free and reduced-price lunch in this Title I school. Class size is approximately 20 in grades K-2, and 24 in grades 3-5. The faculty includes 24 classroom teachers; three special education teachers; two computer lab managers; one coordinator for technology, parents and other volunteers; a full-time librarian; a guidance counselor; and a physical education teacher. Area specialists teach art, music, and foreign language classes. Reading takes top priority at Alexander, and the inviting library explains why students often break records for prolific reading.

The school, a charming, inviting place, even though it has seen years of usefulness, serves as a model for special education inclusion and Title I services. All of Alexander's bright, cheerful classrooms boast Internet access and accelerated reader capabilities. Alexander teachers extend the school day for at-risk students and provide a rich variety of instructional materials throughout the school day for all learners.

Staff development plays a large part in the life of the school. Training in AEL's QUILT program (Questioning and Understanding to Improve Learning and Thinking) has been provided for all teachers; parenting and technology training are provided by a full-time coordinator.

What makes this school work for students? You can spot Alexander students wherever you meet them, because they know they are special! Wiman instills in each faculty and staff member his belief that all kids are special and all kids can learn; he and his staff communicate that belief and that energy to the students. This translates into a student body that radiates self-confidence and enthusiasm, and celebrates success joyously.

Atenville Elementary School

Darlene Dalton, Principal
Route 2, Box 28
Harts, WV 25524
304-855-3173
Fax: 304-855-3713

Atenville Elementary School in rural Harts, West Virginia, is a school with a vision—and a school with a faculty that refuses to take failure as anything but a challenge to work harder and do better. This small (192 students) pre-K to 6 school provides a plethora of services that enriches the lives of students and their families in a community in which the only two major employers are the coal mine and Wal-Mart. Principal Darlene Dalton reports that free and reduced-price lunch participation, although high, is down from 83 percent to 73 percent since Wal-Mart came to town! Attendance is good at 94 percent, but Dalton and her staff think it should be better and have initiated a plan to keep kids in school. The 15-member faculty works diligently to find added resources and approaches that succeed in raising the expectations of the students.

Two programs in particular have enriched academic and social life at Atenville. The school currently enjoys the benefits of a 21st Century Community Learning Centers grant for *After-School Smarts in Harts*, which provides academic enrichment while expanding cultural horizons and sharpening technology skills for children and their parents. The school also has embraced the MicroSociety program as an umbrella for learning practical skills that will follow the children into the workplace as they grow older. Students report increased enthusiasm for learning as a result of participating in both programs.

Cave Spring High School

Martha Cobble, Principal
3712 Chaparral Drive, SW
Roanoke, VA 24018
540-722-7550
Fax: 540-772-2107

Cave Spring High School in Roanoke, Virginia, serves grades 10 through 12 with an enrollment of about 1,250 students. Operating on a traditional seven-period schedule, the program of studies consists of more than 300 courses. In addition to core curriculum classes, instructional areas include labs for technical education, work and family studies, marketing, science, and vocational education, as well as instructional and performance areas for band, chorus, fine arts, and physical education, and a media center. Cave Spring houses several countywide special education programs. Some Cave Spring students are dual-enrolled in the Governor's School for advanced studies in math and science, or at the Burton Technology Center. Four administrators and 100 faculty staff the school.

Cave Spring serves a predominantly suburban, middle-class community, with a substantially homogeneous student body. Approximately 6 percent of the students are identified as minority. Enrollment is fairly stable, with a rate of student mobility approaching 10 percent. Three percent of students receive free and reduced-price lunch; and 15 percent participate in special education programs. The drop-out rate is reported as less than 2 percent. Approximately 95 percent of graduating seniors enroll in postsecondary programs. The SAT (Scholastic Aptitude Test) scores for Cave Spring are the highest in the county (Verbal=539, Math=533). Parents actively participate in school programs.

Central High School

C. B. Haskins, Principal
Route 2, Box 63
Victoria, VA 23974
804-696-2137
Fax: 804-696-1322

Central High School, located in Victoria, Virginia, serves a rural population of 575 students. According to Principal C. B. Haskins, the area is so isolated that no major highways pass through the town, which boasts only one stoplight. The students (51 percent White and 49 percent African American) represent families in which there is extremely high unemployment and severe economic depression. Fifty-seven percent of Central students receive free and reduced-price lunches. Class size averages 22.

Despite the fact that the area offers little opportunity for economic advancement, these students perform well on standardized tests and on the state-mandated SOLs (Standards of Learning). Principal Haskins credits a "super dedicated faculty" that takes extra time after school to help students and a strong guidance department for much of the school's success. Central High School teachers are totally student oriented, and they support students in both academic and social endeavors. Central and South Harrison High School, both Quest participants, have adopted one another as sister schools.

East Dale Elementary School

Janet Crescenzi, Principal
Route 3
Fairmont, WV 26554
304-367-2132
Fax: 304-366-2522

Principal Janet Crescenzi proudly announces that East Dale Elementary in Fairmont, West Virginia, boasts the greatest quantity and the most up-to-date technology of any school in her county. This K-6 school, with an enrollment of 593 students (less than one percent minority), also faces some of the problems reported by other rural Quest schools—high unemployment among parents due to the shutting down of the coal mine and high free and reduced-price lunch participation (50 percent).

The remarkable thing about East Dale, however, is that, despite the socioeconomic status of its community, the school has forged ahead to acquire the things students need to succeed. Crescenzi points out that the school raised the funds and built its own hands-on science/math lab for students. With that acquisition as an impetus, East Dale applied for and received a $386,000 Dwight D. Eisenhower Mathematics and Science Education National Program grant to equip and train teachers. (This grant is part of more than $1 million in grants the school has earned over the past 10 years.) Community partners First Exchange Bank and Mont Levine Steel Producers assist the school in providing resources for students and teachers. All teachers receive intensive training in the use of technology as a teaching/learning tool. As a result of East Dale's dogged persistence in seeking to enhance school offerings, 77.5 percent of its students rank in the top two quartiles of the SAT-9 test scores. The school has been named a National School of Excellence and a West Virginia University/Benedum Foundation Professional Development School.

Highland County Elementary School

Randy Hooke, Principal
Meyer-Moon Road
Monterey, VA 24465
540-468-2181
Fax: 540-468-2184

Located in Monterey, Virginia, immaculately landscaped Highland County Elementary School shares its campus and building with Highland County Middle School and Highland County High School. Located in an area that is almost entirely national forest, Highland is the sole K-5 school in the county, with a total enrollment of 161 students. The Highland County community is considered middle to low income, and 32 percent of Highland students receive free and reduced-price lunches. The student population includes no minority students. Three to four percent of the students receive special education services. The average class size is 18 students.

What strikes the visitor to Highland County Elementary is the closely knit community, the sense of family that defines the school. No one can doubt that Highland County students benefit from warm and caring teachers who nurture their progress gently and lovingly throughout their academic careers. The annual Maple Festival, which celebrates the harvest of maple syrup each spring, draws thousands of tourists into the school and provides financial as well as cultural benefits for the students.

Lumberport Elementary School

Norman Van Meter, Principal
P. O. Box 417
Chestnut & Lydon Streets
Lumberport, WV 26386
304-584-4010
Fax: 304-584-5943

Lumberport Elementary School in Lumberport, West Virginia, one of 25 Harrison County schools, serves 337 students who come from predominantly middle- to low-income families. Sixty-three percent of the students receive free and reduced-price lunches. The school population is 100 percent White, and 29 percent of the students qualify for special education services. The school staff includes a principal, 15 teachers, and eight full-time specialists and resource teachers. Eight part-time professionals and 10 support personnel complete the staff.

As a result of Lumberport's participation in Quest, the school leadership team decided to take a long, hard look at what was actually happening in the school. The resulting video, when shared with the faculty, provided the impetus for real inside-out change for this school, as faculty realized their school offered a combination of rich traditions and exciting innovations to celebrate as well as practices in need of improvement. The faculty and staff that have emerged have formed tight bonds and strong vision in the quest for revitalization of this school. One exciting showcase for highlighting student work is Lumberport's "morning meetings," which give students and teachers a chance to share their successes with the entire school community.

Man High School

William Carter, Principal
800 East McDonald Avenue
Man, WV 25635
304-583-6521
Fax: 304-583-6566

Like several other Quest schools, Man High School in Man, West Virginia, represents a small town where school is the hub of the community. Each day 384 students in grades 10-12 travel from outlying areas to attend Man. The school reports low minority enrollment (less than 3 percent); high free and reduced-price lunch participation (49 percent), good attendance (94.6 percent), and a low drop-out rate (2.5 percent). The staff of 32 full-time teachers, two itinerant teachers, two administrators, a counselor, and a dean comprise the instructional staff. Parent involvement in this small-town school is incredible, with 84 percent of parents working in some fashion with the school program.

Man High School focuses on developing each student to his or her fullest potential, on maximizing talents, and on providing support systems to help students make good choices. In a community that reports high percentages of tobacco use and no nearby entertainment for teens (the nearest movie theater is 15 miles away!), the school has developed an amazingly strong community service program to keep students busy and to teach them to care for their fellow citizens. Programs such as Meals on Wheels and the Community Lab provide opportunities for students to earn a total of 60 hours of community service (10 hours in ninth grade, 10 hours in tenth, and 20 hours each in eleventh and twelfth grades) in order to graduate.

The newly adopted school curriculum also mandates higher expectations for students. All tenth-grade students must complete Applied Communication, a writing, speaking, and listening class. All Man students now choose an academic cluster, or major, which prepares them for the Professional Level (college prep), Entry Level (business), or Skill Level (vocational/business). Each student receives services from SAT, the Student Assistance Team, which monitors and assesses students in planning and tracking their progress throughout their high school years.

Natcher Elementary School

Connie Allen, Principal
1434 Cave Mill Road
Bowling Green, KY 42104
270-842-1364
Fax: 270-842-1563

William H. Natcher Elementary School in Bowling Green, Kentucky, serves a middle- to upper-class population of 800 students in grades pre-K through 6. The lush surroundings, complete with hiking and exercise trails and a Monet pond, welcome visitors to the school. The cozy atmosphere prevails, from the living-room feel of the lobby throughout the 33 classrooms and numerous special subject instruction areas. Two administrators, 30 classroom teachers, 18 full- and part-time specialists, 11 instructional assistants, and 15 support staff members make their indelible contributions to the nurturing environment for youngsters.

Natcher serves students from an economically diverse area, with approximately 22 percent of the students eligible for free and reduced-price lunch. Sixteen percent of the students represent racial or ethnic minority groups; less than 3 percent are considered Limited English Proficient; and approximately 9 percent receive special education services. Average class size is 24. Average daily attendance approaches 97 percent.

The thing most characteristic of Principal Connie Allen and her staff is their fierce dedication to continuous improvement. Allen's philosophy: We've never "arrived." We must always seek better ways to help children.

The halls form a virtual gallery for the display of student work. The "we celebrate our students" message reverberates into every corner of this school. Today, Natcher stands as a shining example throughout the state of a school that has responded to the Kentucky Education Reform Act (KERA) not merely as an outside mandate but as an opportunity to bring about improvement from within.

Our Lady of Fatima School

Marcia McDonald, Principal
535 Norway Avenue
Huntington, WV 25705
304-523-2861
Fax: 304-525-0390

The Diocese of West Virginia established Our Lady of Fatima to serve K-8 students in the Huntington, West Virginia, area. Fatima's enrollment is just under 200 students, with one classroom per grade. Most students come from professional families of middle- to upper-middle income; 96 percent are White. Principal Marcia McDonald shepherds a young staff of nine classroom teachers, a computer lab manager, art teacher/librarian, and part-time music and physical education teachers. Class size varies from 18 to 26; and performance on the SAT-9 ranges from the 74th percentile (grade 3) to the 89th percentile (grade 5).

What makes Fatima so special? The community that nurtures it supports both school and students in a powerful way. Parents and church community involve themselves in every aspect of the school's academic and enrichment programs, working diligently to raise additional capital to provide the extras that make a child's learning experience memorable. It is not unusual for the PTO to deposit more than $25,000 in the school enrichment account in a year; gifts from the community often add even more. This is a school community where school *is* community; and community *is* school.

Fatima also strives to instill in all its children the importance of love for family and respect for country. Teachers and principal alike never miss the opportunity to teach traditional values of good citizenship, respect, honesty, kindness, and gentleness. A visitor to Fatima comes away with the feeling that this school and its inhabitants epitomize the old phrase "sweet spirit."

Sewanee Elementary School

Mike Maxon, Principal
P. O. Box 696
209 University Avenue
Sewanee, TN 37375
931-598-5951
Fax: 931-598-0943

Sewanee Elementary School occupies a unique place in our line-up of Quest schools. Located in Sewanee, Tennessee, home of The University of the South and the children of its professors, the school also serves a community that is rural and somewhat isolated. The K-6 school enrolls 235 students, with two classes at each grade level. Fourteen classroom teachers, along with five education assistants and special-subject teachers, provide the core academic curriculum, art, music, physical education, and special education classes. This charming school, constructed in 1924 and often expanded and renovated, boasts a stable faculty, nearly half of whom have earned advanced degrees.

Racial diversity (2 percent) and free and reduced-price lunch participation (27 percent) are low at Sewanee. Class size averages 18, and attendance is good (95 percent). Students test in the upper ranges (72 percent of fourth-grade students performed at the competent level or higher on the 1998 writing assessment). The greatest challenge faced by the Sewanee staff involves meshing the needs and wants of a university community with those of the outlying rural community.

Over the years, grand traditions have enriched the learning environment at Sewanee. The Castle of Learning supplies one of the most spectacular points of interest in the school. Located in the center of the school, this "real" castle promotes the learning theme of the moment. Here, children gather to celebrate and learn about each new season in their learning cycle as they view elaborate displays and "teasers" that entice them to expand their natural curiosity. The Castle of Learning represents the Sewanee teachers' dedication to promoting individual inquiry and responsible learning habits in every child.

South Harrison High School

Jerry McKeen, Principal
Route 1, Box 58
School Street
Lost Creek, WV 26385
304-745-3315
Fax: 304-745-4292

South Harrison High School in Lost Creek, West Virginia, serves students in grades 9 through 12, and reports an enrollment of 480 students. This 32-classroom school houses labs for home arts, computer science, business, music, and physical education, in addition to core curriculum areas. Two administrators, 36 teachers, eight specialists, 16 support staff, and one paraprofessional staff the school.

Student population is homogeneous, with less than one percent minority enrollment. The students live in predominately rural, low- to low-middle income homes; and 40 percent are eligible for free and reduced-price meals. Attendance is good (96 percent) and the drop-out rate is low (2.2 percent). Eighty-five percent of recent graduates continue their education, with 55 percent attending four-year colleges or universities.

When South Harrison decided to adopt the block-scheduling concept, administrators and faculty knew they wanted additional professional development to make classes more interesting and engaging for students. Embracing Quest wholeheartedly as a means for studying hands-on learning and cross-disciplinary curriculum integration, the school sent two teams of teachers to rallies. These teams, dubbed the "dynamic duo" by their Quest colleagues, returned to South Harrison with fire in their souls as they kindled an energy and a passion to infuse vitality into a tired curriculum. Out of their enthusiasm, programs such as SHOlympics, which celebrates academic success, and the Appalachian Festival, which honors the local culture and history, have translated that energy into student learning and leadership at South Harrison.

University School

Don Gresso, Principal
East Tennessee State University
Box 70632
Johnson City, TN 37614
423-439-4333
Fax: 423-439-5921

East Tennessee State University established University School to provide a laboratory setting for students who are enrolled in its School of Education. The K-12 school, with a student body of approximately 550, has established a reputation for its willingness to explore and implement innovative teaching practices and its school climate of mutual respect among students and staff.

University School operates on a year-round schedule, with numerous and varied intersession activities for students. One of the strongest intersession programs, the Learning Academies, provides skill-strengthening classes for those students who wish to use school break to hone their skills in one or more areas.

Woodbridge Senior High School

Karen Spillman, Principal
3001 Old Bridge Road
Woodbridge, VA 22192
703-497-8000
Fax: 703-497-8117

Woodbridge Senior High School, Virginia's largest senior high school, serves 3,000 students, grades 10-12, in its 125-classroom setting. Scattered throughout the school complex, labs for computer science, technology, business and vocational education, and home arts, as well as instructional and performance areas for band, chorus, fine arts, and physical education, tell the visitor Woodbridge offers comprehensive services to its students. Seven administrators, 201 teachers, eight teaching assistants, and 55 classified staff complete the Woodbridge "family."

Woodbridge boasts great diversity in its student body. Sixty-five percent of the students are White, non-Hispanic; 20 percent are African American, 10 percent Hispanic, and 5 percent Asian/Pacific Islander. Because the school serves a large military installation, student mobility is high (19 percent). Many students participate in special programs, including special education (7 percent), ESL (3 percent), gifted (9 percent), and work-study (2.5 percent). Eighty-two percent of the students choose vocational education courses.

The average class size in core academic subjects ranges from 19-25. Average daily attendance approaches 92 percent.

It takes only a moment for a first-time visitor to sense that this is a school *for* kids. Happy kids, eager kids, excited kids feel comfortable in the "skin" of their school because they know they have their say when decisions are made. At Woodbridge the byword is *student empowerment*. Teachers and administrators do not need to "patrol" the halls and common areas because the kids simply take care of their own business. Strikingly, for a school of such size and diversity, graffiti does not exist at Woodbridge!

The Woodbridge learning environment does not close its doors when the last afternoon bell sounds. All over the campus, focused, disciplined student groups—band, sports, student government, clubs—stake out their turf and hone their skills. Woodbridge offers ways for every student to enrich the educational and social experience.

Quest Scholars

Quest Scholars

Connie Allen
Principal
William H. Natcher Elementary School

Pamela Brown
Former Principal
Woodbridge Senior High School

Darlene Dalton
Principal
Atenville Elementary School

Cheryl Dingess
Speech Pathologist
Atenville Elementary School

Maria Fernandez
Parent
William H. Natcher Elementary School

Mary Ann Hardebeck
Assistant Principal
Woodbridge Senior High School

Vickie Luchuck
Teacher and Parent
Lumberport Elementary School

Jackie McCann
Teacher
Atenville Elementary School

Barbara McFall
Parent
Cave Spring High School

Randy Meck
Teacher
Cave Spring High School

Alice Phillips
Teacher
Sewanee Elementary School

Katherine Ralston
Teacher
Highland County High School

Angela Simms
Student
Woodbridge Senior High School

Ann Watkins
Principal
Sewanee Elementary School

Stacy Watson
Teacher
Alexander Elementary School

Brenda Williamson
Principal
Man High School

Earl Wiman
Principal
Alexander Elementary School

Sample Observation Forms for Data in a Day

Observed Teacher's Initials: _____ Observer's Initials: _____ Time of Observation: _____

Grade Level of Observed Class: _____ Subject: _____

Describe Lesson Observed (What's happening in the classroom?)

Other observations about the classroom environment:

Possible examples of **"Student Behavior Conducive to Learning"**	Observed examples of **"Student Behavior Conducive to Learning"**	
	+ (Positive) examples	- (non-examples)
Classroom rules are clear and posted		
Students are following classroom rules		
Students are paying attention—listening, looking at teacher, not fidgeting		
Students show respect to one another and to the teacher		
Students doing assigned work		
Students in seats or other appropriate location		
Students answer questions		
Students ask questions		
Students participate fully and eagerly		
Students actively engaged in learning		
Students get along with others in group work		
Students listen to other students' answers		
Consequences are posted and consistently enforced		
Positive feedback given for appropriate behavior		
Students earn points for good behavior		
Doing what you know is right (self-discipline)		
Not talking when others are talking/raising your hand for permission to speak		
Smooth transitions—moving from one task to another is not disruptive		
Students working and discussing in groups appropriately		
Students participating in "fun" learning projects		

Possible examples of "Positive Culture for Learning"	Observed examples of "Positive Culture for Learning"	
	+ (Positive) examples	- (non-examples)
Student work and art are displayed		
Students are engaged in work and at least some of it is "fun" work		
Students participate in discussions		
Positive energy in the school		
People are smiling and friendly		
Teachers have sense of humor		
Teachers happy to help; answer students' questions		
Students and teachers respect one another		
Teachers use a positive tone of voice and positive body language		
Students ask questions; ask for help when needed		
Staff are friendly and approachable		
Colorful, creative bulletin boards and posted materials—related to subject under study		
Lots of books and other resources evident, related to topic of study		
All students are included; no student is ignored		
Staff has a "can-do" attitude		
Staff interact with one another		
The principal is visible around the school, interacting with others		
Plants, animals, and other living things in school		
School people respect the building—no trash, dirt, mud, etc.		
Classroom arrangement is best for learning		

Possible examples of "High Expectations for All Students"	Observed examples of "High Expectations for All Students"	
	+ (Positive) examples	- (non-examples)
Teachers ask questions that cause students to think		
Teachers pose questions that call for creative response modes		
Teacher "reaches" for in-depth answers, prompting and probing—not just settling for the first response		
Work makes students think; it is challenging and interesting		
Teachers show confidence in students and believe they can do the work		
Teachers make sure students understand		
Teachers give extra help when needed		
Students are given the opportunity to re-test as needed		
Students tutor and help other students		
Teachers and students review tests		
Students ask questions		
Teacher has positive attitude; not bored with work		
Students do their best work, not rushing or being sloppy		
Students don't seem frustrated		
Teacher interprets and rephrases textbook		
Teacher expects all students to participate; calls on everyone, even shy and reluctant students		
Students are actively involved in "hands-on" activities		
Classroom aides reinforce learning		
Lessons correlated with state standards and state testing program		
Teachers give good directions/provide adequate time		
Teachers accurately grade assignments and offer appropriate and challenging feedback		

Possible examples of "**Teaching and Learning Strategies That Reach All Students**"	Observed examples of "**Teaching and Learning Strategies That Reach All Students**"	
	+ (Positive) examples	- (non-examples)
Cooperative learning/working in groups		
Hands-on activities/use of manipulatives		
Peer tutoring (students teaching students)		
Reteaching		
Use of computers/technology		
Team teaching		
Not all students get the same assignments		
Students learning in different ways: listening, looking, talking, doing, moving, creating (art)		
Active student engagement/participation		
Students and teacher have a high energy level		
Students assess own work		
Teacher gives students some choice, beginning with what students know		
Teacher checks for understanding		
Teacher brings humor and fun into class		

Possible examples of "Appropriate Student Behavior"	Observed examples of "Appropriate Student Behavior"	
	+ (Positive) examples	- (non-examples)
Classroom rules are clear and posted		
Students get along with others in group work		
1,2,3 Magic used		
Rewards and reinforcements used for good behavior; used consistently and fairly		
School motto taught and used		
Positive student interactions, for example: waiting before speaking, respecting diverse opinions, not making fun of wrong answers, helping others, sharing, keeping hands to selves, not disrupting others who are working, listening, showing respect in tone of voice and words used		
Teachers treat students respectfully: listening, being open-minded, using sincere praise, being positive, (not sarcastic, critical, or belittling)		
Doing what you know is right (self-discipline)		
Not talking when others are talking/raising your hand for permission to speak		
Students learning from one another (modeling appropriate behavior)		
Environment is orderly/people know what is expected and are doing it		

Possible examples of "Culture for Learning/ Academic Focus"	Observed examples of "Culture for Learning/ Academic Focus"	
	+ (Positive) examples	- (non-examples)
Celebrate successes/awards, etc.		
Display student work		
Things are posted in the classroom related to academic learning (bulletin boards and displays not just for display)		
Physical environment (building and classroom) conducive to learning		
Learning centers are utilized		
Classroom arrangement is best for learning		
Students are comfortable "being themselves"/differences are respected		
Students are open to ask questions		
Teachers encourage students		
Teachers praise academic success		
Teachers are creative/use storytelling and other "nonboring" strategies		
Students are doing their work/on-task		
Students obey rules in halls, not just classroom		
Teacher creates atmosphere of warmth, friendliness, caring, and concern		
Lesson objectives written on board		

Possible examples of "High Expectations for All Students, with Appropriate Academic Support"	Observed examples of "High Expectations for All Students, with Appropriate Academic Support"	
	+ (Positive) examples	- (non-examples)
Teachers ask questions that call for student to think at higher levels		
Special services teachers provide help for all students		
Lessons correlated with state testing program		
Use of brain research: warm-ups (activities to get ready for learning); providing breaks		
Teachers show confidence/believe students "can do"		
Teachers give good directions/provide time		
Students take good work to office		
Students show pride in their work/seem to do their best		
Students are self-confident		
Students learn from mistakes		
Teacher uses wait time for all students		
Work is challenging and interesting		
Teacher gives clues/doesn't answer own questions		

SMART Parenting
Excerpts

SMART Parenting

Below are excerpts from a SMART Parenting Series that appeared in Natcher Elementary School's newsletter, *Jaguar Tracks*.

Author Shannon Gottke and Natcher both grant permission to reprint these columns in your own school newsletter with appropriate credit. Questions about these resources may be e-mailed to ShannonGottke@hotmail.com.

Column 1: Becoming SMART(er) Parents

Your child's environment is vitally important to his or her ability to become a SMART learner. For instance, the atmosphere at the table during mealtimes is almost as important as what your child eats. Along with providing healthy, well-balanced menus, a SMART parent will attempt to provide a haven in which true conversations and exchanges can take place.

What can we, as parents, do to ensure that? In this column we will attempt to answer that and other questions. To start with, parents, take away that Game Boy, unplug those headphones, turn off that TV, put away the books and newspapers, and **communicate**—or chat, blab, bump your gums, pontificate, verbalize, rap, even tattle (as long as it's done without malice aforethought!). Classical music turned down low is the only suggested accompaniment to the sound of the voices of your family calmly and encouragingly discussing the day's events. In today's busy society, that time is more precious than ever. When I was a child, lingering around the dinner table was a natural occurrence. It was the time of day when we gathered and shared the day's experiences. Laughter was abundant. Who knew then that what came naturally was going to enrich our brain's capability to learn?

We all know that we can't survive without water, but do we know what role water plays in the learning process? Are we aware of the importance of exercise for increasing and maintaining the high energy and low stress levels needed for optimal learning? And how do we fit it into the busy lives that we all lead these days? What attitudes should we try to instill in our children and how do we go about it? How do we instill a love of reading in our children, and why is it so important?

Column 2: Becoming SMART(er) Parents

The "S" in SMART represents "Successful." As we all know, the normal measures of a student's success are test scores and grades on a report card. This means that someone other than the student is deciding whether he or she has been successful in a learning task. However, neither parents nor teachers can make a student successful. A successful learner must learn to take charge of learning and also participate in evaluating his learning.

People's beliefs about their abilities have a profound effect on those abilities.

—Albert Bandura

One of the most important factors in student success is self-efficacy. Simply put, this is the student's belief that she has mastery over the events of her life and is capable of meeting the challenges that may arise. She must believe that she is the master of her own fate (educationally speaking, that is).

Many parents have probably experienced the fears of children preparing to begin a new school year. A lot of that fear stems from the unknown and the belief that they will be called upon to prove knowledge that they don't yet possess. We, as parents, can help calm that fear by reassuring them that they will be provided with the tools to learn, that it will be up to them to use those tools in the most efficient way, and that we will be there to help them with their choices. In our house it has always helped to voice confidence in their abilities to make good decisions. Discuss the choices that they will face and, if you believe that your children are capable of making good decisions, tell them. When they believe they can do it, they will do it.

This may also lead to a discussion of cause and effect. Sure, it's a theory that we all study in science class, but it's also a concept that needs to be applied to every area of life. For instance, if the "cause" is staying up all night watching a Scooby-Doo marathon and eating Little Debbie Nutty Bars for breakfast the next morning, then the "effect" might be failing the spelling test and, possibly, alienating all your friends with your grouchy mood. It doesn't take long for the concept of cause and effect to take root. At two years of age, my daughter, Jordan, figured out that since Santa came (effect) only after she went to sleep (cause), she would hasten his arrival by going to bed at 3:30 p.m. Even at that age, her reasoning was sound. Children are never too young to learn the principle of cause and effect, and this is especially true in an educational setting. All students can enjoy success if they are willing to make the right choices.

Another important factor in learning success is dealing well with change. Interestingly, a study of people who have lived over 100 years reveals that this is a trait that they all have in common. They learned at an early age to "roll with the punches." It seems to come naturally to some while others have a much harder time adopting this attitude. Some children "think around" a change while others seem to "hit the wall" when something unexpected takes place. We will get into this area more as we discuss the remaining components of SMART.

While we, as parents, cannot *make* our children successful, there are some areas over which we can exert some measure of control. You might wish, for the sake of peace in the house, to call it "gentle persuasion." We can gently persuade our children that an apple makes a better snack than a bag of Count Chocula. We can gently persuade them that taking the dog for a walk would be more beneficial (for both the children and the dog) than watching a rerun of *The Brady Bunch*. We can ever so gently suggest that it might be more productive to study social studies at the dining room table where it's quiet than to set up a study area within five feet of the radio, which is churning out the magic of 107.5.

We can talk to our children and communicate to them that the choices they make on a daily basis will determine their success, in school and in life. We believe in them. Let them know it and help them believe in themselves. Help them understand that their education isn't a huge, scary task to be mastered all at once; it's something that will be accomplished in small steps that they are equipped to take. And we will be right there beside them.

Column 3: Becoming SMART(er) Parents

We have worked our way to the "M" of SMART, and this column will deal with the "motivated" element of the equation. It's easy, as parents, to fall into the habit of over-rewarding our children. Children who receive a reward for every little effort can become dependent on it, and it can sap their intrinsic motivation.

Using behaviorism to control learning is like using an umbrella to control the weather.

—Steven Nordby

There's a huge difference in how the human brain responds to rewards for simple and complex problem-solving tasks. Short-term rewards can temporarily stimulate physical responses, but more complex behaviors, such as learning, are usually impaired, not helped, by rewards. We sometimes make this mistake very early on. I remember, in potty training one of my children (for her sake, I won't mention names), I promised her a sucker "as big as her head" if she would just use the potty. Sure enough, this promise eventually produced . . . shall we say, results. I thought we'd had a huge

breakthrough. However, when nature next called, I quickly realized we were back to square one. Though common sense and fear of cavities told me I couldn't continue down that road, it's hard to walk away from something that works. What I found was that instead of producing results, the promise of rewards began to produce agitation. It was only when I dropped the reward system and began to encourage her in other ways that we got permanent results.

Studies find that simple novelty is one of the greatest motivators. Curiosity or the mere pursuit of information is a reward in itself. We've all seen the delight on the faces of our toddlers when they learn something new. Remember the look on your child's face the first time he wrote his name for you? There's no reason for that delight to diminish as they age. When my eldest daughter was in kindergarten, I was a Daisy Scout leader. One day, as we took on an arduous task, they asked what they would "get" if they did well. Candy? A pencil? A sticker? I told them, no, they would get the "satisfaction of a job well done." After I explained to them that meant they could be proud of themselves for working hard and doing well, they went back to work and rewards weren't mentioned again. Upon completion, I had a roomful of happy, satisfied Daisies.

In education, we have both long- and short-term rewards. Long-term rewards are good grades, pleasing others, and graduation; short-term rewards might be test grades, privileges, and choices, for example. Short-term hooks appear to work well with students who are temporarily unmotivated. If a student goes in and out of "motivating" states and occasionally engages in learning, it's probably temporary. There are many possible causes, but solutions are relatively easy. Learned helplessness, the more chronic and severe demotivation, is very different. For the purposes of this column we will discuss the causes and possible solutions for the more temporary lack of motivation.

One reason for temporary lack of motivation is association from the past. These memories are stored in the middle of the brain and, when triggered, cause the brain to react as if the incident were occurring at that moment. All the same chemical reactions are present. It may be as simple as a teacher's tone of voice or a gesture reminding the student of a previous, disliked teacher. Past failures or embarrassments can be re-triggered by a much smaller event. We all know the feeling. I once made a devastatingly embarrassing comment to the mother of the groom at a wedding and ever since I've been filled with dread when I approach a reception line.

A lack of motivation may also be present-time and environmental: unsuitable learning styles, lack of resources or choice, poor nutrition, etc. These can be addressed individually. If your child is a visual learner, show him as well as tell him what you want him to remember and help him convey his learning style to his teacher. If you don't have access to the resources of the Internet, provide access to the library. Give her a cereal bar instead of a Hershey's bar. You can eat the Hershey's bar! There are many things you can do to help remedy a temporarily unmotivated child.

Thirdly, a temporary lack of motivation

can be caused by the student's relationship with the future. Does the student have clear, well-defined goals? If not, perhaps you could help him or her set some. The learner's belief that he has the ability to learn a subject, in this class, with this teacher, is also critical.

Neuroscientists tell us that the brain makes its own rewards in the form of chemicals that are used to regulate stress and pain. They can produce a natural high. Students who succeed usually feel good and that's enough for them. Rewards are received differently by different children, but when a learning experience is positive, nearly all children respond favorably. Remember that there's a difference between reward and celebration. "Do well and you'll get some M&Ms" is a reward. "You've done so well that I think we should have some M&Ms" is a celebration. Studies have shown that the use of rewards damages intrinsic motivation, but an occasional celebration never hurt anyone!

Provide the proper and necessary tools, help your child set goals, eliminate sarcasm and embarrassment, provide more quality feedback in a variety of ways, and encourage good nutrition. These are the steps to helping your child become and remain a motivated learner. Praise instead of reward, and when you do, be specific. Instead of saying, "That's the most beautiful picture ever drawn," try "I love the mustache on your valentine!" It shows you're paying attention, and it's also reason to celebrate because one important characteristic of a motivated learner is that he's not afraid to take a risk. And what could be riskier than a bearded valentine?

Column 4: Learning to Become SMART(er) Parents

We are now up to the "A" in our exploration of the SMART acronym. As I'm sure we're all aware now, the "A" stands for autonomy. Our goal is to help our children become autonomous learners. Another word for autonomy is "emancipation." Our children can become emancipated from dependence on adults for control and directions. This does not mean that they work in isolation, but they are curious and able to set their own goals for learning. They know how and where to gather the information that will help them solve problems.

Have you ever noticed how much easier it is to do something yourself rather than show another person how it's done? To show how is to risk consumption of your precious time as well as the erosion of your patience. How many of us have washed up, picked up, and put up after our children just because we could accomplish it so much more quickly and easily? It might take us five minutes to pick up a room but take 45 minutes to guide a child through the same process. It's tempting to save the time and trouble, but each time we do it, we rob our children of a potential lesson in independence.

In order to develop autonomy, it is imperative that children be allowed to "muddle through" on their own. A little guidance or "tweaking" on your part may be necessary, as well as a lot of encouragement. This will help them begin to develop confidence in their abilities. Picture this scene: You're sitting on the floor with your very young son and what seems like half an acre of Duplo building blocks. He wants to build a dinosaur, and he wants to "do it by myself." Now, you, with your vast experience and superior knowledge, can see trouble in the making. You know that, as a rule, Duplo dinosaurs require at least two legs in order to stand erect, and it's painfully obvious that this dinosaur is missing something vital to its balance. Keep your hands to yourself and hold your tongue, unless he asks for advice. He will figure it out on his own, and the next time, he'll not only do a little better but he'll have the pride that goes along with having learned a lesson on his own. Praise and encourage the process, and he will grow to enjoy it more and more.

Try to remember and to remind your child that "there's more than one way to skin a rabbit." When our daughters were in first and second grade, they brought home problem-solving projects to be done by the family. You can imagine the scenario: Dad's an engineer and Mom's a . . . well, Mom! (Though I feel compelled to interject here that in some circles I'm known as "Mechanical Mom.") Our approaches to the problems were completely different, but, lo and behold, the problems got solved! The projects were designed to teach exactly what they did teach: there are many approaches to a problem, and the end result is all that matters. That's a life lesson that we all need to be reminded of sometimes. Think around it, over it, under it, or straight through it . . . just think! Knowing that she doesn't have to "hit the wall" at the first sign of trouble enables your child to relax and approach a problem with more confidence.

On another note, some of you probably remember when your children came home talking about the importance of drinking enough water during the day, and you may have noticed water bottles appearing on student desks throughout the building (something strictly forbidden when I was a student). Well, all of us know that we need water to live. It's also had many other claims to fame for everything from curing bad breath to flushing away cellulite. But, until I started reading *Teaching with the Brain in Mind*, I didn't fully realize the connection between water and learning. Because it was such a revelation to me, I want to take a minute to share it with you. Thirst is, of course, a drop in the water content of your blood, resulting in a higher concentration of salt. This higher concentration causes the release of fluids from cells into the bloodstream. That, in turn, raises blood pressure and stress levels. Within five minutes of drinking water, there's a marked decline in corticoids and ACTH, two hormones related to elevated stress. Additionally, where water is available in the learning environment, the typical hormone response to stress (elevated corticoids) is "reduced or absent." This suggests a strong role for water in keeping learners' stress levels down. It will also help reduce lethargy and impaired learning in the classroom. Many children need more water; juice, tea, and soft drinks will not take its place. In this case, only good old H_2O will do!

There's so much to learn about learning if we are just willing to do so. As parents, we want to give our children the best start in life; and, in order to make them good learners, we should never stop being learners ourselves!

Column 5: Becoming SMART(er) Parents

This month's column deals with the "R" in SMART—responsibility. This is a big one, parents, whether you're talking about education, work, or life in general. The ability to be responsible will affect every aspect of your child's life.

You cannot function without discipline.

—H. G. Pratt

SMART learners demonstrate responsibility by, among other things, understanding and accepting their own limitations. This doesn't mean that they overuse the generic "I can't." It simply means that they explore their abilities enough to become familiar with their strengths and weaknesses. They understand that weakness in one area doesn't necessarily translate into a weakness across the board. For instance, if you've got a child who's naturally a good speller, she will likely know that she needs to spend the time saved on spelling to study an area where she needs more work, such as math. Support your child in this by maintaining open lines of communication with teachers, understanding their expectations, and then helping your child develop good work habits. This helps her take responsibility for monitoring her own progress and allows her to take pride in it.

Responsible learners also respect the property of others. This begins with respecting their own property and taking care of it. You can begin this at home by discussing how your child came to possess this property. Where did it come from? How much did it cost? What would happen if this property were to be destroyed and not replaced? Many times, it's an awakening just for the child to realize that not everything is replaceable, that you're either unable or unwilling to replace it. Doing without can be a strong incentive to behave responsibly.

Children need to learn to take care of themselves and their belongings. Though it would not seem to affect their schoolwork when they don't hang up their clothes or wipe their feet, it's an issue of self-reliance. Once they become self-reliant at home, it can't help but carry over to the classroom. You could start with something as simple as having them pick out and prepare their clothes for the next morning. Not only will this teach responsibility, it will alleviate some of the stress of the morning. Find ways to help your child learn to be responsible. Decide where their school papers and backpacks belong and let them decorate a box to hold all of it so they will know where to find things.

We have to be careful not to undermine our own good intentions in helping children learn responsibility. We naturally want to protect them and, in doing so, sometimes become responsible for them. I know that I have been guilty of it! When I was a student, if I forgot a paper, it might as well have been on the moon for all the chance I had of getting my hands on it in time to turn it in! I still remember the fear I felt! For the first few years of my children's education, I never failed to take these forgotten items to them at school. One Thursday, I realized that I'd been to school every day that week; and, not only were

the kids not overly grateful, they were starting to look upon it as my job to find what they'd forgotten and deliver it to them! I couldn't believe I'd let it happen! So I thought back to my own experience and realized that, while that fear I'd felt was bad, I'd forgotten very few assignments over the years. Not only was I creating a nuisance for myself, I was undermining my children's sense of responsibility and, also, the lesson that the teachers were trying to teach them! The next morning, and for a few mornings thereafter, I reminded them to take a final look around because I wasn't making any trips to school. I'm happy to report a drastic decrease in forgotten assignments!

Talk to your child about what happens when people don't do what they're supposed to do. What if the piano teacher decided to take a day off and just wasn't there when you showed up for your lesson? What if your soccer coach decided he didn't really want to make 15 phone calls to let the players know what time the game started? What would happen? Would it be fair to everyone? Would it be responsible behavior?

We all want to be good and do good things, and children must be supported in their impulse to do right. We, as parents, are the most important source of that support. We need to talk and let our children talk openly about the issues facing them and the best ways to handle them. We also need to let them see us acting responsibly. Remember that with everything you do, you're setting an example. Even bragging about breaking the speed limit undermines a child's respect for the law. My five-year-old son is a terrible backseat driver, always watching the speedometer and nagging me if I'm going at all too fast. I let him. It not only holds me accountable, it teaches him that the law is the law no matter who is making an issue of it! Even if the person happens to be only five years old!

Once the children and I were in line at a fast food restaurant, all starving and cranky, and when I'd finally paid for the food and was pulling away, my oldest daughter said, "Mommy, didn't she give you too much money?" Did I glow with pride at her mathematical abilities? No. Full of dread, I counted the money and realized that, yes, I had one dollar bill too many. One look at my daughter's face told me I had no choice. I had to stop the van, get out, walk back to the window, interrupt the person who had been behind me in line (for an eternity) and return the money. Even the cashier looked at me like I was crazy as she thanked me. But I was able to get back into the van and look my daughter in the eye, knowing that I'd done the honest thing and that she would remember it. Wow, did I ever feel virtuous!

Underlying everything that I've written is one word, one concept that will sum it all up: consequence. There are consequences for everything that we do in life, beginning when we are children. If we can make our children understand that, they will have a strong foundation upon which to build. When Jordan and Ashley were three and four years old, my neighbor marveled that they didn't run out into the street while playing in the yard. She asked me how I kept them from it. I told her that she didn't give them enough credit. All I had done was explain to them

that, in a contest between a 2000-pound car and a 42-pound girl, there really was no contest. Did they want to be dead? No. Well, that would be the consequence of running out into the street. Maybe the car wouldn't be there the first time but, eventually, they'd pay the consequences. Thus, having decided that they wanted to stay alive, they never ran into the street. Any child who can grasp the concept of consequence—cause and effect—will be able to make smart and responsible choices. We, as parents, must help them understand that consequences do exist and what they will be.

The man I quoted at the beginning of the column is my father. If I've heard that statement once, I've heard it five thousand times, and I'm happy to finally be able to use it in print! As in most cases, he was right!

Column 6: Becoming SMART(er) Parents

We have reached "T", which not only stands for "thoughtful" but also stands for "the end" of the SMART acronym. What are the qualities of a thoughtful learner, and what can we, as parents, do to promote thoughtfulness?

In becoming thoughtful learners, children must recognize two things about themselves: Do they have the confidence that they can solve most problems? Are they open to the ideas of other people? This calls for a measure of self-awareness, and on that topic I feel compelled to make an admission that will not surprise the people who know me. I am not a teacher. I do not have the gift of teaching. Because of that, I have great respect for teachers and the things that they accomplish.

I grew up with a father who is a teacher and can easily transfer knowledge on any level. I also grew up with a mother who was unable, we always said, to teach you to scratch your nose. She lacked the gift. But there were things she could do and, thankfully, did do that helped us become more thoughtful learners.

Did we believe we could solve most problems? My mother was very creative; although she would rather do something herself than teach someone else to do it, she did manage to illustrate that by far the greatest part of problem solving lay in the trying. I always thought she could do anything because she was willing to try everything. That was the example she set for us. Were we open to the ideas of others? Well, if you have children, you know that sometimes the ideas of others are the last things they want to hear. But we can help them learn the value of listening to others by listening to them. I remember being listened to by my parents. It made me feel respected and thus inspired self-confidence. After all, if my parents were willing to give my thoughts and ideas real consideration, then my thoughts and ideas must have merit! It gave me credibility. We can all do that for our children!

When I was growing up, my parents made a deal with their four children. If we heard them misuse a word and pointed it out to them, they would pay us a dollar! As far as I know, I never collected a penny, but the idea that we might catch them in a mistake and get paid for it was so intriguing that we became avid "grammar police." More important, it told us that our parents were willing to engage in a give-and-take situation. We were more willing to be corrected because they were willing to be corrected. It made us think.

"Mommy, what's that?"
"A cow."
"Why?"
"Why what?"
"Why is it a cow and not a horse?"
"You know what? I think you should ask your grandfather!"

A thoughtful learner questions others' assumptions. Hey, no problem there! Most kids want to question everything! While it can be exasperating, it can also be an opportunity to help our children become more thoughtful learners. Allow them to question you and take the time to explain your answers, unless of course your brain short-circuits as mine did during the above exchange with my daughter. And if they have a different opinion, take the time to listen to it. When I was young, I used to read a humor column, "At Wit's End," to my mother while she prepared our Sunday lunch. We would share a laugh and share some time and share an appreciation for each other's sense of humor. I sometimes cringe when I think of the opinions I expressed during these times, but my mother never ridiculed them and always seemed to give them thoughtful consideration. I don't know how she managed to keep a straight face but, again, I felt respected, valued, and credible. Even though she wasn't much of a teacher, the woman could make me feel good about thinking!

Does your child use quiet time to reflect on what he's learned? Is he comfortable with silence for thinking? Sometimes our tendency is to keep talking until our children give us a visible or audible clue that they understand us.

Try tossing out an idea and letting them think about it for awhile. Let it brew and see what comes back to you as a result.

A thoughtful learner reflects on accomplishments in order to set new goals. Encourage your child to plan and evaluate his own learning. "Retention, understanding, and the active use of knowledge can be brought about only by learning experiences in which learners think about and think with what they are learning."

We've all had the experience of memorizing something for a test and, a week later, drawing a blank when we're questioned on the subject. That's because we failed to relate the new information to our past experience and knowledge. We can help our children avoid the trap of "rote memorization" by helping them make meaning out of what they learn in school. Sit down, look them in the eye, listen to what they have to say, ask them questions and respect their thoughts, ideas, and opinions. Anyone can do it!

Summaries of de Bono's Six Thinking Hats